The Price Waterhouse Change Integration® Team

THE PARADOX PRINCIPLES

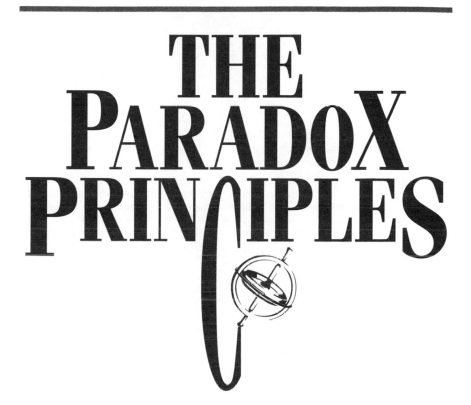

How High-Performance Companies Manage Chaos, Complexity, and Contradiction to Achieve Superior Results

 *IRWIN*
Professional Publishing®
Chicago • London • Singapore

© Price Waterhouse LLP, 1996

All rights reserved. No part of this publication may be reproduced, stored in a retrieval system, or transmitted, in any form or by any means, electronic, mechanical, photocopying, recording, or otherwise, without the prior written permission of the publisher.

This publication is designed to provide accurate and authoritative information in regard to the subject matter covered. It is sold with the understanding that neither the author nor the publisher is engaged in rendering legal, accounting, or other professional service. If legal advice or other expert assistance is required, the services of a competent professional person should be sought.

From a Declaration of Principles jointly adopted by a Committee of the American Bar Association and a Committee of Publishers.

Irwin Professional Book Team

Executive editor: *Amy Hollands Gaber*
Editor-in-chief: *Jeffrey A. Krames*
Marketing manager: *Tiffany Dykes*
Manager, direct marketing: *Rebecca S. Gordon*
Managing editor: *Kevin Thornton*
Project editor: *Amy E. Lund*
Production supervisor: *Pat Frederickson*
Assistant manager, desktop services: *Jon Christopher*
Designer: *Matthew Baldwin*
Jacket designer: *Barry Littman*
Compositor: *David Corona Design*
Typeface: *11/13 Palatino*
Printer: *R. R. Donnelley & Sons Company*

Times Mirror
Higher Education Group

Library of Congress Cataloging-in-Publication Data

Price Waterhouse (Firm). Change Integration Team.
    The paradox principles: How high-performance companies manage chaos, complexity, and contradiction to achieve superior results / The Price Waterhouse LLP Change Integration Team.
    p.   cm.
    Includes index.
    ISBN 0-7863-0499-5
    1. Organizational change—Management.   2. Organizational effectiveness.   3. Performance standards.   4. Industrial efficiency.
    5. Personnel management.   I. Title.
    HD58.8.P74   1996
    658.4'06—dc20   95–23346
Printed in the United States of America
1 2 3 4 5 6 7 8 9 0 DO 2 1 0 9 8 7 6 5

Contents

PART TWO

PART THREE

PART FOUR

PART FIVE

The Fourth Paradox Principle:
True Empowerment Requires Forceful Leadership 133

PART SIX

PART SEVEN

Fifteen Rules: A Manifesto on Managing Paradox   265

Foreword

by James J. Schiro, Chairman, Price Waterhouse, LLP

I write this introduction from a very personal perspective. As Chairman and Senior Partner of Price Waterhouse, my own challenge in the next five years will be to guide our firm into the next century. And I know that a key element of our success will be the thought leadership that we bring to our clients. Such leadership in the marketplace of ideas begins with a culture in which the quest for new ideas and the unceasing development of business wisdom are valued and visible. One of my prime objectives will be to perpetuate this climate at Price Waterhouse.

In developing the ideas underlying this book, the Change Integration® Team conducted a prodigious and comprehensive research effort. Our senior consulting partners from the United States and Europe carried out in-depth interviews with executives from many of the most prestigious multinational corporations, questioning them about the challenges they face. These interviews were analyzed and filtered through the lens of our own client experience and were supplemented with case study and literature research to compare our findings with the best thinking in business today. Finally, in order to "reality check" our conclusions, we conducted a survey of employees from some 200 business organizations.

As the ideas from our research began to emerge, I found them to be at first interesting, and then fascinating. Indeed, I have found the idea of paradox—the tough, enterprisewide problems with no perfect solution—and its relationship to managing in an environment of increasing complexity to be both intriguing conceptually and yet quite practical in its application. Paradox is a powerful concept to hold onto. It tells us that contradictory forces and values *are* going to clash. This is to be expected and needn't surprise us. The issue is how to *manage* paradox, not how to erase it.

The book speaks to the importance of achieving a synthesis or integration of contradictory forces—and doing so again and again, as the environment changes. There is no question that meeting our objectives at Price Waterhouse will require us to learn how to integrate and synthesize the distinct needs of our different disciplines, geographies, and markets.

Speed of execution is critical to our success, as well. And thus, we must continue to build upon our strengths of entrepreneurship and initiative, responding with flexibility to the needs of our clients. At the same time, we must *balance* that entrepreneurial spirit with the reality of a global practice in which clients are due the best collective thinking from across the firm and around the world.

Like you, I know I must continually search for new thinking—ideas to build upon. In this book, I think you will find very sound advice, advice worthy of the challenges ahead. I will keep it close at hand. I hope you do as well.

Preface

. . . the paradox is the source of the thinker's passion, and the thinker without a paradox is like a lover without feeling; a paltry mediocrity.

Søren Kierkegaard (1813–1855)
Danish philosopher and theologian

Writing a book is an acceptable form of obsession, to which we have again fallen prey. Our curiosity pushed us into a research effort in which we soon found that we were not so much looking for "the answer" as asking why satisfactory answers were not manifest in the conventional wisdom of our day. Early in our research, it became clear that the transformations that have taken place over the past decade should cause us all to rethink how we lead and manage our organizations in the decade ahead.

A new millennium is close at hand. The opportunities are enormous, but in many ways our world has turned upside down. We need a different way of thinking about things, new tools, a new perspective.

In the last decade, an explosion in management doctrine has been visited upon our organizations in pursuit of improved performance—a virtual feeding frenzy of programmatic change. And at the head of this food chain, this offensive is being led by a profusion of consultants, management gurus, and New Age theorists, all having discovered "the answer" to world-class performance. All manner of technique and methodology have been employed to restructure, redesign, rehabilitate, and, yes, reengineer the companies we serve. Unfortunately, the passion with which these programs have been implemented has too often been matched by their narrow-mindedness, their intolerance for real-world ambiguities, and the discontinuity in their application. Train the team, pledge steadfast allegiance to the new theology, get the team out on the field wearing the right colors—and wonder why things aren't better in four months.

Speed is critical. We agree. Focus is key. Who would not agree? Results are the bottom line—no question about it. But is "truth" so neatly packaged? Must the answers appear overnight? Must gratification arrive this week?

This is a book about the past, present, and future. We expect it to challenge at least some of your beliefs as it provides a genuinely new framework for management. But it also contains plenty of experience-tested, pragmatic advice. It is a book that should both arrest your thinking and drive you to action. And it is written for both the CEO and the shop steward, who share more concerns than you might think. One may drive a Mercedes to work and the other a Ford truck, but they hit the same parking lot each day and can't prosper without each other.

This book is about searching out smarter ways of leveraging the capabilities of the human resource. It is about capitalizing on the whole of the individual and allowing each to maximize his or her potential across both work and family dimensions. Our objective is to awaken and rekindle that centuries-old ember in the human spirit, to recover what we heard someone call the "Jurassic spark" in us all, which so often goes untended in our organizations today.

We have written about intersections—the most important intersections that run through our organizations. For example, there is an intersection between the manager/coach and his or her employees where chaos can be reduced to something manageable, complexity can be simplified, goals can be adjusted in real time, and the contribution of the individual can be maximized. By dismantling now-dated structures, we can achieve greater flexibility. In a world moving at warp speed, the challenge is to be broadly right and to avoid being precisely wrong.

We have also written about courage. This is a book for the manager in the messy middle, faced with disorder, confusion, and environmental complexity. The population in the messy middle includes CEOs and shop stewards, middle managers and the directors general of European and Asian subsidiaries. The courage we have in mind has somewhere toward its center the ability to act on the basis of what you know to be right rather than on the basis of what you have been told is right. It is a capacity to focus attention upon and even embrace your own company rather than trying to remake it in the image of various "cult" companies that receive the lion's share of praise and publicity.

Throughout this book, you will find evidence of the problems that managers are attempting to solve, first by leaning on one of the many theoretical "crutches" available, then by throwing away those crutches and daring to walk and think on their own.

When we began our research, we started—as have many— with a theory in search of evidence to prove it. We had the view that the horizontal corporation is the wave of the future. Gradually, however, we began hearing something different from the managers we interviewed. They were fed up with theories. Sometimes the theories worked, more often they did not. We realized that these managers were actually facing a group of fundamental paradoxes that prevented the theories from working.

However, they hadn't allowed the paradoxes to stop them from succeeding. They learned that through balance, synthesis, and integration, and by calling on the courage inside each of them, they could achieve extraordinary results. Out of their courage and intelligence, they developed an abundance of common sense grounded in business fundamentals rather than new theories.

These managers are, for the most part, not the ones you read about in the papers. Few if any have been the subject of seminars or talk shows. But they *are* recipients of praise and respect from their company peers. They are recognized as the ones who have had the courage and resourcefulness to succeed. We think you'll find their stories fascinating. Their insights have catalyzed our own to generate what we believe is an original body of management thinking.

What we offer here is not a crutch. It is a model of the new business reality that leaves managers with more to observe and think about than before, and with greater demands on their intelligence, sensitivity, and decisiveness. It exemplifies managerial effectiveness within that new business reality. Paradoxically, much of what we have to say may be new to you, but you'll quickly see that you've been thinking about these things for some time.

In preparing this book, we were perhaps moved most by a single comment. It occurred in a meeting of managers and employees, the purpose of which was to reconsider and affirm a collective vision, mission, and purpose for their organization. While the organization's strategic direction was clear to most of the participants, right-minded senior executives wanted the group to be involved in the articulation of mission and so forth.

During the discussions, which at times grew intense, a young manager stood up. What he said stilled the group at once. The dialogue had been focused on how best to articulate the purpose of the organization. This young man jumped in to confess confusion. He spoke eloquently, never whining, about a succession of 60-hour weeks and working weekends, about being on the road half the time, about a growing anxiety that his kids hardly knew him. Each of the participants listened carefully, full of the empathy that arises when one person speaks for all. And then he closed his soliloquy with a stunner of a question: "How can I come up with *our* purpose here, when I'm not clear as to my own?"

Were this an isolated account, there would be little concern. It is no such thing. Many of those employed in the world's greatest corporations today feel just as he does.

They deserve help. But it is an error in perspective to write "they" when all of us are fighting the same battles. We *all* deserve help in managing the near-chaos of our business climate today. We deserve help in battling the daunting complexities posed by today's competitive environment. We deserve help in dealing with the host of contradictory pressures facing managers today.

Tomorrow's best leaders will face these issues head on. The organizations they lead will be battling paradox at the end of this century. For this reason, they will endure well into the next.

Bill Dauphinais (New York)
Colin Price (London)
Paul Pederson (Dallas)

The Authors:

Bill Dauphinais

Colin Price

Paul Pederson

Hank Adamany

George Bailey

Saul Berman

Debbie Cohen

Randy Dalia

Andy Embury

Matt English

Jim Holec

Charles Kalmbach

Dan Keegan

Richard Moran

Kevin O'Laughlin

Cedric Read

Bill Reeves

Bob Russell

John Singel

Acknowledgments

T here could be no more collective and collaborative book than this. It has engaged at length the energies of the author group listed on the previous page. More temporarily but no less definitely, it has engaged the following group of Price Waterhouse professionals, from whom we have received both cases and counsel:

Kevin Bacon, Tom Britton, Carolyn Carlson, Tom Colberg, Don DeLuca, Bob Eiler, Bill Ek, Glenn Galfond, Nicole Gardner, Tig Gilliam, Ed Goll, Rick Guior, Kurt Janvrin, Ruth Klewans, Marilyn Miller, David Pettifer, Susan Pieper, Rabia Rahman, John Scharlacken, David Schneider, and Ken Toombs.

At Irwin Professional Publishing, the editorial, marketing, and design groups have been effective collaborators from the beginning. Jeffrey Krames and Amy Hollands Gaber have guided us with intelligence and care on the editorial side. Tiffany Dykes has helped us think about our book not only as a work in progress but as a market presence. Doug Dickson added great value to our effort researching issues, by synthesizing case material and bringing his own unique perspectives to the book. Marion Cochran Lunt, our friend and designer, gave generously to the look of the book and its art. And our firm's director of external communications, Roger Lipsey, contributed mightily as editor, counselor, and friend to the project as a whole.

PART ONE

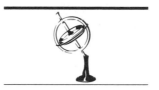

Chaos, Complexity, Contradiction: The New Corporate Reality

The way of paradoxes is the way of truth.
Oscar Wilde (1854–1900),
playwright, toast of London, convict

One

The Five Paradox Principles

Seek simplicity, and distrust it.

**Alfred North Whitehead (1861–1947),
mathematician and philosopher**

T*he pressures on today's managers and employees are un-precedented. For many of us, the sum of our institutional learning took place in an environment much different than we will face in the decade ahead. The playing field was level, if not pitched to our advantage. Many of the rules were obvious. Structure was our friend. Hierarchy provided context and orientation. Time helped, and there was enough. Uncertainty was to be avoided.*

It's not that the rules have been tinkered with. We're in a different game! We've honed our cricket skills and suddenly find we're in a basketball game, where little more than gravity can be counted on. It's not simply that the pace has increased. Our "velocity"—mea-sured in air miles, e-mail messages, and meetings—is approaching some point beyond which human beings should not go.

It's time to take measure, to pause long enough to examine what's behind all this. It's time to bring some clarity to the patterns emerg-ing out of the tumult of the last decade. The new millennium is not far off. Our approach needs work if we're to arrive in one piece.

Nearly a hundred years ago, Oliver Wendell Holmes Sr. observed: "I see it all perfectly; there are two possible situa-tions—one can either do this or that. My honest opinion and my friendly advice is this: do it or do not do it—you will regret both." Of course, this was an irony. He found an intriguing way to observe that there is rarely a perfect course of action. In a broader sense, he touched on a problem that has troubled humanity since philosophers first began trying to make logical sense out of what often seems wholly illogical: the paradoxes in our lives.

The dictionary defines *paradox* as a "seemingly contradic-tory statement that may nonetheless be true." Paradoxes, or contradictory statements, have been used in eastern religions, especially Zen Buddhism, as a teaching device to develop a student's discernment and intuition. At a distance from the Zen monastery but still recognizably related, Hegel's dialectic pitches two opposites vigorously against each other—thesis and antithesis—to develop a synthesis that is not merely a compromise but a new solution. All these things point in the same direction, toward ourselves. In our businesses today, contradiction often follows from seemingly logical and straight-forward premises. A conclusion reached "by the book" can clash with common sense. Little or nothing is perfectly clear.

Today's environment is more like a white-water kayak race.

Each day things get just a little more complex. Each day there are new contradictions. Each day new paradoxes emerge. Each day edges toward what feels more like chaos. You have certainly heard very bright people use sailing as a metaphor for business—they find interesting parallels in strategy, teamwork, tactics, and such. But the metaphor doesn't work anymore. Today's environment is more like a white-water kayak race.

And at the finish line are your customers. Customers today demand simplicity in their dealings with your organization. But providing customers this simplicity creates endless complexity in systems, structures, and processes. Battling this complexity requires a new approach. The paradoxes in this environment require new perspectives.

In his book *The Age of Paradox*, Charles Handy made the case that business paradoxes will only increase in number and kind. Handy's advice to managers when faced with a paradox: "[Managers] can, and should, reduce the starkness of some of the contradictions, minimize the inconsistencies, understand the puzzles in the paradox, but [they] cannot make them disappear, solve them completely, or escape from them." We share this view.

What's Ahead

This book illustrates how some of the best managers in the world are achieving new levels of performance in the turbulent 90s—the age of paradox. It began with a series of interviews with over 200 senior-level corporate executives in a variety of manufacturing and service organizations. Work continued by examining the knottiest problems these managers face and how they achieve high performance under conditions of chaos, complexity, and contradiction. It ended with the writing of this book.

As members of an international consulting organization, our practitioners are continually called on to help managers improve their operations. Many of the assignments we're asked to undertake have a "programmatic" character; that is, our clients are typically predisposed to use one of a variety of management techniques or programs such as TQM, reengineering, empowerment, culture change, horizontal organization, benchmarking, and others. These techniques have sound underpinnings; they can help thoughtful managers achieve their objectives.

However, we often encounter another, darker side—virtual hysteria regarding "the newest management program." As each new management theme emerges, the volume goes up, the hyperbole accelerates. Making matters worse, the rush to install these new programs tends to add to the chaos of change all around us. As a result, managers lose one of their very best qualities—their doggedness. They become easily discouraged when things get tough and results are not immediate. The temptation to move swiftly on to the next expedient becomes overwhelming. And throughout their efforts to institute positive change, they are asking their employees to focus more on the theory of the new management technique than upon fully implementing the sound principles of programs past. In the worst circumstances, organizations come to resemble a beaten prizefighter, reeling about the ring, lurching and lunging at shadows that appear to be their target, but are not.

What to Do?

Clearly, things are out of balance. Managers are pushing technique and theory to an extreme, when what they need is a better synthesis of facts and ideas, a better integration of seemingly conflicting concepts—and better balance. Our experience suggests the following overall perspective:

1. The challenges managers face have escalated. Chaos, complexity, and contradiction are common in today's business environment.

2. Those achieving the highest levels of performance do so through deftly *balancing* the conflicting demands or "tensions" created by the paradoxes inherent in developing, operating, and continuously transforming any large enterprise.

3. Managers in the decade ahead will acknowledge and overcome this chaos and complexity not with some set of formulae or rigid management doctrines but by working flexibly—and with uncommon intelligence; by managing paradox itself.

We have found these things to be true in high-performing organizations. Instead of applying particular techniques or theories across the board and to excess, managers in the best organizations focus on the paradoxes in their markets, organization, and business model. Each is trying to make sense out of organizational and competitive situations that seem plainly illogical or vastly inconsistent with the past and with expectation. Each is trying to come to grips with the inherent contradictions and tensions of their organization. Each is attempting to achieve enduringly superior performance by managing paradox.

The first difficulty for many managers is that mission-critical "solutions" today are not always available through traditional, rational analysis. The questions facing them do not conveniently yield to deterministic methods—and this denies the science of management as practiced for almost a century. Since Frederick Taylor first applied precise data-gathering techniques to the workplace, we have wanted management to be more science than art.

The second difficulty is that the newer management techniques do not succeed automatically. By our count at least 55 distinct management programs or techniques (such as reengineering, self-directed teams, etc.) are in use today, many with mixed success. Increasingly, managers are realizing that there is often a gap between even the most attractive general theory or technique and their specific problems. They identify what seems to be the right formula, input their particular variables—and hope that the output will be a smashingly elegant, effective answer. Unfortunately, management techniques are not universally true mathematical formulae. They can yield answers, but those "answers" may spawn more chaos, complexity, and contradiction.

It would be absurd to suggest that managers should turn their backs on focused management programs. Much can be gained through intelligent application of the principles underlying, for example, reengineering and TQM. At the same time, we must all now face something for which we have not necessarily been trained: life in the messy middle, somewhere between answers A and B, at the point of tension where contradiction and complexity are the norm.

We are not suggesting that management will be overwhelmed. Nor are we suggesting that management approaches need be as messy as the situations they address. But managers must learn to balance the free exercise of their intelligence and experience against the programmatic, often false, security of the latest management techniques. We are not MBA students learning the next technique. Our actual role resembles scientific investigation, with its emphasis on trial and error, probing and testing, synthesis of results, fact-finding and data gathering, and intelligent case-by-case judgment.

Courage is at the center. Integrating and synthesizing the best ideas is the objective. And high performance is the result.

That position in the messy middle is not the proverbially uncommitted "middle of the road." It has nothing in common with watered-down, conciliatory solutions. Unwarranted caution and timidity usually result in lowest-common-denominator concessions. Those who successfully manage the paradoxes and tensions discussed in chapters to follow are men and

The Mighty Gyroscope

The central icon celebrated throughout *The Paradox Principles* is the mighty gyroscope. It is a worthy model for tomorrow's leaders, primarily because its movements manifest a marvelous synthesis of competing forces. The physics governing its varied capacities lie beyond the scope of this book. On the other hand, the lessons it teaches as one relaxes and experiments with it are at the heart of this book.

The gyroscope was invented in 1852 by Jean Bernard Foucault, a French physicist. Truly a thing of beauty, the device brings many dynamic forces into balance: high-speed rotation, centrifugal and centripetal forces, forces that temporarily offset gravity and magnetic fields. Most impressive are the gyroscope's grace and balance. It hums along perfectly in all sorts of precarious positions when the balance of forces is just right.

The uses to which the gyroscope has been put strengthen the metaphor. It has long served as the nucleus of navigational systems. It has helped to guide and stabilize 19th-century ships and 20th-century rockets. It is both a toy that prompts wonder in children of all ages and a venerable tool serving critical objectives.

women of courage. For them, courage, not disheartening compromise, is at the center. Integrating and synthesizing the best ideas is the objective. And high performance is the result.

The New Business Environment

If our observation that managers are facing a greater number of contradictory situations is valid, we shouldn't fail to ask the next question: Why is this happening now? We believe that seven primary forces have reshaped the business environment and impose the need for new management approaches and insights. Each of these forces has been at work for some time, but each has become so strong and evident in the 1990s that virtually no one can overlook them and still conduct business.

Among these forces, *global competition* is our reward for managing the aftermath of World War II so astutely that our former enemies could rebuild into innovative industrial

Solutions through Synthesis

A great success story of the latter half of the 20th century concerns Royal Dutch Shell, one of very few oil companies able to anticipate and profit from the dramatic increases in oil prices following the OPEC oil embargo of the early 1970s. Unlike almost every other company inside and outside the oil industry, Shell was on top of the price increases. It was the first company to look for and evaluate the potential of alternative energy sources, the first to have a planned response.

Since then, in the usual rationalist manner, Shell's method of managing through this point of tension has been studied and restudied in order to find the one answer that would allow other managers to move as adroitly in meeting their own business challenges. The fact that Shell used a series of extremely sophisticated scenario forecasts was unearthed and thought to be the key to its success. But like so many other techniques, scenario forecasting has not taken hold. Many companies lost interest when they discovered the financial investment and degree of intellectual sophistication needed to apply this technique.

The key to Shell's success, however, was not the scenario technique but rather something that Shell discovered about its managers as they worked on their scenarios. In 1985, the chief analyst in Royal Dutch Shell's planning function at that time, Pierre Wack, told the story of Shell's effort in a two-part series in *Harvard Business Review*.[1] He pointed out that before the development of the new technique, the managers at Shell—some of the most highly paid and analytical minds in the corporate world—practiced the fine art of rational prediction and forecasting by quantifying obvious alternatives and projecting equally obvious results. Despite the beauty of their technical orientation, they were getting nowhere. Shell's breakthrough occurred when these managers recognized the paradoxical situation in which they found themselves.

> The way to solve this problem was not to . . . [perfect] techniques. . . . Too many forces work against getting the right forecast. The future is no longer stable; it has become a moving target. No single right [answer] can be deduced from past behavior. . . . The better approach . . . is to accept uncertainty, try to understand it, and make it part of our reasoning. Uncertainty today is not just an occasional, temporary deviation from a reasonable predictability; it is a basic structural feature of the business environment. . . . [The key is to] structure uncertainty [and] change the decision makers' assumptions about the way the world works and compel

---

Solutions through Synthesis *(continued)*

them to [reorient] their mental model of reality. . . . [Such a] willingness to face uncertainty and to understand the forces driving it requires an almost revolutionary transformation in a large organization. . . .[2]

Wack goes on to explain that Shell's managers recognized the primacy of uncertainty with a starkness that had previously escaped them. Only then could they reorient their approach and address uncertainty directly in their formulation of possible and probable scenarios. From this flowed the decisions that put the company in such excellent shape.

---

democracies. Entrepreneurial nations around the Pacific Rim and elsewhere have followed suit by creating successful, competitive economies. In the 1990s, global competition has been democratized: It is no longer just the Big Three automakers and certain high-technology sectors that must contend with it; all of us contend with it, all the time.

It is also more than obvious that *new computer technologies* have reworked how we accomplish tasks from the simplest to the most complex—from typing and editing a document to managing the complexities of an international business and operating factories. The impact has been incalculably great on what we do and who does it, never more so than in the 1990s.

New markets worldwide also represent a powerful business preoccupation and opportunity of the 1990s. The Iron Curtain is no more, and numerous societies in Eastern Europe and elsewhere are applying for full membership in the world economy. The opportunity is vast; the attendant chaos, complexity, and contradiction are as vast as anyone could want.

The *new financial system,* including a host of financial markets and investment vehicles, is the offspring of new information technologies and the global economy. The increase in computational and analytic power and the expansion of markets and capital resources have generated massive complexity, and there is no backing away from it. This is again a trend peaking in the 1990s, when a young trader on one side of the world can bring down a financial institution on the other side of the world that had been doing well since Mozart's era.

New demographics have both enriched the workplace and added layers of social, psychological, training, scheduling, and equity issues that require not just policy and procedure but communication, sensitivity, and good judgment. In the 1970s and 1980s this was new, and many mistakes were made. There is an opportunity in the coming decade to learn from all that and get it right or nearly right.

New psychological requirements make today's manager and employee markedly different presences in the workplace than 10 or 15 years ago. New concepts of lifestyle and definitions of personal well-being have found their way out of the books of Abraham Maslow and other humanistic psychologists to become a shaping force in the business world. People don't prosper in environments that ignore or downplay their psychological requirements. This introduces new complexities and subtleties, as well as new promise.

Finally, *new communication networks* and a new emphasis on communication have enormous implications. Again, this is the offspring of technology, but that is not the main point. The main point is that people in their private lives are now accustomed to a nearly overwhelming wealth of communication, and they do not leave that expectation at the office or factory door. Communications allow your manager in Australia to talk shop with his or her peer in Holland, and to report jointly to you in Chicago via videoconference. Communication systems not only allow this, they make it inevitable and productive.

More and more managers now understand that their own corporations are subject to all these forces, which are breaking down the corporate structures built so carefully since the turn of the century. These bureaucracies, some with roots in the 19th century, were built to structure, control, and concentrate the unbridled innovation of industrial progress. They carried us through many decades, but now, at century's end, the pendulum has swung back to a second era of innovation and creativity. The bureaucracies and controls put in place (and reinforced to take care of social problems during the Depression) are becoming obsolete. Economic power is not going to be based on how much control you put in place but rather on how you lead, manage, and empower.

Communications

Defining Communications: Elements of the Mix

"Perhaps the most important single change in human consciousness in the last century . . . has been the multiplying of the means and forms of what we call 'communication.' "

Daniel Boorstin, *Democracy and Its Discontents*

The historical development of communication provides clues about today's tensions and paradoxes. On the one hand, for centuries communication meant transmitting *information* from person to person, across time and space, in order to exchange, to exert control, or to ask a question and receive an answer. This definition still holds today: Technological innovations (e-mail, voice mail, etc.) are mere efforts to extend that sphere of exchange, control, and questioning over greater distances (space) more quickly (time). On the other hand, communication also supports *rituals of sharing,* participation, and "community." It can create or strengthen the participants' faith in who they are, what they believe, and what they do.[3]

The implication is clear that communication can—and we believe, must—be used for more than disseminating information to and through the organization. It can create a common faith—a unique corporate culture that drives performance. The paradox of communication is that the more technology has extended the breadth and reach of communications, the less we are actually communicating with one another. The danger is a human sense of isolation.

What are the elements of communication? In the broader definition that encompasses both control and community, these elements must all be considered:

- Content
- Voice
- Tone
- Message
- Audience
- Medium
- Frequency
- Consistency

Information, the actual content of the communication, is only one part of

Communications

Defining Communications: Elements of the Mix *(continued)*

an effective communications effort. What gets heard—and, more important, what is perceived and believed—will be as much a function of who delivers the message, in what tone, by what means, and so on. All these aspects must be considered for a communication to achieve its dual mission of informing and igniting.

As we explore the Paradox Principles, we will highlight with anecdotes and suggestions how various types of communication can be deployed to build community and commitment and to achieve organizational objectives.

How Have Managers Responded?

Of course, this is not the first time that the business world has been affected by macroenvironmental trends, and these particular trends have been driving change for more than a decade. But the response of today's managers and their organizations has been unique. Today as in decades past we are all Taylorists—and we are all something else that is just emerging. We share a tradition, in place since the work of Frederick Taylor, of attacking management problems rationally. The rise of the MBA since World War II is a long testimony to our commitment to rationalism. Many managers simply *expect* the optimal solution to emerge from concentrated, quasi-algorithmic analysis. We tend to respond as Taylorists, and then to doubt what we have done, often with good reason. Among the issues of riveting interest to managers today are these:

- **Our legacy of structure and organization.** Huge bureaucracies and organizations are in place and functioning according to a variety of metrics. The result of this era of "white-water" change and, we believe, management creativity will not be an immediate overhaul of the traditional approach or a complete surrender of power. Too many stalwart barriers exist, both in our organizations and in our minds. The new structure will be something else. We are beginning to see its outlines, but no one as yet can fully describe it.

- **Our need to simplify.** As complexity increases, we seek to simplify. We resist paradox. It bothers us, requires us to live with two opposites that coexist. Simplicity is a natural instinct in the face of the accelerating pace of change. We all gravitate toward it when confronted with too little time, too many choices. In its place, simplicity is unquestionably a worthy management principle. It is also dangerous around paradox. Choosing quickly between contradictory but seemingly valid alternatives can be seductive—*and* destructive.

- **The rise of the charismatic management guru.** We have witnessed over the last several decades an unprecedented increase in the number of widely publicized management gurus. Many are engaging—indeed, almost evangelical in their sermons espousing reengineering, TQM, customer intimacy, teams, even chaos. Prior to this phenomenon, managers read the teachings of a very few learned but relatively low-key intellectuals—Drucker, Taylor, Weber. A lecture by Peter Drucker is still immensely rewarding and leaves you with many intriguing questions. However, your employees today are pouring out of seminars *calculated* to create a frenzy of obsession and single-mindedness about one doctrine or another. Some of what they hear underscores sound management fundamentals. Some of it is over the top, out of balance. One manager with whom we've spoken thinks of these doctrines as *focus pocus*.

> Simplicity is a natural instinct in the face of the accelerating pace of change.

- **The age of the cult company.** Yesterday's companies truly were the *private sector:* They went about their business without much publicizing how they did what they did, and no one apart from management professors was peering over the wall to find out. But something has changed in the last 10 years. Managers are now fascinated with how *particular* companies achieve their goals. The trend has developed well beyond normal benchmarking into an obsession with certain *cult* companies. We're sure you know them: L.L. Bean, Federal Express, Home Depot, GE. Certainly, benchmarking and the search for best practices are to be applauded. But they become a problem when managers believe that their own operations should be facsimiles. "If I just find out how that cathedral of best practice operates, the answer *here* will be obvious . . ."

> **Today, employees are pouring out of seminars *calculated* to create a frenzy of obsession and single-mindedness about one doctrine or another.**

Managers today are experiencing an unprecedented era of corporate reawakening and what often feels like psychoanalysis. Companies are struggling in every industry to find out what they are, who they are, why they are. Few executives caught in the middle of this frenetic activity and soul-searching fully understand what it all means. One sign of their struggle for understanding is the growing number of organizational change programs instituted since the late 1980s.

While techniques differ among companies, the need to respond is universal. Figure 1.1 illustrates this phenomenon through management literature. On the subject of change alone, more than 800 books were published in the five years ending with 1994! Authors and consultants are falling over each other trying to think of the best new and trendy term for what is going on. They are advancing "innovative" concepts and methodologies in an attempt to provide a solution for all problems through one Big Idea. Managers are attending change management seminars and executive-training programs in record numbers so as to be able to guide transformations by the latest methods.

But the innovation in these conferences is often more apparent in the new label than in the ideas and principles behind

Figure 1.1
Mounting Management Fads

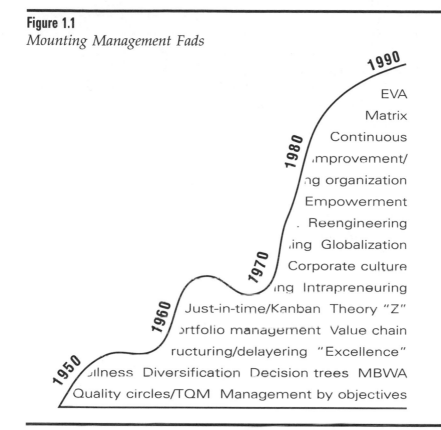

it. And for every senior executive you might find who es-
pouses a particular management theory, you can easily find
five asserting that they tried it and it
didn't work. Our research and client
work indicate that the key to success
in the decade ahead will *not* be still
another technique. In fact, we believe
that many managers need to be
deprogrammed, weaned from the
next wave of theories, and convinced
that they should not expect the "next
program" to make it all happen.
Nothing is that simple. Like the
power of new computer hardware,
the half-life of each new technique is shorter than the one
before it.

One sign of the struggle for understanding is the growing number of organizational change programs instituted since the late 1980s.

Every management doctrine contains not just future opportunity and greatness but current challenges and deficiencies. The more impassioned and evangelical the sponsor, the less likely that these challenges and deficiencies will be exposed. As a result, such programs and the managers in charge of them are running headlong into powerful points of tension and daunting managerial paradoxes that threaten to undermine their efforts and perhaps damage their organizations.

Principles for Managing Paradox

Today's managers are under enormous pressure to balance the tensions from all sides. Consider just one aspect of our new environment: the diversity of our workforce. We are asked to celebrate diversity—and we should. But executives today know that they walk a tightrope when they articulate the needs of a selected group. Reference to the characteristics and needs of one group can be interpreted as bigotry by some, stereotyping by others, and favoritism by still others. The best solutions are not obvious. With a predominantly white male executive team and mostly male workforce, past U.S. employers could more predictably direct and motivate their organizations than they can today.

Management over the past five decades involved clearer choices, fewer choices. This is not to say that managing has ever been a trivial task—far from it. But the transformations taking place and the competing tensions that result bring a new level of complexity to the game. They mandate a new way of thinking for tomorrow's managers. A new "science" of management is emerging in response. Its laws are only now becoming clear. The need for tomorrow's managers to have technical and analytical skills, perseverance, and functional expertise won't go away. But they will have to augment these competencies with instincts for balance and integration, and the ability to recognize and master nuance.

The key to success in the next decade will be a balanced approach to management, which does not ignore or explain away the existence of contradictions and uncertainty—the existence of paradox. Intelligent managers will face in that direction. They will learn to balance deftly the paradoxes or points of tension that run through the development, operation, and continual transformation of their enterprises.

In our research and interviews, we have begun to identify the principal paradoxes that seem to most trouble today's executives. In the chapters ahead, we explore them and shed light on how high-performing managers are dealing with them. We also assemble 15 fundamental guidelines for managing paradox. The result, we hope you'll agree, is an effective field guide for managers facing the operational and competitive environments ahead. It is also a manifesto. We have not been untouched by the paradoxes we describe. This book is not the work of a lofty consultant who somehow never loses the shine on his shoes. We too have struggled with these issues.

> **Intelligent managers will deftly balance the paradoxes that run through the development, operation, and continual transformation of their enterprises.**

We focus on five paradoxes facing managers today:

The First Paradox Principle: Positive Change Requires Significant Stability

Rampant change in the absence of key elements of stability is chaos. Uncontrolled change fathers turmoil, not solid performance. Managers need stakes in the ground to guide change. Where such guideposts are missing or wobbly, change can be nothing more than a free-for-all—plenty of activity, too little real performance improvement.

In leading transformation, successful managers identify the critical sources of stability such as culture, community, and a stable vision, mission, strategy, and core competencies. These beacons of stability are necessary to guide you through the turbulent waters of change.

The Second Paradox Principle: To Build an Enterprise, Focus on the Individual

More is being asked of each of us by our organizations. At the same time, we are being given less to rely upon, less security. A decades-old quid pro quo is gone and must be reinvented if we are to maximize our collective potential. To create a global organization, you must recognize that its fundamental building block is the individual employee. To ring true and act accordingly, you will need to revise and integrate your thinking about the individual, unique among all others in his or her skills and aspirations, and the organization of which he or she is a part. You will have to look upon the majority and see the one. You will have to optimize performance in the aggregate by maximizing the potential of each part.

The Third Paradox Principle: Focus Directly on Culture, Indirectly

Managers today understand the importance of culture. They recognize the powerful leverage gained when behaviors and decisions firmly reinforce an organization's strategy. And they are aware that their organization's culture is a strong determinant of employee behavior and decision patterns. But culture change does not result from a focus on culture itself, nor does it flow from training programs, wish lists of values and beliefs, or instructing people to care about customers. Such initiatives don't work. To reshape culture, managers must focus on the six important "levers" that create and shape culture: (1) leadership actions; (2) vision, purpose, and strategy; (3) performance measures; (4) structure; (5) people practices; and (6) competitive context.

The Fourth Paradox Principle: True Empowerment Requires Forceful Leadership

Without forceful, directed, and purposeful leadership, empowerment will not happen. New Age theorists are wrong when they advocate that employees run the workplace. Employees want and expect leaders to set direction and determine the business focus. But they also want new latitude to achieve objectives. A new interactive model of leadership is emerging—one that relies more on the power of *influence* than of command and control. It is based on mutual respect, reinforced by effective communication skills. Its aim is to balance an increasing need for bold leadership with each person's instinct for freedom and initiative.

The Fifth Paradox Principle: In Order to Build, You Must Tear Down

We have invested much of our lives in building the organizations we manage. We are all highly vested in the seductive notion that what we have built will continue to flourish. But the force of change today is so dramatic that many of the solutions and business models we have created no longer work. They will not support competitiveness in the decade ahead. We must face up to the things that require dismantling in order to start anew. Complexity—now rampant in our systems and structures—demands that we do so. And the age-old paradox of "less is more" has never been so true.

Conclusion

In the chapters ahead, we explore the tension and paradox surrounding many elements of the business model: leadership, empowerment, performance measurement, human resources management, culture, information technology, strategy, and the individual employee. The ideas in these chapters represent our collective experience. They also incorporate the best thinking we have heard from executives just like you. Pondering the future. Looking ahead. Squinting, perhaps, as we all do when something's not quite clear. Nonetheless, discovering patterns that make tremendous sense.

• • • • •

The quest for certainty blocks the search for meaning.
Uncertainty is the very condition to impel man to unfold his
powers.

Erich Fromm (1900–1980),
psychiatrist and author

Notes

1. Pierre Wack, "Scenarios: Uncharted Waters Ahead," *Harvard Business Review*, September–October 1985, pp. 72–89, and "Scenarios: Shooting the Rapids," *Harvard Business Review*, November–December 1995, pp. 139–50.
2. Wack, p. 72. "Scenarios: Uncharted Waters Ahead."
3. Taken from writings of John Dewey, as discussed in *Communication and Culture*, James W. Carey (Unwin Hyman, 1988).

PART TWO

THE FIRST
PARADOX PRINCIPLE:

Positive Change Requires
Significant Stability

---

*Wisdom lies neither in fixity nor in change, but in the
dialectic between the two.*

Octavio Paz

Two

Change and Stability

Only the wisest and the stupidest of men never change.

Confucius

C hanging markets. Changing employee demographics. Changing foreign competition. Changing technologies. Had enough? The idea of change so permeates business and society today as to be absolutely withering. It's beyond fashionable to have a major transformation under way in your organization. In business, we seem consumed by change. Count the books and magazine articles on strategies for managing change that have appeared in just the last three years. (We gave up at *150!*) It's as if nothing will ever be the same.

Managers who have learned to master change, who channel its impacts to advance their objectives, also manage its limits.

Don't believe it. Yes, we can expect change to be a constant in our lifetimes—just as it was in our ancestors' times. Indeed, the pace of change will accelerate. But it is just as clear that those managers who have learned to master change, who channel its impacts to advance their objectives, also manage its limits. They grasp the importance of constancy. In short, they understand the first paradox principle:

• • • • •

Positive change requires significant stability.

• • • • •

Rampant change in the absence of key elements of stability is chaos. Uncontrolled change of this kind generates turmoil rather than a new level of corporate excellence. Managers need stakes in the ground to guide change. Buoys that mark the course, constellations that it takes only a sextant to read, a lighthouse—stable reference points. Absent such guideposts in the corporate world, change programs have the feel of a free-for-all—significant activity but not enough real and little positive change.

The frenetic pace of change can wither employees challenged to churn out work in newly downsized organizations. In the worst circumstances, the result of a decade of corporate change efforts is a climate of fear and uncertainty. Many managers we interviewed recognize that a never-ending cycle of change in recent years has generated skepticism and hobbling frustration. One initiative doesn't produce results quickly enough; another program is tried; it fails and another is tried. At the same time, current operations suffer as panic sets in when intended improvements don't materialize.

Managers need stakes in the ground to guide change.

The successful balancing of operations and transformation requires *flexibility*—flexibility to the point that change does not "rattle" the organization. Accomplishing this requires stability of vision, culture, or purpose—steadiness greater than the turbulence met along the way to lasting change.

Not long ago, we were called upon to assist one of the largest service organizations in the United States. The organization was valiantly attempting broad transformation against the huge odds of a legacy of poor strategic decisions in a fast-changing market. While profitable of late, the company was under great pressure to improve its performance. Its executives knew that meaningful transformation would have to include changes in organizational structure, culture, and major

---

Better Balance

Figure 2.1
Gyroscope

Place a spinning gyroscope on your fingertip. The magical little instrument maintains uncanny balance. The high speed of its spinning wheel is part of its secret of stability. Speed, change—*and stability.* Quite a combination. Would it be so impressive if it were wobbling wildly out of control? If its characteristics were chaotic? We think not.

Consider this.

processes. They knew, as well, that in order for the transformation to succeed they needed to involve and engage most, if not all, employees.

Management seemed pretty thoroughly enlightened. They had recognized and wished to address many of the crucial components of broad-based organizational transformation. Before our arrival they had engaged professional help to craft and carry out workshops to engage employees and convert them into agents of change. *Engagement* they achieved: They unleashed a torrent of enthusiasm for change. Meeting upon meeting was held to explore the subtleties of organizational change.

However, some of the meetings and the environment supporting them were eerily melodramatic. Charts and slogans were visible everywhere. Wall hangings communicated the latest expressions of enthusiasm for the new organization. Yet not much was getting done. A huge proportion of the company's energy and investment was actually being wasted in a chaotic, futile search for "truth" about organizational transformation.

What was missing? Focus. Hard-nosed objectives. Structure. Some of the time devoted to discussing organizational change would have been better spent in examining exactly which service behaviors were driving customers away; in implementing purposeful new performance measures; in reengineering core processes with specific cost, quality, and speed objectives; and in creating systems to reward decisiveness. Driven by their desire to change, few executives and employees asked, "Change what?" and "What should remain the same?" It is the second question that echoes through this chapter. To lead change efforts, successful managers identify and leverage sources of stability. This is the paradox. The stable elements are organizational lifeboats, able to ferry the community through the turbulent waters of change.

Successful managers identify and leverage sources of stability.

Communications

Consistency Propels Change

To bring about real change, you have to get people on board. You have to really engage them. Dynamic leaders understand the importance of consistency in communicating with their organization. A consistent message can both stabilize and motivate change. CEO Michael Bloomberg of Bloomberg L.P., the financial and business news service organization, put it this way:

"Consistency is key. Ronald Reagan was not the smartest guy in the world. But people thought he was a great president because even if the ideas weren't his own, even if they weren't complex, at least he used a consistent set of flashcards. He'd pull out the same set every day. He knew exactly what he stood for and what he wanted to do. What people look for in a leader is consistency."

A Fabric of Trust

Many of the managers we interviewed for this book mentioned trust as a fundamental prerequisite to successful transformation efforts. Trust should be at the top of your agenda. If you ever lose it, you'll soon discover that you need it more than ever—and by then it may be beyond reach. Trust is not just a "nice-to-have." It's crucial to organizational efficiency. And trust is a key result of stability. People know what they can count on and what they can anticipate as a consequence of their actions.

Even in an environment of turbulent change, certain constants promote trust: The boss can be fair in the treatment of managers who take legitimate risks and fail; managers can be consistent in their relations with employees; employees can earn the confidence of their managers by continually developing their skills and knowledge of the operation. Significant change requires an unwavering and resolute management style. Successful organizations do *not*

Trust catalyzes action and promotes decisiveness.

have the feel of an "ad-hocracy." While many issues are treated flexibly, there is also a confident understanding that the issues will be addressed in a straightforward and logical fashion. Managers know the histories of certain problems and of efforts to address them. They understand what it takes to make a decision and what they have to do to get the organization to buy into their decisions.

A stable foundation of trust is prerequisite to speed and effectiveness. Trust catalyzes action and promotes decisiveness. Without a foundation of trust, empowerment is limited. Employees operate within a constricted code that keeps them "safe" and "in bounds," but a repressive atmosphere and undertows of anxiety do not support a high-performance environment.

The CEO is the focal point of trust in any organization—the principal source of stability and purpose. A tall order, because he or she must also be the chief agent of change. If the CEO has set the right tone, defined clearly the mission and purpose of the company, and created a culture of trust, the organization will have a very real source of stability. Without this, leading change will be difficult, bringing about successful transformation impossible.

An Environment That Mandates Change

The search for stability will not be easy. So much in our world today *is* changing. Zones of the right kind of stability within companies are difficult to identify, let alone harness to corporate purpose. Both the external and internal environments seem to defeat stability and disguise its importance. Entire industry segments, at one time evolving over decades, now appear almost overnight: managed care in the health care industry, home shopping networks in retail, video-on-demand in entertainment. But even in these high-growth niches, the paradox of change and stability will assert itself. Behind the scenes in explosively successful companies there are sure to be some managers with an instinct for stability.

As complexity increases, change becomes exponentially much more difficult. And today, customers are shifting the burden of complexity to you as never before. This experience is universal. Every industry sector has been affected. Supervising a group of bank tellers in 1960 was simple compared to managing today's global network of ATMs. Yesterday, a gas utility could count on very stable, long-term contracts for its supply of gas. Now they're having to develop sophisticated energy management systems to help stay on top of volatile markets and shifting sources of supply. A basic range of three or four products two decades ago has ballooned into thousands of unique offerings. Today, a company like Anheuser-Busch knows its market will not be satisfied with a simple choice of Budweiser, Michelob, and Busch. Their offerings now must include a wide range of highly differentiated products. But getting "Bud Light in a 'shorts' 12-pack, Christmas-theme packaged with promotional tags for the Houston market" to the right customer at the right time is a huge challenge.

Figure 2.2
Change Curve

Successful transformation is always a challenge. But change can be accelerated by providing your managers and employees with meaningful sources of stability.

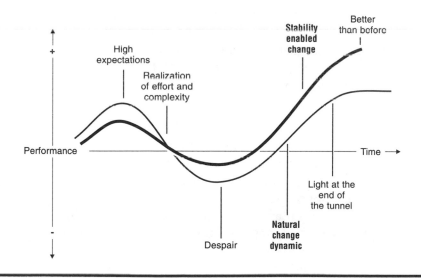

In virtually all industries, managers are under increasing pressure to deliver short-term results, although their better judgment may tell them to ignore this quarter's results in favor of the long term. Pressure comes from all angles—shareholders, regulators, employees. Most organizations face stiffer competition in markets undergoing unprecedented change, all of which leaves scant time to think about sources of stability. Few of the short-term indicators of performance (e.g., sales, quarterly profits, current stock price) provide a reservoir of stability.

Managers are under pressure for another reason, in some ways more surprising: the sheer scope of global opportunity for new business. The world market was growing at a real rate of 3.5 percent in 1995, as this book went to press—the fastest yearly growth since 1988. Interest in foreign stock ownership has soared since the late 1980s. Since 1990, U.S. exports have increased by more than 25 percent, and the United States is increasingly looking toward the so-called Big Emerging Markets (China, Mexico, Indonesia, India, South Korea, Turkey, Poland, South Africa, Brazil, and Argentina) to provide the major markets of the future. Across the developing world, some three billion consumers are beginning to integrate into the world economy. Trading blocs are proliferating, as countries cooperate to create pan-regional markets attractive to global companies. Austria, Finland, and Sweden are now poised to join the European Union. NAFTA is a reality, and the United States has promised membership in 1996 to Chile. In December 1994, all of the countries of the Western Hemisphere (except Cuba) vowed to create a single free-trade zone by the year 2000.

Managers who can analyze and master opportunities on this scale are always in demand. The more your organization invests in its people to help them become effective knowledge workers in the global marketplace, the more valuable they become—not only to you but to other potential employers. The best are highly marketable "free agents." The result is increasing turnover and, yes, instability. The deal *has* changed. And your employees know that loyalty is a two-way street.

Stability amidst Chaos

It is hard to imagine any organization in the world that operates as effectively under conditions of chaos as a U.S. Army rifle platoon. The ground-level tactics of the U.S. Army have long been considered the most innovative and flexible of any major world army. A rifle platoon's ability to react to traumatic change—such as the incapacitation of its leader—relies on four primary sources of stability: its culture, a clear and present strategy, its people, and its community.

The culture of the rifle platoon is deeply rooted and governed by a clear set of well-accepted norms and values. What one can expect from another soldier—even amidst the confusion of conflict—is drilled into the team. Soldiers are continually rewarded for acquiring and exercising certain characteristics critical to success in combat, such as initiative, determination, endurance, courage, resourcefulness, and esprit de corps.

There can be few better examples of a clear and present strategy than the Army's so-called five-paragraph field order. Every platoon leader is adept at composing and delivering this standard order. It begins with a clear and succinct account of the current situation. There follows a statement of mission in succinct, unambiguous terms. Next come operating instructions for each part of the platoon, which cover the timing of the operation, the support on which the unit can count, and how to access that support if necessary. It also includes instructions concerning command and communication, including contingencies should the leadership be compromised. Through repetition and training, a platoon member responds almost viscerally to each element of the order. The order contains a clear statement of intent that guides the actions of the platoon. This clear focus on mission, coupled with instructions regarding boundaries and support, allows the unit to improvise effectively in the chaos of battle.

Two other elements—people and community—are also essential to the effectiveness of this fighting unit. From the platoon leader through the sergeants down to the squad leaders, there is a clear set of roles and responsibilities for every person. Each is trained extensively in his specialty and in at least one other as well. Each is expected to maintain his specialty. The platoon is a tight-knit community. While there is a formal command-and-control structure within the unit, the ability of these units to endure trauma and shocks of change, yet operate effectively, relies just as much on extensive cross-training, frequent maneuvering as a unit under chaotic conditions, and that famous five-paragraph field order. Knowing what they can count on enables rifle platoon members to deal with the chaos around them.

In the final analysis, these pressures orient management away from a careful search for sources of stability toward quick-fix solutions. Pressures do nothing to help a company determine what corporate stakes it can and should fix in the ground. Quite the contrary. Pressures help pull up stakes faster than they can be found.

Too Many Dots

The problem with quick fixes is not that they don't work but rather that they multiply as high-initiative managers reach for the latest technique to improve performance. You've heard your employees groan about "management by magazine article" or "technique du jour." In our book *Better Change*, we speak of this problem in terms of a management discipline missing in many companies. We call it "connecting the dots."

The phrase "connecting the dots"—derived from the children's drawing game—struck a chord with most of the managers we interviewed. It brings to mind the satisfaction of making sense of something that doesn't make sense in its current form—something that is supposed to show a clear pattern but displays instead only a blurred outline. Many managers face an undisciplined collection of change programs that together make little sense. Taken together, the programs don't reveal a rational pattern or integration of objectives. The "dots" are unconnected.

Such a situation can be counterproductive. Your employees and managers know instinctively when change programs go forward without sensible links to one another. Problems surface as rival programs compete for resources, contend for senior management attention, and seek conflicting objectives. It is the job of senior management to monitor these programs and weed out those that don't align with strategy, objectives, and available resources. When the dots aren't connected, it only adds to the chaos and instability.

When the dots aren't connected, it only adds to the chaos and instability.

Figure 2.3
Crossword Puzzle

There is a management discipline that is missing in many companies. Senior executives who create in their organizations a coherent and integrated portfolio of initiatives, and the project champions who help them do so, will be the winners in the serious game of large-scale organizational change.

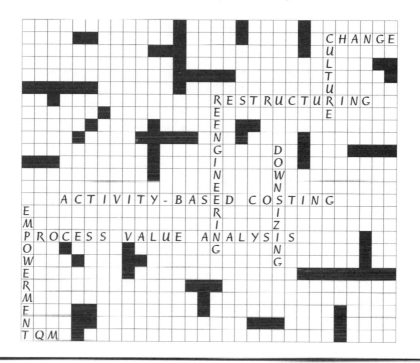

Leaders Do It

As we conducted our research, this paradox emerged like a lion into our agenda of issues. Many of the leaders we interviewed voiced frustration with both those who resist any change and those who want to change everything. One CEO, having taken over a large multinational company during a period of turmoil, said, "I spent the first four months here talking to people and searching out what in our organization and its past could be counted on as we ready this company for the next century." Oddly enough, he found his answer in a decades-old document describing the company's mission and objectives. He was thrilled to be able to pull complete phrases from this enduring script in rearticulating their mission and vision for the future. He recognized the power of drawing on their rich traditions as they create their plans for the year 2000.

We interviewed other senior executives using this very same technique—drawing upon decades-old "legacy" manuscripts describing the traditional strengths of their organizations in order to articulate anew their vision for the decades ahead. Their goal was to focus attention on what is enduring in their heritage, to build pride in their past.

> **Change, almost always painful, can be carried out nonetheless with dignity and with pride in one's past.**

And let there be no mistakes, these leaders are carrying out *major* transformations—restructuring their organizations and repositioning them in their markets. There is no confusion among their employees about the need to change. There is little risk that anyone will see these actions as an excuse to drag their feet. Change is under way. Major change. And it is being carried out in the most positive manner possible. Painful, yes. But with dignity and pride as well.

The Way Ahead

We hope to have sparked your interest in the relationship between change and stability. And we trust your instincts support the idea that positive and aggressive change can be magnified by building upon effective sources of stability. What remains, then, is to explore what elements of your business model you might count on to support vigorous change; what aspects of your organization can you use as stepping stones over the white-water turmoil of our business environment in the decade ahead.

Three

Fortifying Change with Stability

So many formulas for success carry a sting in their tail.

Charles Handy
in *The Age of Paradox*

Six Sources of Stability

For all of the reasons we have been discussing—not least to manage change effectively—smart companies have begun to value the anchors of stability that are almost always present, if you look for them, even in rapidly changing circumstances. From our research and our work with clients, we have identified six potential sources of stability that can help balance the change/stability paradox and allow change programs to succeed. The following pages discuss these six factors, the foundations upon which to promote positive and lasting change. But first, we want to make two recommendations that have emerged from our client work:

> **Search out and identify those elements of your business model that will not (should not!) change.**

1. Search out and identify those elements of your business model that will not (*should not!*) change as your company undergoes transformation.
2. Use that stable foundation as a source of confidence, of initiative, and of courage to create really dramatic change where you need it.

It is of course unlikely that all six of the following elements of your organization can serve as a foundation for change. Indeed, some may have to undergo substantive change. Consider each carefully, as well as other fundamental characteristics of your organization. In a world becoming more chaotic each day, successful transformation will depend on your ability to skillfully integrate them into a solid foundation for change.

1. Culture

Organizational culture has a major impact on employee behavior. While a change in culture is often desirable, some elements of almost any organization's culture are sources of stability. (For a complete discussion of culture, see Part Four of *The*

Figure 3.1
Six "Stepping Stones"

There are at least six potential foundations upon which to promote positive and lasting change.

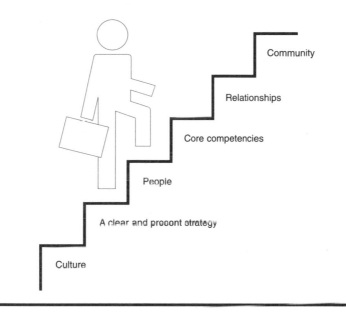

Paradox Principles.) Companies with successful change programs identify, communicate, and build on elements of culture such as deeply held beliefs, accepted norms, and commonly rewarded values that need not change and will almost certainly support change programs. In some companies, innovation is an enduring value; in others, intimate knowledge of the customer; in still others, employee development. Winning companies have definable core values that every successful employee acts on, consciously or not.

It is important to understand these values and to reinforce even their smallest manifestation in the company's everyday life. These values must be real, commonly held, and deeply felt if they are to have real impact on behavior. Genuine values are not often violated. When they are violated, high drama can be the result. If deeply rooted values are openly questioned and tested, fireworks often result and messages are sent by management to the workforce—or by the workforce to management. The result can be positive. It can also be a very rough patch for all concerned.

Some organizations bring in an outside CEO or top management group to drive change from what appears to be a neutral position: no company baggage, great track records. Unfortunately, this strategy entails a serious risk. Will the outsiders be able to recognize and abide by long-established values of the culture? William Agee's much discussed dismissal at Morrison-Knudsen in February 1995 serves as an illustrative "worst practice." As the news stories unfolded, we noted a detail, nothing more than a detail, that spoke worlds. Just as Agee was pressing his managers to stretch themselves, he was also eliminating a cultural icon by replacing the portrait of the much-respected company founder at corporate headquarters with a $10,000 picture of himself and his wife. His fellow managers were offended—as they should have been. Imagine the resistance to change that *this change* aroused. The message was vastly counterproductive.

A company's culture provides a crucial template against which managers and employees can measure their actions. The template includes an often unwritten series of management/ employee covenants, as well as norms of personal behavior and professional performance. These guidelines are easily recognized in organizations such as Nordstrom's and Wal-Mart, where strong cultures create a framework that empowers individuals. Without such guidelines, complete freedom soon degenerates into anarchy. When the template for management and employee actions is so well understood that it is all but second nature, a change effort can proceed more quickly and participants' responses are likely to be more flexible.

> A company's culture provides a crucial template against which managers and employees can measure their actions.

Building on a Culture

Kerm Campbell was the first CEO of the furniture manufacturer Herman Miller to be recruited from the outside. He was brought in to reverse a period of declining revenues. While he was in tune with the company's culture from the beginning ("It was essentially the culture I would have built myself had I been given free rein") he took swift action to change it somewhat to accomplish two important strategic goals—expanding international sales and getting product to market faster. Doing so did not require a complete transformation but rather limited changes that reinforced a unique company asset: its employees. Campbell restated the company's mission to read as follows: "To liberate the human spirit of all people at Herman Miller so that we can furnish environments to our customers that help them achieve their full potential." As Campbell said in a speech before Peter Drucker's class at Claremont College:

"Times have simply gotten too tough for any company to allow even the slightest amount of talent or skill or knowledge available to go to waste . . . [so] we have made several changes to try to release more of the potential I see in all the people there. Instead of a small executive committee, we now have a large business operations team. Instead of limiting certain information to officers and directors, we have opened up the group to include all 'key communicators,' no matter what their rank. 'Cross-functional teams' are now the norm . . . several teams have formed and— more important—have disbanded . . . ."[1]

The results of the two-year program spoke for themselves: while total sales increased 11.4 percent, net income rose 83.1 percent and return on assets doubled.

2. A Clear and Present Strategy

Mention strategy to many managers and they think "strategic plan." They conjure up a burdensome annual rite, relevant in some ways but ponderous and detached from the realities of the business. In a competitive environment that shifts monthly, a highly structured plan seems almost beside the point, and it is true that many plans today aren't built with enough flex.

But here we are speaking of *strategy*, not the strategic plan. The right strategy has nothing to do with a plan, everything to do with providing a baseline that allows the organization to change before the environment forces change. A good strategy is dynamic (not static), focused on the external environment (not inward), explicitly stated (not kept in the head of the leader), and lean enough to be held in the mind, heart, and gut all at once. A good strategy is consistent with experienced managers' assessments of the organization's capabilities. No fluff: We can execute this strategy. A good strategy doesn't take years to develop. And it is most certainly prerequisite to successful organizational change.

There is an old saw in business about the value of planning: "A good plan is worth developing, even if you throw it away the minute it's completed." The point, of course, is that the planning process leads to worthwhile insights. True enough—except when those insights are the sole possession of a few senior managers and staff planners. Integral to strategy is a vision that connects with your employees. Tom Stewart of *Fortune* magazine wrote recently to this point in an issue covering the demands on today's leaders. Stewart explored a paradox facing senior executives: the need to maintain a stable, enduring vision while at the same time initiating major change and addressing those problems that can defeat you long before a vision is achieved. Stewart notes:

> **A good strategy is dynamic, focused on the external, explicitly stated, and lean enough to be held in the mind, heart, and gut all at once.**

> **Without taking his eyes off the horizon, the leader must watch where he steps.** . . . Nothing cripples an army faster than stony details like pay policies and information systems; leaders rightly fear niggling distractions. The solution, says AT&T's Jerre Stead: "Work backwards from the vision." Don't just preach the vision, manage it: Measure your followers by their concrete progress toward realizing the vision, and insist that they do the same.[2]

Figure 3.2
Strategic Alignment

All organizations have a strategy. Many fewer achieve a really powerful alignment of all components of their business model, as is necessary to bring about large-scale change.

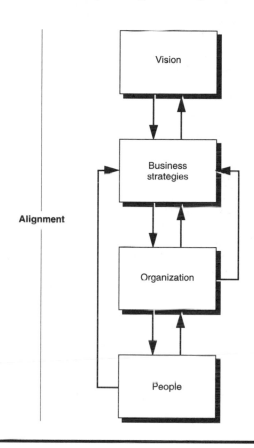

3. People

Under Kerm Campbell, Herman Miller, Inc., sponsored some very innovative research on its workforce, which identified four basic types of employees:

- The Visionary
- The Catalyst

- The Cooperator
- The Stabilizer

Visionaries and Catalysts act as change agents. Visionaries are creative individuals who conceive and communicate an inspiring but attainable whole out of the disparate materials of organizational aspirations, resources, and experience. The best Visionaries bind the possible with the heretofore unimagined. They are not romantics but realists who believe in the power of progress.

Catalysts move the organization forward. True dynamos, they are constantly thinking about possibilities and the need for growth. They spark the organization into life, again and again.

Change is facilitated by the Cooperators. They work to bring people together, harmonize efforts, and build consensus. They also pull the laggards through the process of change.

This is a set of engaging insights. But we believe that the rarest insight of the Herman Miller study is that it recognizes Stabilizers. They, too, play a critical role in change processes. Stabilizers are not stragglers blocking change. On the contrary, they facilitate change by continually creating and communicating models to interpret the changing environment and promote understanding. They act as beacons, shedding light on clarity and structure and articulating what can be counted on. Basing their opinions on logic and information, they create successive versions of order that are persuasive and stabilizing as the process moves forward.[3]

Organizations with visionary, catalyzing leaders can be high performers—but only when Stabilizers are in place. Make sure you have a few in positions of influence as you undertake major change.

With the retirement of chairman Edwin L. Artzt, Procter & Gamble recently selected John Pepper, its president, to succeed him. As *The Wall Street Journal* reported, this surprised some observers who believed the choice would be the reportedly

---

Stability-Enabled Change at Price Waterhouse

In 1988, our current vice-chairman for consulting services assumed his position. While we had a satisfactory consulting practice, he knew that sweeping change was necessary to position us for the inevitable industry consolidation of the decade ahead. Without question a relentless agent of change, he is the sort of man who is constantly in the field stirring things up, breaking down barriers, challenging us to do more. And he has been successful in bringing about a wholesale transformation in our practice.

The change process he produced, which at times felt like a close brush with a moving freight train, would have overwhelmed any group of professionals without the stabilizing influence of a key lieutenant. This Stabilizer provided structure by working relentlessly to document and refine the developing strategy, enumerate goals and performance measures, and clarify decision rights. This was crucial as we developed a more focused approach to key markets. It gave us just enough stability to guide and channel our efforts.

---

more aggressive Durk Jager, who will become president and COO. Pepper is known for his strong skills in managing people and for his ability to build consensus; Jager is perceived as a forceful agent of change. We can guess the board's logic in creating this team: a forceful agent of change coupled with the stabilizing influence of a leader who can help make it happen.

The CEO wields appreciable influence and is free to move among these roles. Clever CEOs can play all four roles. They are expected to be the chief Visionary and Catalyst. And those who understand the difficulties of large-scale organizational change know that they need on occasion to step into the Cooperator role to overcome resistance. They can also be Stabilizers. Whereas Jack Welch at GE and Michael Eisner at Disney have expedited positive change over the last decade, the story is often much different at companies no less intent on change but led by a succession of bosses. A new boss brings new direction. Too many new bosses can generate enormous swings in strategy and style. Change, yes, but with it missteps, lost energy, frustration.

4. Core Competencies

The concept of core competencies, introduced by Gary Hamel and C. K. Prahalad, is good theory.[4] It provides a useful way of thinking about organizations and sheds light on a primary source of stability. Core competencies are *integrated bundles of skills* that enable a company to deliver a particular benefit to customers. For example, one of Sony's core competencies is often termed "pocketability." That organization has developed world-class expertise in miniaturization—so much so that all of us can at once picture a Walkman and a portable CD, and all of us assume that Sony can and will produce further market-leading innovations in miniaturized consumer electronics.

We referred earlier to Michael Eisner's success in transforming Disney. Eisner carried out this exercise in managerial brilliance in part by carefully building on the Disney magic of prior decades. The folks at Disney describe one of their core competencies as "imagineering." For decades they have brought to life the fantasies of young and old on film, in records, and in theme parks. Their special "imagineering" competency is a distinctive integration of creative, engineering, and marketing skills. Somehow these men and women manage to fuse their left brain to their right brain and connect directly to the soft spot in our hearts.

Yet when Eisner took the helm, company performance was off. The stock price was languishing, a takeover was not out of the question. As Eisner transformed Disney into an international powerhouse of creative production, he and his managers were careful not to walk away from the core skills integral to "imagineering."

Spread competencies too thin and you may wish you hadn't.

The "best practice" of leveraging core competencies is powerful. But you must be careful. Correctly evaluating core competencies is crucial. Impose too narrow a focus, and you can overlook or even destroy competencies. Competencies tied to a specific product can produce the illusion of flexibility, of potential applications where in fact little can be accomplished. Spread competencies too thin and you may wish you hadn't.

Caring for Competencies: The International Division, Caremark, Inc.

Active in seven countries on three continents, the International Division of Caremark confronts daily the challenge of developing entirely new and highly regulated businesses in the most diverse health care environments of the world.

When Caremark was spun out of Baxter International, the International Division had only a few months to get its arms around its newly independent operations worldwide. The sense of sudden change was profound. Caremark units were leaving a large, well-established, nationally centralized infrastructure and entering a truly international organization. Just as significant was the change in focus from making and distributing products to delivering health-related services. There was little common culture, no sense of community, and no common strategy. The division leader, Michelle Hooper, focused on competencies and relationships as she built short-term strategies and assembled a cadre of people on whom she could depend.

In every country in which Caremark operates, it has to create the alternate health care site market. This requires deft maneuvering among government regulators, entrenched traditional health care providers, and large funding institutions like insurance companies. The company brings to the market its recognized competencies in alternate site and home health care and its ability to obtain and manage outcomes data. There were, however, no strategies on the local or international level that built on these core competencies.

Hooper identified the core capabilities needed for the organization as a whole and where they had to be located in order to be effective. She identified owners of those capabilities at each level and got the country managers to agree to a contract of performance between herself and them. This focus on core competencies allowed her to circle back quickly to each of the countries and make explicit the strategies the organizations had been following implicitly for some time.

A key stake in the ground for the International Division from its very beginning has been its relationship with the medical community in each country where it operates. Its immediate successes in Germany and immediate problems in Japan were directly related to the strength of its relationships with key medical professionals. Where it succeeds, Caremark is closely connected—if not fully integrated—with its business partners.

The business environment of Caremark International changes daily. Opportunities and threats are constantly evolving. Worldwide operations keep the division open for business 24 hours a day. The division's ability to grow and prosper as it has over the past three years is evidence that it can master change by carefully maintaining stability in key elements of the operation.

It is possible in the course of a large-scale transformation to destroy competencies that took decades to develop. One context in which this can occur is "postmerger integrations." Large organizations undergoing a merger and preoccupied with negotiations and political positioning seldom have a sound plan for integrating operations immediately after the deal is done. Sometimes only years after a merger is formally concluded will integration begin in earnest. When disparate cultures, unique resources, and foreign capabilities are thrust together, core competencies can be overlooked. If so, they may wither and—in the worst case—become so polluted by noncompetencies as to die altogether.

We witnessed this pattern in the merger of two large service organizations. The merger was built around conventionally sound logic: additional scale, access to each other's unique markets, and so on. However, core competencies were overlooked. The organizations were shoved together on day one with few precautions to safeguard competencies such as the high-end, high-quality service capabilities—with customers to match—that were a major asset of one of the merged entities. As management positions were assumed by people with no clue about the needs of these high-end customers and no resources to serve them, quality faltered to the point that customers left in droves.

It is also possible to think about your organization's core competencies in a way that is too narrow or product-specific. This mistake can lead you to abandon capabilities that actually have a future. 3M does not view its core competency as the manufacture and distribution of Scotch tape. The company wisely views its competencies more broadly: solving problems and creating solutions with adhesives. Similarly, in 1975 Hewlett-Packard was an industry leader in instrumentation. Had the company viewed itself solely in that light, however, you might not be using that HP printer on your desk.

BF Goodrich decided to leave tire manufacturing. It understood its core competency was not manufacturing tires but rather its ability to engineer polymers in a variety of ways and develop flexible production capabilities to fit customer needs.

BF Goodrich is now an aerospace and specialty chemicals company. And its Specialty Chemical Division offers a shining example of the power of that company's transformation based on core competencies. It includes three groups—Specialty Additives; Specialty Plastics; and Sealants, Coatings, and Adhesives—each delivering value based, in part, on those core competencies developed over years of tire production. The transformation continues, but on a stable foundation of skills, resources, and organizational wisdom built over decades.

Seen too broadly or spread too thin, core competencies can lead you astray. Many companies have misread their capabilities or overreached, only to have to retrench quickly after failing at a new venture. Following the 1970s oil price scare, oil companies were among the greatest offenders in reaching far past their core capabilities. They defined their competency in the broadest possible terms—"finding and exploiting energy sources"—and entered a maze of new ventures that had little or nothing to do with petroleum exploration, refining, and selling. The new ventures included everything from solar energy to coal. In the 1980s, many of the companies exited these businesses and refocused on core competencies, more strictly defined—but applying these competencies on an aggressively global basis.

Eastman Kodak, as well, is finding in its core capabilities a source of strength as it rebuilds. Since 1994, CEO George Fisher has been guiding a major transformation. Its central theme (and, we believe, a productive one) is a move back to this century-old company's core market: photography. By 1992, Kodak had acquired a host of operations far from this long-successful market focus, such as those selling cleaning products and aspirin. Fisher is revitalizing the company by sharpening its market focus, streamlining operations, and updating technologies and product development capabilities. We should add that no company in today's fast-moving environment can "move back" to a former competency as if that competency has remained just where it was. Kodak is moving *forward* to reassert its command of core competencies where they are today.

5. Relationships

An organization's network of relationships is a critical component of today's business model. It should not be overlooked as a source of strength and stability. The ability to deliver great value, maintain flexibility, and keep costs to a minimum is driving all of us to build a web of relationships with our customers, our suppliers, and, in a few cases, even our competitors. None of us can afford to fully integrate within a single organization the array of capabilities and assets needed in our complex business world. Confederation, collaboration, or close integration with business partners is imperative; it is also a source of stability.

> **Confederation, collaboration, or close integration with business partners is imperative; it is also a source of stability.**

The Japanese business model is a powerful example of the network as a source of stability. The vast network of supplier relationships maintained by Japanese manufacturing giants such as Matsushita and Mitsubishi is an enormous competitive asset. Change as they must and as they will, these great enterprises will maintain the ties they have developed with hundreds of suppliers and service providers.

Among your organization's relationships, none may be of more value than your core customers. The value of enduring customer relationships has focused the energy and concern of many of our clients in the last decade as each has discovered the special rewards possible with repeat purchases.

Stable customer relationships more than facilitate change. They can drive change. Bringing long-term customers directly into the change process (seldom done, despite its compelling wisdom) can speed change and focus your efforts directly on what will add greater value to your selling proposition.

The process of involving customers in creating change requires a different approach to the relationship. Managers need not just "listen to the voice of the customer." They need to relentlessly pursue the *evidence* customers rely on to purchase

A Stable Network—a Source of Strength

Honda of America has emulated the Japanese example in developing what is arguably the most successful supplier network in the United States. First begun in the late 1970s, before most of the other Japanese transplants, it now includes some 300 companies in 15 states, as well as other relationships around the globe. What ties this network together is not a binding contract: it is the hard core of mutual economic advantage, nurtured and reinforced time and again. The key building blocks of the relationship are:

1. **Tangible incentives and benefits.** Honda provides consistent business and the long-term possibility of export opportunities. The company has paid its bills so consistently over time that one executive stated flatly, "If Honda asked us to build a certain plant to accommodate a long-term strategy, I would start tomorrow. That's how certain I am of their sincerity and track record." Honda passes along the insights of its productivity improvement program (termed "BP") and sends trainers into each supplier to teach it. Suppliers are so happy with the system that they have asked Honda to teach it even in their factories with no direct Honda business. Eventually, the relationship evolves to the extent that suppliers help out with future strategy: Some suppliers are currently working with Honda designers on future models that will be sold after the year 2000.

2. **Clear articulation and reinforcement of standards.** Honda's expectations are high. Standards are translated into a system of performance measurement that ensures a connection between the purchasing network and Honda's long-term strategy. In addition, Honda requires suppliers to use only subcontractors it certifies.

Honda has worked long and hard to make certain that the level of involvement with its suppliers is deep and long-lasting, extending from the purchasing relationship into shared strategic planning and product development. Its technology transfer program is two-way, with ideas flowing back and forth. And the benefits and insights of the program are so well known and far-reaching that suppliers are teaching them to their own suppliers, thus expanding the network beyond the original group.

This network provides Honda of America a formidable source of strength, a competitive advantage—but also a foundation for future transformation.

and then repurchase. The best practitioners use sophisticated survey work to ferret out just how and why customers make purchase decisions. Casual customer surveys are inadequate because many customers don't easily articulate why they buy.

Stable customer relationships more than facilitate change.

Innovative organizations are also positioning customers as stakeholders in change programs by giving them influence over just what changes are made in products and processes. If you want to turbo-charge your change effort, invite a few key customers to the next meeting at which change is discussed. We guarantee that it will be a very different meeting. Use your stable customer base to propel change.

6. Community

Managers are continuing to experiment with varied organizational structures in response to more fluid competitive and market environments. They are also finding that they need to think about changing their approach to structural experimentation. More flexibility is needed than in the past; flexibility must be built into the very *concept* underlying a structure. Further, more awareness of employee needs is required in order to stabilize the business. Structure has more to do with attitude than with impressively rationalized "org" charts. As rigid structures retreat, community gains importance.

Given the pace of change in many of today's markets, companies are discovering that they fare better with fluid organizational structures. To undo a rigid organization only to create another rigid organization that briefly matches new competitive conditions is not the future of management. The time-honored formulae—decentralization, centralization, functions, processes—do not meet the need if they are taken as independent and comprehensive.

Yet the employee demand for some sense of permanence— a sense of *community*—has become far more explicit in recent years. This demand intensifies the need for structure. Here again we encounter the core paradox of this chapter: change and stability. Stripped of all sense of community, organizations become sour places to spend one's day. On the other hand, employees benefit from fluid structures because such structures can confer a greater sense of personal responsibility. And yet again, employees want to know that when they look up from their work, the organization around them will not have been reconfigured beyond recognition. They need some sense of permanency to shore them up.

Building Cohesiveness and Community at Chiat/Day

Chiat/Day, the advertising agency highly regarded for its creative work (and that was recently purchased by Omnicom's TBWA Advertising unit), recently chose to create a *virtual organization* as a mechanism to help enable its strategy—*create great creative.* And it didn't make the mistake of ignoring the issues that can arise from a more fluid, loosely structured organization in which employee interaction and collaboration are not a natural consequence of the traditional office environment. It recognized the need for interaction, a sense of cohesiveness, and community.

One example: Chiat/Day builds "project rooms" (almost like war rooms) for each major account. Project rooms serve as the central body of knowledge about a client, as opposed to a traditional agency where knowledge is dispersed into functional units—creative, market research, and so on. In the project room, the account team shares all information, from research files to meetings to creative concepts (some even plastered on bulletin boards). Employees are using less written correspondence and more personal contact. They tend to go to lunch in groups of four or five rather than running out alone or with one other person. Since no one sits in a "department" any longer, there are more cross-functional friendships, leading to greater productivity.

Interestingly, the project room also provides a comfort much like your "homeroom" did in school days. According to Lori Coots, director of administration, when teams are facing tough issues with clients, there's a sense of familiarity and security to be gained by gathering in the project room along with fellow team members. Alternatively, when employees are feeling more adventurous and willing to take greater risks with clients, there's a greater inclination to venture, literally, into newer territory—spending more time at the client's office and simply linking back into the office via technology.

Balancing this paradox requires a new approach to organization. It starts with the same goal: to maximize the potential for peak performance. But it works to achieve a dynamic middle ground between the poles of the paradox. If structure must be decreased, then alternative forms of community must be increased along lines that are functional, robust, and persuasive. The most sophisticated organizations are beginning to realize that structural change must be accompanied by creative actions to maintain an ongoing sense of community.

Putting Your Stakes in the Ground

Successful organizations use a combination of these six sources of stability to allow meaningful change to occur despite seemingly chaotic conditions. The managers we interviewed point out several keys to deciding which strengths to build on and how to go about it. The goal is to understand the organization's strengths, build all available certainty and stability into your change effort, and align the organization around your strategies and objectives—while the organization is operating at speed and accelerating.

Know Thyself

Drawing strength from stability and using it to promote change is not an automatic sequence. You have to know your business intimately. External points of reference are crucial in managing change well—for example, keeping a market-focused perspective and letting customers drive your transformation. On the other hand, examining your core—a sort of corporate introspection—cannot be safely neglected.

Look at the history of your organization as a pageant of past triumphs and a source of current strengths. Legends of the corporate world, such as 3M, literally dote on their past. Their attitude suggests almost a secular religion. This embrace of the good things of the past is a source of real strength and, paradoxically, helps the company move forward. The easiest explanation for 3M's dynamic culture is an ingrained taste for innovation. But that doesn't quite say it. At 3M, it is generally agreed that there are no boundaries to what can happen.

Change without Introspection

Novacare, a rehabilitation services provider, recently restructured its field operations. Management sought to significantly change how its therapists conduct their work. However, the leadership neglected to do some fundamental introspection.

The company had grown by acquiring small, independent rehabilitation clinics. The therapists in these clinics were naturally accustomed to working, and working well, without the constrictions of a corporate structure. In its earlier years, the company attracted many therapists because it left them alone to do their daily work yet provided the advantages of a large corporation, a steady income, and benefits. However, as the company grew, management decided to bring increased standardization and control into the clinics. Changes were made without considering their impact on a crucial source of strength and stability, the independence of the therapists.

The changes were far-reaching. The results were lamentable. The turnover of therapists approached 40 percent; the stock price fell almost 50 percent. Had management thought more deeply about the stable values and expectations of the therapists, much of this pain might have been avoided. John Foster, the CEO, admits: "Candidly, last spring we tried to do too much too quickly, and that caused some paralysis." To stabilize the business, management doubled back to strengthen relationships with field personnel and intensify their training in ways that they welcomed. These steps have reduced the company's attrition rate and put it back on the right path.

Elements of your next winning strategy will almost certainly be found in many different quarters. In the past, that shining past, there will be inspiration. Among the smaller-scale strategies being implemented by line managers, you may discover the source of your organization's next market-leading competitive advantage. By constructing scenarios of the future of each competitive field in which you are engaged, you are likely to surface some of your best management thinking.

Look to daily operations to understand sources of strength. In thinking about change, management often forgets to consider first what it already does well as the basis for the next move forward. The strengths and stability of daily operations can be lost from sight by management groups that have succumbed to endless corporate psychoanalysis. Moreover, just as small emergent strategies can help management find larger strategies that work, so small changes within operations may provide insights into how larger transformation activities can be effective. After all, operations are almost always in transformation.

Look for the best managers within your organization. Which departments or functions seem to do well despite the odds? Which managers seem to have the most perceptive vision of the future? When asked to be part of a transformation exercise, which are best able to balance their operational duties with their roles on the transformation team?

And, finally, confront reality. It is easy to delude oneself. We're all highly vested in the companies we've built. The emperor's clothes are strewn all over the landscape of today's organizations. Unfortunately, the pain and hard work accompanying real change require a level of candor that too few executives exercise. While there is lots of talk about slaying sacred cows, most die of old age. In deference to hurt feelings or employee morale, some managers deny reality, avoid confrontation, and communicate with spin control in high gear. Honesty and openness are fundamental in identifying your strengths and other sources of stability.

Confront reality. It is easy to delude oneself.

Create Certainty Where You Can

Most of the managers we've interviewed believe this to be true: *People detest uncertainty.* We find that employees are better able to accept and deal with bad news than with uncertainty. Change is frightening. Worse, it's debilitating. It saps the initiative of employees as they fret over worst-case scenarios. People need something to grab on to before they will let go of their old behavior. Often they seek sanctuary in work—Maslow told us that years ago. Safety is our primary motivation.

Use that instinct. Tell your employees what you know rather than the abridged version, except in very delicate areas where you will clearly know what can and cannot be said. Better yet, tell them what you *all* must do to succeed and clearly define the results for which they are accountable. Then the changes you seek become the safe way, the path to certainty.

Surprisingly enough, benchmarking can be a source of stability. World-class companies, traditionally more willing to look beyond their confines for best practices, are relying more on it. By sifting data and experience from a rich corporate sample, such companies identify a best practice and institutionalize it, initially on a pilot scale, then companywide if that makes sense. This approach generates stability in three different ways. In the first place, the commitment to investigation—to figuring out, objectively, what is best—can become a standard operating mode: managers and employees simply know that this is "how we do things around here." Secondly, benchmarking reveals that the grass is not always greener and more fragrant elsewhere. Concepts and processes within the organization may meet the test of benchmarking or come so close that everyone feels, with justice, that the company is grounded in excellence. Third, benchmarking can reveal shortcomings. But here again, the process generates certainty because people now know the direction.

Your employees detest uncertainty.

Conclusion

The change/stability paradox offers an intriguing challenge to managers today. At a time when we are bombarded by the message of change, when management gurus get rich with books advocating *chaos*, when "adhocracy" is seriously discussed as an alternative to "command and control," it seems almost cowardly to talk of stability, long-held values, core strengths, enduring relationships. Champions of stability have lost legitimacy in some management circles.

We disagree with this attitude emphatically. Resolutely.

Look for what is admirable in your organization. Build upon what is solid. Combine many lesser strengths into real competitive advantage. And, of course, change what must be changed. The paradox of change/stability is productively lived by keeping each side of the paradox intact.

Notes

1. Kerm Campbell, "Changing the Meaning of Management," presentation at Claremont College, October 1993.

2. Thomas A. Stewart, "How to Lead a Revolution," *Fortune*, November 28, 1994, p. 48.

3. Cecil Williams, David Armstrong, and Clark Malcolm, *The Negotiable Environment: People, White-Collar Work and the Office* (Ann Arbor: Facility Management Institute, 1985), pp. 27–39.

4. Gary Hamel and C. K. Prahalad, "The Core Competence of the Corporation," *Harvard Business Review*, May–June 1990, p. 79.

PART THREE

To Build an Enterprise,
Focus upon the Individual

A man must make his opportunities, as oft as find it.

Francis Bacon

The nail that sticks up, will be hammered down.

Japanese proverb

Four

One Individual at a Time

Comrades! We must abolish the cult of the individual decisively, once and for all.
Nikita Khrushchev, February 25, 1956

W hat of ourselves? The role of the individual within the organization has changed dramatically since World War II. The "organization man" of the 1950s was seen—and often saw himself—as a minor cog in a clockwork of function, procedure, hierarchy, and structure. In his place is today's harried manager, male or female, asked to move at warp speed, piling up frequent flier miles like an airline pilot, lacking security and structure, challenged to get it done with little influence over many who determine his or her success.

> **Today's harried manager moves at warp speed, piles up frequent flier miles, lacks security and structure, and is asked to get it done with little influence over many who determine his or her success.**

Similarly, the plant worker of decades past who left his brains at the gate in order to survive the mindless repetition of Taylorism gone mad is soon to be history as well. Today's employees are invited to participate, challenged to think, asked to create, pushed to improve continuously, and encouraged to manage themselves. At both the top and the bottom of the organization, accountability for results is increasing. The pressure is on. The stakes are high. Another restructuring, another CEO sacked—these are the headlines almost daily.

The changes have been bittersweet for the individual. Over the last decade, the importance of people in achieving organizational goals has been reaffirmed and celebrated. No one— not even the contrarian management gurus—doubts the rich potential to be tapped when talented people are better employed. Most managers today applaud the employee as *the* key resource. Unfortunately, they also want fewer of them. As one manager put it, "We're creating better jobs for fewer people."

The classic deal—individual loyalty in return for lifetime employment—is a thing of the past. It has died in the downsizings. A key reality of our New Economy is written on the "pink slips" given to hundreds of thousands of individuals displaced, downsized, and now departed from organizations from which they expected to retire.

How Things Compare to a Few Years Ago

Our Survey Research Center asked a national sample of employees how their jobs have changed over the past few years. Here are some of the findings:

More	Same	Less	
72%	22%	4%	Importance of multiple, diverse skills to my success
69	25	5	Importance of specialized skills to my success
68	24	7	Responsibility in my job
52	32	16	Job stress
48	30	19	Meetings attended
42	42	16	Hours worked

The biggest changes are the need for more diverse and specialized skills and for increased responsibility. If it sounds as if the business environment is putting more pressure on the individual, you're right. The statistics reflecting greater job stress and longer hours at work tell the same story. Other data gathered in the survey concerning the balance between work and personal life, clarity of job responsibilities, rewarding work, and job security show little improvement over the past few years.

A different cut through the data shows that the situation is gloomier at larger companies. Individuals at companies with over 1,000 employees are more likely to report that their responsibility has increased, the balance between work and personal life has not improved, and their jobs are both more stressful and less rewarding. Further, the past few years have been more difficult for those below management ranks. While reporting nearly the same increase in hours worked and job stress as managers, this population is far less likely to report that jobs are more rewarding, more secure, or better defined.

There is more than a touch of schizophrenia across the business world. Senior executives speak passionately about people making the difference—while the employee base is cut back to 40 percent of its size just a decade ago. Managers talk admiringly about "their team"—while health care benefits are quietly scaled back. Reengineering task forces use dazzling new analytical methods, but the result is too often familiar: payroll cuts and the same old tasks piled on those who remain. The message seems to be: "We really like those of you left standing."

The Paradox

A cause of cynicism is that individual accomplishments do not typically get as much notice as those of teams. Individual accomplishments are still applauded in occasional bursts of recognition, but for many this is rare. One plant worker resentfully put it this way: "Yesterday I was a [expletive deleted] from the union; today I'm a *team associate*." The importance of people has been celebrated, but only in the context of valuing teams. There has been much of this. Maybe too much. Today the success of an individual's career is sometimes viewed as the sum total of team victories of which he or she has been a part.

Based on our collective experience and on manager interviews (each an individual), we believe that single-minded focus on teams is about to be turned on its head. Teams don't think. Organizations don't act. Groups don't decide. *Individuals* think, act, decide, produce, and serve customers. They do all these things *together*, no question about that, just as they have for centuries. But too much today is routinely attributed to teams, with the result that the real source of success is overlooked. Every outstanding team gathers talented, motivated *individuals* with good social skills, who work together to achieve an objective.

Teams don't think.

Organizations don't act.

Groups don't decide.

The larger team—the organization itself—begs still another question about the welfare of the individual. By and large, the organization is doing well. Companies that have undergone aggressive transformations often show greater profits for their effort. The many stories trumpeting the success of reengineering are impressive: costs reduced dramatically, cycle times collapsed by 75 percent, even some revenue gains. But behind many of the successes is a workforce pushed to the brink, people pouring too much of their lives into the job, workers worried about their kids at home while working late, individuals who are out of balance and know it. One employee with whom we spoke had listened recently to a less-than-inspiring presentation by his CEO about change and the "need to get on the train before it leaves the station." This individual told us that his newly reengineered job gives him the impression he's *strapped to the front of the train.*

When they feel free to speak with candor, most managers recognize this trend and know that things must be made right. Many of us know deep down inside that we can't keep pace forever with the change around us. Work is becoming something that could consume us. Managers recognize that better balance is critical. But few are ready to go public. One CEO we interviewed had recently discovered just how confused people are about the level of commitment expected of them. After he published a piece on work/family issues in the company newsletter, employees asked him whether he really meant what he said—was it really OK to put family first? He responded sharply that this was *his* priority.

Figure 4.1
In the Crosshairs

All of us sit in the crosshairs today. We are subject to many organizational pressures — not the least of which are exerted by the hierarchical and the horizontal components of our organizations.

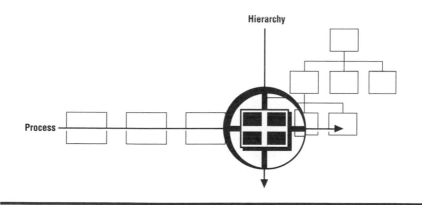

This chapter seeks a better understanding of what all this means for professionals in large organizations. We are people in the middle, and *sometimes in the crosshairs.* The chapter explores how best to manage the tension between individuality and integration, how best to balance individual good with the good of the team or organization. We seek some understanding of the optimal overlap. The paradox?

$$\bullet \ \bullet \ \bullet \ \bullet \ \bullet$$

"To build an organization, focus on the individual."

$$\bullet \ \bullet \ \bullet \ \bullet \ \bullet$$

This paradox points to the mind-bending task of creating a global organization—perhaps one with tens of thousands of employees—while remembering that the building block is the individual. Your employees, one by one, are the most critical components of the organization. The greatest leaders in the decade ahead will look upon the majority and see the one. They will set a vision for the whole that engages the many. They will understand the organization by knowing its people. And they will optimize performance in the aggregate by maximizing the potential of each.

> **The greatest leaders in the decade ahead will look upon the majority and see the one.**

A Contrarian View of Teams

The thought that teamwork is important in business is not new; since we evolved from the single craftsperson to the small enterprise, effective teaming has been important. What *is* new is the dialogue about the use and effectiveness of teams. The hyperbole is not unlike that surrounding any other management doctrine, pushed to the extreme by consultants and theorists who claim teams can work anywhere and amplified by business media that find in this topic both human interest and organizational change. What's more, the term is abused. Ten years ago, the guys from the second shift would point out a recurrent paint spray booth problem. Today, Production

Team 2 raises the issue in a quality circle meeting. There is more ideology than before, but the reality is little different.

We are *not* suggesting that teams are just another fad, soon to lose favor. The benefits of experienced, highly integrated teams are obvious. We needn't repeat all that here. As with every fashionable management theme, however, there is a raft of conventional wisdom about how effective teams are. Our work turns some of this conventional wisdom on its head. Not all teams are successful. And when there is success, it is not all due to teams. Much is simply *assumed* about a team's ability to agree, to decide, to take initiative. One manager put it in starkest terms: "We've formed our teams. Now what?"

The hyperbole about teams is not unlike that surrounding any other management doctrine.

There is, naturally, a mixed history of failure and success. Many teams succeed. But for every well-documented success, there are many small undocumented failures. Responsibility is given without the back-up of money. Teams are formed with no clear purpose. Groups of employees are "empowered"— but with few decision rights. And all of this undermines the effectiveness of individuals *and* teams. One CEO told us he would know that teamwork was fulfilling its promise when teams not only achieve their objectives but form and disband spontaneously. This is happening in few organizations.

There is no question that teams can be a powerful integrating force. But one has to wonder how long the obsession with teams can last in the face of all the changes impacting tomorrow's corporation. Will the highly accomplished, multiskilled individual replace teams? Can you imagine a world in which teams form, perform, and disband so frequently that the notion of teams is lost altogether? Perhaps these thoughts represent a walk on the wild side but, at a minimum, effective teams in the real world will need to be engineered faster than before. They will have to be more event driven, as roles and tasks become more fluid. And stabilizing factors such as a strong culture will become much more important as organizational structures become more fluid.

Five Problems

Team are pervasive. According to a recent survey, 68 percent of *Fortune* 1,000 companies were using self-managed work teams in one form or another in 1994. But not everyone sees teams as effective. Here are some common problems:

1. **Teams assigned to inappropriate tasks.** The greatest error of all is to form a team as a knee-jerk reaction to a problem that an individual ought to tackle. Teams too often reflect a manager's reluctance to take action or to empower some*one* to "get it done." Teams are not appropriate for all tasks.

2. **Inadequate commitment to a clear performance objective.** The single most important determinant of team performance is that each member understand clearly the team's performance goal and that each be fully committed and mutually accountable for its achievement. This is seldom the case. Many teams are simply patchworks of people who would like to achieve an objective but who have no unifying obsession to *get it done.* An important corollary here is that team goals should be explicitly connected to significant issues—and this connection must be ratified by senior management.

3. **Inadequate (and inappropriate) training.** By and large, team training is a mess. People come into teams with diverse experience, technical abilities, and—most important—social skills. Seldom is the training crisply focused on what *this* team needs to know. Training is abundant but often unfocused and unproductive. When we asked one interviewee what he had learned from a series of sessions on self-directed work teams, he responded, "I learned that you need an agenda for meetings"—and in so many words, he added, "and not much else."

4. **Unrealistic management expectations.** When management sees teams as a way to transform the organization beyond the teams' specific goals, the use of teams is likely to disappoint. There is little evidence that teams have changed whole cultures or radically altered employee attitudes toward the organization. Most teams are groups. We've been working in groups for decades amidst cultures strong and weak.

5. **Indecisiveness.** Teams are rarely as decisive as the individuals who make up the team. How *can* they be when they're struggling to gain consensus, make everybody happy, and craft a compromise solution? Teams should produce better ideas. But those ideas will be of little use if they arrive too late.

The Individual

The importance of the individual becomes evident when one examines organizations and teams that are effective and those that are not. We find, for the most part, that ineffective organizations and impotent teams are brimming with dysfunctional individuals. The reverse is true as well: Good people make good teams. Since "dysfunctional" is a tough word, let's clarify its meaning at once in this context. We are not suggesting that ineffective teams are made up of individuals who lack the requisite functional and technical expertises. We are suggesting that individuals in ineffective teams are often unprepared for the social interaction required.

Ineffective organizations and impotent teams are brimming with dysfunctional individuals.

Individuals understand that adding value in a business environment requires two broad areas of skill: (1) technical,

---

Team Efforts

Our Survey Research Center conducted a nationwide poll of employees to gain a better understanding of problems they typically encountered in teams. These were the issues they stated most frequently:

- People with poor communication skills
- People who don't work hard
- People who are difficult to get along with
- People unwilling to tackle the tough issues

Factors directly under employers' control such as resources, time, and authority to do the job were among the least frequently cited problems. *The biggest problems noted by respondents relate to the human element.* Other cuts through the data provide further detail. Management was more likely to cite lack of resources, lack of time, and inability to reach consensus as the primary problems of teams. Those outside the management ranks were more likely to cite lack of hard work, lack of authority, people who don't trust each other, and unwillingness to face tough issues.

functional, or subject matter skills and (2) social skills. The majority of jobs today require both. The assembly line worker who clocked in at 7:00 AM, placed left door panels on car bodies all day, paused to talk with friends at breaks and lunch, and clocked out at 4:00 PM is becoming a thing of the past. Today's workforce and managers spend—and must spend—more of their time working with their peers. Today's business goals cannot be achieved by the quiet technicians of yesterday, toiling away as an integral but isolated element of the process. The flatter, more fluid, process-based structures we seek require much more *effective* social interaction than in the past.

Business organizations have always been social systems. But in the quasi-military hierarchies of the past, communication patterns were less fluid and mostly one-way—down. Much of the interaction that *did* take place, even across functional or organizational boundaries within the same enterprise, was more formal and ruled by a prescribed structure and norms. Informal, mix-it-up negotiation and power sharing were just not as important. As one manager said to us, "In the past, we always shipped grain to the plants on *our* schedule. Today, I need to understand in detail the needs of 10 plant managers and work out shipments with them every few days. I *know* these guys now. I even know some of their families!" This was, we should add, not a voice of regret; he viewed the new situation as more alive, more engaging, better for business.

Teams and the Individual

Understanding individual needs in the context of teams is essential today. As the pace of change increases, teams will form, do their work, and disband much more often than in the past. In fact, the aging model—forming, storming, norming, and performing—will probably have be collapsed to near-nothing. As this pattern begins to prevail, training any *specific team* becomes less efficient. However, developing *individuals* with the right technical skills, a clear sense of strategy, a strong sense of urgency, and good social skills becomes a most important goal. Employees cast in this mold will be able to move freely and effectively from one team to another. In the most volatile environments, team effectiveness will need to be nearly

Whither the Individual?

The role of the individual, like many of our business organizations, is changing rapidly. What one could count on in the past is no longer reliable. This begets tension. Here is a sampling of issues, tensions, solutions.

The Individual versus the Team

Perhaps the greatest tension is that of the individual versus the team. Without any doubt, the relation can be mutually beneficial. But despite all the sloganeering, this may be the toughest one for each of us to manage day to day. We are, in the end, individuals—with individual values, work habits, goals, and aspirations. The best teams draw upon, integrate, and harmonize the aspirations of each team member. But this can only go so far. When the individual's best interest does not coincide with the team's best interest, we're back on that balance beam.

Self-initiative versus Involvement of Others

High-performing individuals maintain a bias for action—this is clearly a trait that supports their success. But never before has there been so much pressure to include others in our decisions, to involve others in our work, and to build consensus. This creates a daily balancing act as we reconcile self-initiative with the need to bring others along and involve them in what we do.

"Be analytical" versus "Be intuitive"

Employers want clear-thinking analysts, but they are also looking for people with another trait—great antennae, natural instinct, keen intuition—that leads to good, speedy judgments. They want you to be both thorough *and* fast. Employers want you to make data-based decisions, but at the same time deal adroitly with ambiguity. This produces tension: Work too long on an issue and you're accused of "analysis paralysis," move too quickly and you're "shooting from the hip." Aren't you?

The Individual versus the Organization

The boundary between organizational life and personal life no longer resembles the Great Wall of China, far from it. Most of our jobs are insatiable in their demands for additional time and effort. You could pour your whole life into work if you're not careful (and you often feel as if you're doing just that, we bet). But is more better? Of course not. As we craft tomorrow's organizations, we need also to craft zones of privacy.

Depth of Skill versus Breadth of Responsibility

Will I need deeper functional or technical skills? Or should I be a generalist? Neither sounds especially appealing in today's world. There is an elusive middle ground—to be a specialist in multiple subjects—and plenty of pressure to achieve that. But who really can? Back to the question of lifestyle: Would the personal cost be tolerable?

spontaneous—that is, so rooted in prior training and experience that team participants know at once what to do and how to form a temporary unity with one another.

Individuals do not forget their wallets and pocketbooks when they enter teams. Money remains an important motivator. A team can't bring home groceries for the family. Ultimately, the most reliable motivator is *individual* compensation and reward. We predict that most of you will avoid the "commune" model in which pay will vary only slightly for individuals who provide vastly different levels of value to your customers, your organization and, yes, their teams. Careful consideration of individual rewards based on individual performance offers a more realistic approach than does setting team and organizational dividends.

> **In the most volatile environments, team effectiveness will need to be nearly spontaneous.**

In the end, how will it be possible to achieve the best of both worlds? How will it be possible to create an effective, integrated organization while making the most of the initiative of the best individuals? Here we are at the heart of the paradox and, as with any paradox, to resolve it we will need to focus our minds simultaneously on the two forces in play: the team and the individual. We know that teams can be effective in integrating the efforts of individuals. We know that high-performance teams are not much more than a grouping of highly skilled, fully developed individuals.

Redefining Commitment and Its Rewards

Amidst all of the changes in business today, one key aspect of the relationship between the individual and the organization is *not* changing—as it must. We are speaking of how to measure individual commitment to the organization. Lotte Bailyn of the Sloan School at MIT provides some of the best thinking on this topic in her book, *Breaking the Mold*. She highlights the imbalance prevalent today:

Further Teachings of the Gyroscope

Figure 4.2
Gyroscope

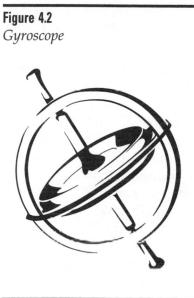

Place a spinning gyroscope on its side. Then place a *second* spinning gyro on the end of the first. They will maintain balance and position. It is marvelous to see. It seems to make no sense. Someone really good at this could probably pile them much higher. The teams of the future will have this delicate poise and temporariness. As long as they are energized by worthwhile tasks, the teams will hang together. When a task is done, the team members will go elsewhere, where again they will need all the poise and energy they can command. The enduring element is the individual.

Managerial definitions of commitment involve more than just good performance while at work. Solid work is not sufficient; commitment to work—an abstract notion, sanctified by tradition—must supersede other commitments. As a manager who had denied permission to an employee to work five hours a week at home remarked: "It's a whole work philosophy. She comes here, she does her work, she does a good job at it. But I know when she goes home, she divorces herself from it all." The employee did good work at the office, but when her manager had to face the realization that she "divorced" herself from work when she went home, he denied her request. Unable to supervise her behavior directly, and uncomfortable with her seemingly circumscribed commitment to the job, he did not trust her with the requested arrangement.[1]

> **To fully resolve this paradox, we will need to focus our minds simultaneously on the two forces in play: the team, the individual.**

Absurd thinking on the part of this manager. Destructive thinking. But this kind of thinking still exists in many office environments. Clock time and other superficial proxies for an individual's commitment to the organization exist in many if not most environments today.

As Bailyn goes on to point out, this view of commitment not only is dysfunctional but undermines the mutual respect and trust we are struggling to establish with our employees. Commitment to the organization, if not kept in balance, can engulf greater portions of one's nonwork life. Some choose freely to devote virtually their lives to a commercial concern. This is their adventure, and it would be a rush to judgment to declare such people to be "workaholic" candidates for a 12-step program. On the other hand, such people do not set the general criteria for dedication and commitment; their choice is individual and adds to the rich texture of individual choices within the organization. When employees are coerced to make a choice along those lines, it indicates a relationship gone awry, an organization out of bounds, and an individual out of balance.

The tragedy of imposing foolish proxies for commitment to the organization is clear when you observe those who are genuinely and passionately committed to their organizations. Get it right and you can inspire individuals and teams to break down walls, do what was thought impossible, achieve remarkable breakthroughs in performance. But this will not happen in an environment where commitment is foolishly gauged. Energy and resources are sapped in fulfilling ritualized representations of dedication that have limited value and, in the end, undermine any genuine passion for work.

Today, equity does not necessarily mean uniformity.

The organization's response to individual commitment is *rewards* or *compensation*. Here, too, less has changed than the changing demographics of our workforce dictate. There is much talk about equal pay for equal work or work of comparable value. But the models used to gauge equity are often vestiges of an era when the workforce was chiefly men with wives at

---

New Structures Require New Perspectives for the Individual: Chiat/Day

As companies move to more flexible, responsive, customer-focused ways of doing business and new structures for accommodating such needs, the impact on the individual employee. (in effect, another type of customer) can be profound and pervasive. The structure not only of the organization but of the employee's life changes. Therefore, along with the structural changes comes a host of behavioral and decision-making changes as well.

Take the case of Chiat/Day, the highly regarded advertising agency. It recently chose to create a *virtual organization* as a mechanism to support its strategy—*create great creative*. This corporate decision, in turn, altered the lives of each of its employees.

For example, the traditional "workday" (versus the "rest of life" day) was thrown out the window. No longer is anyone expected to be in the office or be working at any set hours. Each individual has to structure and compartmentalize not only his or her "workday" (which managers have always been required to do in the corporate world), but the *entire* day. How much is work? Where to work? When to work? Along with the traditional "How to work?"

This can provoke anxiety at first, but eventually becomes quite liberating. According to Lori Coots, director of administration and the person charged with operationalizing Jay Chiat's virtual vision:

> Much more difficult than mastering the new technologies of our virtual structure is the fact that virtualness removes the traditional structure of the workday, and therefore, people must learn to restructure their lives. They must wake up and determine what they need to do today (both work and nonwork), figure out how to do it, and then determine if they need to go to the office. Virtualness requires not only mastering new technologies, but mastering time, and human interconnectedness—knowing how and when to connect with whom you need to in your work and in your life.

With technology, the ability to work anywhere, anytime means that one could literally work round the clock. While innovations such as virtualness create flexibility to balance work and family/personal life, they also create a new responsibility, on the part of both employee and employer. Employees must make very personal decisions about how to discipline themselves and balance their lives. And their employers must now, more than ever, pay attention to balancing long-term productivity with short-term effort.

home tending to the kids or elders. By this dated model, equitable pay amounts to *uniform* pay. Today's much more diverse workforce requires us to rethink pay equity. Equity does not necessarily mean uniformity.

Employees are thinking differently about compensation. The simple pay structures of the past are narrow in comparison to the alternatives that might be attractive to them in the next decade. Flexibility will be of greater value; so too will location (as in telecommuting or teleworking). Health care options will become increasingly important. The simple one-dimensional pay structures of the past (basically, a check every two weeks) are not enough to attract, retain, and equitably compensate tomorrow's workforce.

So What to Do

For ourselves, the individuals writing this book, this may be our most meaningful chapter. It opens up a dialogue—in part with ourselves—on an important set of issues. And our concerns are certainly not just focused upon the stress each of us faces in today's business environment. We really believe that managing paradox effectively demands that we seek two sometimes polar ends at once.

Yes, we seek to make the most of our own potential. But we also seek to maximize the value our institutions create. We aim to make the whole much more powerful than the sum of its parts.

This will not be easy. Imbalance is the norm. But read on. For in the next chapter, we will explore the best ideas put to us by those we interviewed for this book. Like you, individuals each. And each facing the challenges you see bearing down upon you and your organization in the decade ahead.

Note

1. Lotte Bailyn, *Breaking the Mold* (New York: Free Press, 1993), p. 106.

Five

Building the Enterprise

Everything has changed except our thinking.

Albert Einstein

The issues explored in Chapter 4 lead us to conclude that tomorrow's managers will more consciously build high-performance organizations around skilled *individuals*, men and women with outstanding technical and functional abilities and, not least, superior social skills. Teams will continue to be important; the organization and its alliances will represent, as they do today, the larger team. But there must be balance, and this means correcting toward a stronger focus on the individual. In the end, it is the single human being with his or her individual perspective and needs that you must attract, develop, and motivate in order to build an organization. The efforts of many individuals will determine your organization's destiny, although they will undoubtedly operate in team structures with team goals.

> **In the end, it is the single human being that you must attract, develop, and motivate in order to build an organization.**

You can take specific actions to ensure that your organization is an integrated network of skilled, committed individuals. Here are ten.

1. Hire Big People

Success comes when management is constantly improving, rebuilding, and working to perpetuate a championship team through its recruiting efforts. Advertising entrepreneur David Ogilvy found a dramatic way to underline this principle. To send a strong message to his team at Ogilvy & Mather about building the organization, he gave each of his directors a set of nested Russian dolls. You know the kind. A painted wood doll. Open it up and you find a smaller doll; open that one up and you find an even smaller doll; on and on. Around the smallest doll he placed a slip of paper with his message: "If we hire people who are smaller than we are, we will become a company of dwarfs. If we hire people who are bigger than we are, we will become a company of giants." A powerful message, indeed.

Figure 5.1
Russian Dolls

Think if all your managers hired someone more skilled than
themselves; more resourceful; with better social skills. What if
they kept on doing this? You *would* become a company of giants!

**If we hire big people,
we will become a
company of giants.**

Hire big people. Hire someone
bigger than yourself—more talented,
better skilled, more creative. The alternative will only perpetuate a firm
of lesser and lesser people. Build an
organization of giants.

2. Turn Performance Evaluation on Its Head

For decades, performance evaluation has been done by superiors as a way to develop their subordinates. This worked in
a "vertical" environment, where we took direction from the
boss and directed the efforts of others. But now we have spent
billions of dollars creating flatter, more *horizontal* organizations. We must in turn reshape our approach to performance
evaluation. Tomorrow's managers will be effective as much
because of how well they deal with peers and customers as of
their skill in directing their staffs.

A Field Guide for Recruiting in the New Economy: Ten Key Characteristics

Managers today are looking at their people much differently than a decade ago. In our world of rapid change—in which individuals must develop fluid portfolios of functional and technical skills—*personal characteristics* are becoming much more important in selecting and evaluating people. Here is what managers are telling us they want.

1. **Integrity**—*Strict adherence to a code or standard of values.* Integrity is clearly *the* most important individual attribute. Imagine working where you couldn't depend upon the integrity of those around you. How demoralizing and ineffective.

2. **Initiative**—*The instinct to begin or follow through a plan or task on one's own.* With integrity, it's the one to look for most closely in evaluating your people. A heavy dose of initiative often more than compensates for shortcomings and generates success after success.

3. **Intelligence**—*Intellect; smarts; the ability to think on your feet.* Managers tell us that their best people have the ability to focus intently and creatively on solving problems. They see vivid patterns of opportunity where others see a dull field. They have the tenacity to follow through on their ideas. And few of them are shy about communicating.

4. **Social skills**—*Not just getting along with people but getting things* done *through people.* Even the most technical projects depend on one's ability to work with and motivate superiors, peers, and subordinates. Communication skills are fundamental to social skills. The very best people today have the instinct to *invest in their peers* and know that they must work endlessly to *influence peers* in order to reach their objectives.

5. **Resourcefulness**—*The ability to act effectively or inventively, especially in difficult situations.* Getting things done in a volatile world will require resourcefulness—particularly when return on assets puts pressure on the levels of inventory, supplies, and capital you have at hand.

6. **Imagination**—*The power of the mind to form a mental image or concept of something not currently real or present.* Peter Drucker was asked what skills one should learn to become a better manager. He replied, "Learn to play the violin." Drucker's point was to suggest a right-brained activity, outside of the business world, that would cultivate creativity. Imagination and hard work are the keys to creativity.

7. **Flexibility**—*The ability to deal with ambiguity and change.* As

---

A Field Guide for Recruiting in the New Economy: Ten Key Characteristics *(continued)*

structures become more fluid, those who need everything defined, rehearsed, and compartmentalized will find their surroundings alien. Some otherwise talented individuals will be less effective unless they can grow.

8. **Enthusiasm**—*Intense feeling for a subject or cause; ardent eagerness; zeal.* Enthusiasm is critical to working well with others. It helps even in routine situations, let alone in once-in-a-lifetime scenarios. Take, for example, a typical business meeting. What is worse than a low-energy meeting? It can be like death. Genuine enthusiasm is infectious. Foster an epidemic.

9. **A sense of urgency**—*Clear recognition of both the gravity and the enormous potential of the situation.* The cousin of enthusiasm, but different. People with a strong sense of urgency are directed and goal-oriented and don't mind breaking some glass to meet the objective.

10. **"World-view"**—*Perceptiveness; the ability to take in, synthesize, understand, and relate to the world.* You want people with a point of view. People who will take a stand. But their value to the organization is much greater if they can also understand those with an opposing view. Attract and develop managers with good "peripheral vision"— that ability to understand and relate to others, particularly their peers. People with perspective and balance are your kind of people.

Most traditional superior-to-subordinate evaluation processes lack candor. Few of us are spotlessly honest counselors.

> **Now that we are flatter and more *horizontal*, we must in turn reshape our approach to performance evaluation.**

Most of us are uncomfortable in counseling unless we're either praising staff or admonishing them for error or failure. Few of us are skilled at giving clear advice about characteristics or skills that need improving— particularly when we like the individual and his or her overall performance is pretty good. These shortcomings can be overcome by a sensible peer or 360-degree evaluation process. Done

---

Communicating Behavior

Consider the value of this simple peer evaluation conducted by a services company group we interviewed.

All members of the group were sent a simple form they were asked to complete and submit anonymously to a third party administering the survey. They were asked to assign *each* of their 75 peers one of the following designations:

A This person has been of great help to me.

B This person helps occasionally.

C This person has at times been a hindrance to me.

D I don't know this person (or rarely interface with them).

The results were compiled and communicated privately to each individual by the third party.

Simple enough—and a means of communicating powerfully to each individual just how helpful he or she is viewed to be by peers. Many had to face the reality of peer perceptions far from their own views. Should you consider an exercise similar to this?

---

anonymously, the process frees up people to be honest about one's work and one's work-related relationships. Those on the receiving end of this input are forced, at long last, to confront the reality of our behaviors, particularly with the help of coaching and individualized follow-up.

3. Consider the Whole Individual

Most organizations have by now reengineered some of their important work processes. In most cases, the target of these efforts has been the work itself; the goal has been to dramatically improve how work is done and add value to products and services. But in our experience, something is missing from the standard analyses—something fundamental to the cost, quality, and speed of work carried out in these processes. Most work reengineering efforts overlook the individuals doing the work.

With its laserlike focus on work, reengineering has ignored the worker. But no amount of streamlining and work redesign will come close to succeeding with a workforce whose lives are out of balance or out of control. If you want to duplicate in managers' work the spirit they show as they coach their child's soccer team or build a new wing on the local church, you will have to consider more than that manager's time on the job. We're not suggesting that you bring all elements of private life into work redesign. We are recommending that you give consideration to the whole individual when highest job performance is the goal.

Most work reengineering efforts overlook *the individuals* doing the work.

Fifty years ago most employee support systems consisted of (in total) a parking lot, a cafeteria, and the men's room. Today, nearly all organizations recognize the huge shift in demographics and the demands each of us faces. They are responding with support systems that make it easier for us to put in a productive day at work. There is no altruism in this. Most executives know that harried employees are not going to deliver what they might, given reasonable support.

These support systems include more than on-site day care or the right to maternity or paternity leave and flexible work schedules. The most innovative companies are *looking* for ways to help individual employees, with "eldercare," affinity networks, or telecommuting. Their approach can be viewed as a subtle return to the paternalism of the early 20th century, when firms tried everything from corporate health care to housing in an attempt to keep unions out. Now the strategy is to provide as much support as possible to maximize the full potential of human beings in the course of their work day. We mentioned earlier the executive who explained his motive in downsizing as wanting to create "better jobs for fewer people." These programs create "better people for the remaining jobs."

For the past 10 years, Avon Products has operated support groups for minority employees and employees who are parents. Funded by Avon, these networks meet regularly and provide information and education for all employees. Annually, each sponsors a week of programs targeted to all employees, including activities, speakers, and videos. Far from least, these groups report to Avon's CEO about problems and possibilities that affect their group more than others.

Engage the Individual

We are beset on all sides by messages. Flip open a pizza box from your local parlor. *Ecco:* an ad from a nearby car dealer. Because of the saturation, getting through to people—really capturing their attention—can be a major challenge. You have to use every trick in the book.

A new plant manager we interviewed knew right away that he had to do something to improve the plant's safety record. The standard safety campaign banners and safety award programs were in place—and ineffective. He had to get people's attention, and fast.

When he thought about his people as employees, most of them impervious to the countless messages put in front of them at work, he realized that it would be difficult, if not impossible, to get through. But as he began to think of them as people—individuals—with family and friends at home, he discovered a way to reach them. Close on the heels of the next plant accident, he documented the trauma in stark terms, put it into a letter, and mailed the letter to the families of each employee. The response was dramatic and immediate. The message struck family members so hard that safety became a frequent topic of conversation at home. Accidents at the plant abruptly dropped off.

4. Build Social Skills through Innovative "Practice Fields"

Some organizations and some people within them could benefit from refining the social skills that count in the emerging business environment. Top CEOs have begun to stress how crucial this is. As Larry Bossidy, CEO of AlliedSignal, puts it: "Today managers add value by brokering with people, not by presiding over empires. . . . Today we look for smart people with an added dimension: they have an interest in other people and derive psychic satisfaction from working with them."[1]

The Learning Center in MIT's Sloan School is uncovering the power of practice. Its research shows the need for managers and employees to *practice*—much as people do in sports, the performing arts, and the military. As managers climb the ranks, they don't get this kind of practice. Classroom role-playing does not qualify. It is seldom realistic or relevant.

The research suggests that we create *practice fields* that let managers and employees hone their skills and gain experience under realistic but risk-free conditions. The "product" of this approach is managers who understand how to create a learning environment for those around them.

5. Create Crystal-Clear Objectives. Insist upon Accountability

Be certain that every team you form has a clear objective, constantly reinforced, and linked to the organization's vision, purpose, and strategies. Research on effective teams indicates that clarity of purpose and strategic linkage are of overriding importance.

Consider the teams in your organization. Were you to ask each team member to write down in two or three sentences the team's goal, how consistent would their answers be? How much disparity would you expect? And then, are the participants *absolutely committed* to their goals? One manager described to us, in memorable fashion, a series of cross-functional team meetings at his company. Imagine, he suggested, a scene with marionettes—team members—sitting at a table discussing issues and working toward team objectives. In actuality, each team member is less than fully committed to the team. Each is controlled by invisible threads leading away from the conference room to a puppeteer hidden away in his or her home department. Each is part of the team—but as soon as issues heat up, the hidden influence of traditional hierarchy overwhelms the result. Lots of easy stuff gets done, but few tough issues are tackled and few cross-functional borders are broken down. Vivid and insightful, we think.

6. Make Initiative and Decisiveness Specific Objectives

One of the most troubling traits of ineffective teams is that they lack initiative and decisiveness. Stuck in a cycle of debate and deliberation in an effort to gain consensus, many teams lack

Measuring Participation

The expansion of teams and teamwork in tomorrow's organizations creates a troublesome question for the individual: "Just what is my 'real' job? How do my team roles dovetail with my daily line responsibilities?"

Norwest Bank has a system of toting points for just about anything—line results, introducing a customer to another division, having lunch with a colleague's customer, making a suggestion to another team. The system, called GEMINI, won MICROBANKER's 1994 first place award for "best in microbanking." The award recognized Norwest's achievement as the first bank to develop a full-fledged client/ server commercial banking workstation.

The bank's chief strategy calls for commitment to relationship management and to maximizing service levels to the bank's best customers and prospects. This strategy required a technology solution that supports team selling. Since GEMINI was launched in 1991, fee/service income has grown 15 percent, and the proportion of fees to total revenue has increased from 40 percent to 60 percent. Each customer is assigned to a team made up of professionals from each business unit— for example, account management, cash management, trust services, lending, and others. All team members use GEMINI to service the customer; GEMINI provides an overview of customers, products and services provided, and service providers that makes it easy to recognize new opportunities. The system and the processes built around it have sharply improved the relationship manager's ability to cross-sell.

Before, much of what officers knew about a given account resided in their heads alone. Now customer information is no longer only a personal asset but a corporate asset as well. In addition, the loan officer assigned new accounts can quickly familiarize him or herself with the relationship and the other players on that customer's team. Service has improved markedly as a result.

The key here is that all employees' participation in any customer-related activity is tracked and toted. This encourages all individuals to contribute to their own team and help other teams. The marketing data that flow out of the system are used to determine incentive compensation. The individual benefits. The bank benefits. The customer benefits.

the decisiveness of the best individuals on the team. Initiative is another victim. Good ideas delivered late are often not worth much.

Many actions must be taken swiftly in business today. Decisions must be made expeditiously. High-performance teams understand that team processes are naturally slower, so they work hard at initiative and decisiveness. They develop informal processes to expose ideas and come to "enough" consensus quickly. Often the trick is to get the team to shift from diplomatic discussion to true dialogue, full of the candor and tension that can move its members to surrender individual ideas and closely held beliefs in order collectively to create something bigger. Intel focuses intently on sharpening this skill. What Intel calls "constructive confrontation" is that company's approach to getting things out on the table. *In the process, it is creating people with more "hide" and greater empathy.* This is just what it takes to achieve decisiveness on the basis of a raw, unfiltered debate of the issues.

7. Measure the Team. Reward the Individual

Constantly measure and recognize team performance. And then *reward the individuals.* Rewards should flow from meeting well-established and clearly stated performance objectives. This seems obvious, but many mistakes are made in this regard. We were asked by several managers, "How do I know if my team is doing well at reengineering?" The question does not even suggest itself when a reengineering effort has measurable goals (preferably based on cost, quality, and speed standards). If a project team's goal is to cut cycle time by 75 percent, cut costs by 30 percent, and maintain product quality standards, will there be any confusion as to whether the team is doing well? We think not.

Measuring team success ought to be easy. Rewarding individuals for that success is not so easy. As mentioned earlier, equitable rewards today are not necessarily uniform rewards. Workers are different, so they need different kinds of rewards. The rewards puzzle has at least three parts: team performance, the individual's contribution to that team, and reward options structured to satisfy different individuals. Solving the puzzle again and again will stretch all of us as we seek to attract, motivate, care for, and reward the individual.

Many companies have begun to tackle this issue through pay-for-performance or variable compensation schemes. In the broadest sense, this means that they try to find a sensible way to base pay on individual contribution or performance. While incentive pay has always been part of a senior manager's compensation, the belief that it should become part of the reward system for middle management and lower-level employees is less widespread—some unions still fight the idea on its merits. These new systems allow much-needed flexibility. Clever managers are tying bonuses to *both* broad corporate measures and narrower individual or team benchmarks.

8. Search Out and Promote Passionate Leaders and Effective Coaches

In successful organizations, a few great coaches—not layers of managers—are the "neural network" linking the individual to the team and the team to the larger organization. Today's managers must coach, train, sponsor, motivate, and counsel. Managers skilled in each of these roles are rare. Fortunately, in today's horizontal, process-oriented, and wired organizations, a very few managers can affect many people deeply. A single great coach can motivate many individuals across a huge organization—contrary to conventional wisdom about span of control.

9. Leverage the Individual and the Team with Technology

Success comes when the organization provides its people with the right equipment for the mission at hand. Moving at warp speed is one thing; doing it without the right equipment or training is quite another. In an age when technology is everywhere, there is no excuse for not equipping your people with the right tools. Why is it, then, that so few companies invest enough to make sure their workforce has access to the training and tools that will *cost-effectively* leverage their skills and desire to excel?

A typical shortcoming is in the area of training. Simple things, such as effective use of voice mail, are neglected. More difficult things are often more neglected still. Training cannot be offered to your people as if it were a set of elective courses; some parts of training need to be core curriculum. Force it—in a friendly sort of way. Were you to enter the homes of many of your managers, you would probably see the VCR with its clock blinking 12:00 . . . 12:00 . . . 12:00. Many of us just don't take the time to learn that extra 20 percent about the technologies available to us. Convince each person that this 20 percent will give both the organization and the individual a handy return.

> Moving at warp speed is one thing; doing it without the right equipment or training is quite another.

10. Expect a Lot. Reward Handsomely

Establish stretch performance targets. People are naturally more motivated when they have a goal. Unfortunately, not every goal presses toward the kind of breakthrough performance most of us want. Demanding stretch goals will provide a powerful signal to everyone that business as usual won't cut it. By targeting an outrageous level of performance, you force everyone to look at the issues in new ways. They will have no alternative. They will know that they can't possibly come up with solutions by relying on past models. On the other hand, if you set comfortable goals, you will be tempting the team to adopt solutions that are already near at hand and not especially effective. Be specific: The goal of becoming "more customer-focused" is vague; achieving 98 percent repeat purchases is anything but vague.

Watchwords

There is every reason to expect that we will continue to downsize our organizations—adjusting, of course, for revenue volumes. The pressure to drive costs down will endure. Global markets will continue to accelerate competitive pressures. For these reasons, the stuff of this chapter is important now and, if anything, more important in years to come.

Maximizing the potential in each of us will be the overriding prerequisite to the success of our organizations in the decade ahead. To accomplish this, each of us will need both a strong sense of individual self-worth and a strong sense of community. Each of us will have to be a competent soloist and a valuable component of the ensemble. And each of us will be asked to be genuinely committed to our jobs—without abandoning commitment to balance in our lives.

Balance and integration are the watchwords: balancing the needs of the organization with those of the individual, integrating the aspirations and skills of each one into a single powerful enterprise.

Note

1. "The CEO as Coach: An Interview with AlliedSignal's Lawrence A. Bossidy," *Harvard Business Review*, March–April 1995, p. 75.

PART FOUR

THE THIRD PARADOX PRINCIPLE:

Focus Directly on Culture, Indirectly

*A belief is not merely an idea the mind possesses;
it is an idea that posseses the mind.*

Robert Bolton

Six

Culture and Performance

Whenever I hear the word "culture" I reach for my revolver.

Hanns Johst

Hanns Johst's sentiment may echo in the hearts of many otherwise law-abiding executives. Although the concept of corporate culture is familiar to all, many of us still regard culture as something the NEA funds, unrelated to management concerns even if some people insist on applying the term to business. There is good cause for this mistrust. The word *culture* is ambiguous, describing on the one hand the arts and education, and on the other hand the values and behaviors that typify collectives such as business organizations. This second usage has more to do with anthropology than art—and the techniques for analyzing corporate culture owe something to anthropologists visiting tribes, interviewing elders, charting kinship patterns, picking up tools and asking "What's this for?" That today's tools are LAN-based PCs with a CD-ROM peripheral and Internet access doesn't nullify the question: "What's this for?" Since we know of no better word than *culture* for all this, we hope that you will holster your weapon and read on.

In this chapter we define corporate culture in two ways—first analytically, then through observation and cases—and we shed what light we can on the core paradox that faces managers who recognize a need to "change the culture." Culture shapes an organ-ization's decision patterns, guides its actions, and drives the individual behavior of all members. Visibly, it is "the way we do things around here." Less visibly, it comprises the beliefs, values, and attitudes that permeate an organization. The durability and embeddedness of corporate culture provide continuity—an important asset—but also make culture difficult to change.

Clues to the prevailing culture are evident in details. Just watch people. How do employees interact? Are customers the main topic of conversation? Are the tough issues openly debated in meetings? Or is everything already decided prior to meetings, so that the formal gathering is something like a play where people say their lines, act their parts, and then "the decision" is made? Do people feel they have to show up for meetings even when they'll have little to contribute to the topic? Do staff members seem to know what to do without being told? Do they interact effortlessly with fellow employees in other offices, even if they have never met? Does the office feel empty or busy? Are the managers' doors open or closed? Do managers have offices at all?

Another place to look for signs of an organization's prevailing culture is its performance measures and rewards. Performance measures codify culture—or at least they should. When a set of measures is established and their importance continually reinforced, strong messages are sent about what counts. Similarly, rewards are another indicator of culture. When carefully crafted, they shape and authenticate the company's values. Connecting these dots could not be more important: Powerful execution of strategy is possible only when performance measures are reinforced by rewards and are consistent with organizational values.

Rewards are a strong indicator of culture. When carefully crafted, they shape and authenticate the company's values.

Many organizations are beginning to recognize the need to reshape their culture. Managers commonly complain that one or another change didn't work because "the culture" got in the way. These managers are aware of the leverage gained when the behavior and decisions of people at all levels square with organizational objectives. And they are learning that the effort to change a culture must be as powerful and deep-seated as the culture itself.

Some companies attempt short-term solutions to change culture: set up a training program, reorganize the infrastructure, instruct people to care about customers. Such initiatives don't work. Managers we have interviewed complain of wasting time in meetings where everybody frets over developing list upon list of new and desirable cultural characteristics—meetings where the premise seems to be that if you wish hard enough and talk long enough, the culture will change. No amount of wishful thinking will help. No amount of exhortation can actually transform the cultural fabric of an organization. One manager commented that such things add up to telling her 18-year-old son to ignore those 18-year-old girls!

So what *is* needed to change culture? In this chapter we look at examples from around the globe to understand some of the ways successful organizations have transformed culture. These best efforts reflect the following logic:

1. In any organization, high performance comes from appropriate behaviors and appropriate decisions on the part of its people.

2. Culture determines behavior and decision patterns.

3. The characteristics of culture and the forces that shape it can be defined.

4. To reshape culture, managers must be aware of these characteristics and shaping forces, and work with them both directly and *indirectly*.

The key concept of indirection leads to the Third Paradox Principle:

• • • • •

Focus directly on culture, indirectly.

• • • • •

It is true, of course, that you will need to assess the current culture and understand whether and how it keeps you from carrying out your organization's strategy. But having done so, don't make the mistake of obsessing about the values, beliefs, or behaviors you would *like* to see. Transform your culture as other successful managers have—by using practical tools such as measures, rewards, and people practices. Change the characteristics of a culture by changing the forces that influence it. Indirection.

What *Is* Culture?

The following six characteristics define an organization's culture:

Values The principles or qualities considered worthwhile by the organization, such as client service or product innovation, candor or collegiality. Values can attach to any element of your business model: customers, employees, shareholders, products, service levels, and the like. Values tend to persist over time, even as the organization evolves.

Beliefs The hypotheses, assumptions, and business model the organization holds to be true. Implying a view of the world in general, beliefs can be true or untrue. Beliefs generate paradigms, i.e., compelling models of what is best for the business and how best to act. Paradigms also can either further or hinder organizational goals. Shared beliefs exercise a tremendous, sometimes unseen influence on decisions.

Climate An organization's feeling or atmosphere, noticeable in the physical layout of work spaces and, far more acutely, in how employees interact with each other, with customers, and with other outsiders. What's it like to work here? Is it a formal or informal organization? Do people worry about who should receive an e-mail message, or do they copy as many people as they believe will be interested or helpful? Do people raise or avoid issues?

Norms The standards and rules that evolve in the organization, such as how hard people work, when they come to work, and when they leave. Norms embrace matters at all levels, from dress code and attitudes toward weekend work to whether or not a slow-growth strategy is acceptable. Norms, often unwritten, affect how decisive managers and employees are. They determine how inclusive or exclusive people are in making decisions and doing their jobs.

Symbols The icons, lore, rituals, and traditions that embody strong messages about what is important. These can include positive events such as annual ceremonies and celebrations, and recognitions such as a special parking space for the employee-of-the-month. Symbols can also be negative—corporate regalia such as wristwatches and rings available only to the Chosen, lavish corporate parties when annual

Figure 6.1
Culture on Two Levels

An organization's culture has many artifacts and manifestations that can be described as climate, norms, symbols, and philosophy. It is, however, the deeply seated values and beliefs that most genuinely influence individual and organizational behavior.

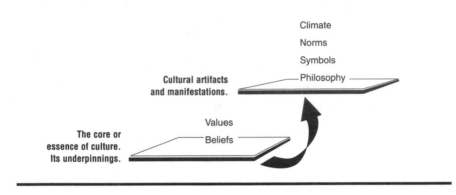

increases for the rank and file have been cut back because of business results.

Philosophy   The stated policies and ideologies that guide an organization's actions toward owners, employees, customers, and all other stakeholders—epitomized by "the HP Way" at Hewlett-Packard. The employee handbook of Nordstrom, the successful retailer, conveys two axioms before all else. First: The customer is always right. Second: When in doubt, refer to rule number one.

What Shapes Culture?

Powerful forces shape an organization's culture:

Leadership Actions   The actions of the organization's leaders communicate their beliefs, values, and assumptions. When the CEO abandons the executive dining room to eat in the cafeteria, spends significant time with customers, and walks the shop floor to talk with line workers, he or she is communicating powerfully. Such actions far outweigh any number of memos and newsletters from headquarters.

The HMS Vanguard: A Cultural Beacon

If an organization's culture is strong enough, people don't need to speak to communicate. Take The Vanguard Group, the Valley Forge, Pennsylvania, mutual fund company headed by investment community legend John C. Bogle. Since its founding in 1975, the symbol of the ship HMS *Vanguard* has been the "beacon"—a symbol so strong that it helps shape behaviors and decisions that have consistently achieved superior business results.

The Symbols

The history of Vanguard's name is a colorful one. The inside cover of a recent report to shareholders states, "The HMS *Vanguard* was the flagship of Lord Nelson during the Battle of the Nile in 1798, and was chosen as the name of The Vanguard Group for the significance of its traditional meaning, 'the advance guard' or 'leadership of a new trend.' "

In creating Vanguard, Bogle set out on a maiden voyage to do what no other investment firm had done before—to "provide performance, price and service beyond all client expectations." With that, he used the battleship HMS *Vanguard* to symbolize all that he hoped to achieve by his vision and to establish a guiding philosophy. " 'The Vanguard Experiment' [is] a test to determine whether a mutual fund complex can succeed, operating independently, on an at-cost basis and solely in the interest of its shareholders. . . . With HMS *Vanguard* as our symbol

and our consistent strategy as 'a star to steer her by' we intend to do exactly that."

As the only mutual fund management company, which is owned by its mutual fund shareholders, Vanguard's consistent, clear, four-pronged strategy is:

- To provide excellent investment performance.
- To provide the highest-quality service at the lowest possible cost.
- To innovate without opportunism.
- To distribute shares directly to investors on a pure no-load basis.

The cost advantage is achieved by the unique organizational structure where all profits are returned to the client/owner.

In addition to a symbol of the leader's vision, this battleship as a logo is one of a host of analogies to voyages, battles, victories, and medals of honor that are used throughout the organization. In written materials, artifacts picture themes of ships and winning battles (medals of honor, war uniforms, peace treaties, etc.). Language is used that discusses how client service is "the Vanguard battle cry" and how a consistent strategy is "the star to steer

The HMS Vanguard: A Cultural Beacon *(continued)*

by." Investment funds are named after ships, following the naming of Wellington, Vanguard's first fund.

Expanding upon the battle metaphor, a videotape that profiles Vanguard's history and mission opens with a panoramic scene of an empty battlefield and type scrolling down the screen that reads, "Valley Forge, PA ... It has a way of testing beliefs .... For this is where two revolutions proved their mettle ... Both were based on little more than mettle. ... Both were waged against great odds ... Yet, in both the greater good prevailed."

All this symbolism feeds the values and beliefs that pervade Vanguard's culture—a sense of mission, a feeling of being a pioneer charting uncharted waters, and the determination to complete a successful voyage and win in an extremely competitive marketplace.

The Behaviors

Vanguard crew members—never "employees"—respect each other and work together to achieve the common goal of satisfying the client. This can be seen throughout Vanguard in its team-based approach, including frontline client service. Every crew member is available for the "all hands on deck" call to fortify the front line by working in the client service center. This periodic experience for all crew members keeps the focus on the client and instills mutual respect for the importance of every crew member's role in the Vanguard voyage.

The common determination to complete a successful voyage and win in a competitive marketplace also instills a bias for action in crew members. When issues surface and action is required there is not a lot of waiting and wondering. Meetings are equally likely to occur in a conference room as on the road or in the campus "galley" (i.e., cafeteria). Additionally, numerous glass-walled meeting rooms surround the galley for quick, action-oriented meetings.

The Results

The above behaviors translate into results for the organization. Vanguard has been awarded "Number One in Mutual Fund Customer Service" by *Financial World* magazine for five consecutive years. *FW* commented, "Vanguard's track record in this study is extraordinary, given the quality of its competition."

To size up Vanguard's culture, you need only take one step into the headquarters building to meet the receptionist. She will greet you with a smile, remember your name, and be more than willing to explain the rich tradition of Vanguard ranging from Lord Nelson's Advance Guard in the Battle of the Nile to Jack Bogle's Vanguard Voyage to "provide performance, price and service beyond all client expectations."

The CEO's actions far outweigh any number of memos and newsletters from headquarters.

Performance Measures Performance measures play an enormous role in determining an organization's culture. What is measured? Are the measures clear? Are there so many measures that their overall effect is diffuse? Do they emphasize individual contributions? Or do they focus on group goals? Do they value short-term thinking, planning, and action, or decisions and behaviors linked to longer-term success? Do the measures reinforce or unknowingly undermine *today's* business strategy?

People Practices People practices include many, many things. Staffing: Are the right people hired with the right skills? Training and development: Are opportunities provided, mentorships established, and so on? Promotions: Do the *best* people get promoted? Is promotion a function of time in job or merit? Disciplinary measures: Does the punishment fit the crime? Are the rules clear? Firings: Are they handled humanely? Are they preceded by constructive counseling? There are so many issues: How are people evaluated and rewarded for their

---

Communications

Backing Up Words with Action at Chiat/Day

When communication is buttressed by action, the messages are received loud and clear. Bob Kuperman, CEO of the West Coast operation at Chiat/Day, lives this principle—accomplished with such small but symbolic actions as his famous "tree meetings." The tree meeting is a vestige from the days of Chiat/Day as a young, growing agency where everyone could fit into one room.

Whenever he had good news to announce, Bob would climb to the top of a ficus tree in Chiat/Day's main lobby, and yell out "tree meeting!" Everyone knew that something important was about to be unveiled. While the actual tree is gone, replaced by a conference room, the tree meetings are still an important leadership tool and means of shaping culture at Chiat/Day.

performance? Are rewards based on professional contribution—or on the symbols rather than the substance of performance? Does "face time" at work matter more than real contributions?

Vision, Purpose, Strategy All organizations play out a strategy—well conceived or not, well communicated or not. In organizations like Southwest Airlines, in which nearly every employee can rattle off the seven-point strategy espoused by its chairman Herb Kelleher, vision, purpose, and strategy strongly influence culture. When an organization's vision and strategies are muddled, its culture will eventually become a muddle.

> **When an organization's vision and strategies are muddled, its culture will eventually become a muddle.**

Structure Organizational structures are not inert containers for culture; they affect it. Structures can be loose, flexible, and short-lived to encourage collaboration and cross-functional problem solving, perhaps at the expense of some functional specialization. Or they can be rigid, formal, and control-oriented to promote functional efficiency at the expense of some collaborative innovation.

Competitive Context "Who are we?" and "Who do we believe to be our competitors?" are key questions. Consider the reputation, financial muscle, market share, distribution, and technology of your own organization and its competitors. Is competition based on price, volume, geography, or product? Is the industry in its infancy, mature, or somewhere in between? Is there regulation governing the industry or product? Are barriers to entry high or low?

Culture Drives Behavior and Decisions

The importance of culture is widely recognized. We have surveyed managers and employee groups about what they believe *must* change in order to achieve their organization's objectives. In 90 percent of the surveys, culture gets the top

Figure 6.2
Culture Model

Culture "shapers" (leadership actions, etc.) create culture, which strongly influences behavior and decisions, which, in turn, help determine performance.

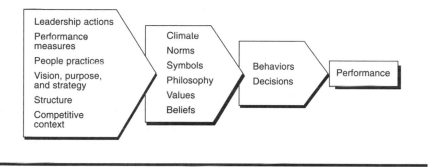

nod. People know almost instinctively that culture drives organizational performance. On the other hand, in the absence of a model, culture change exercises degenerate into woolly-headed, touchy-feely workshops full of exercises unrelated to corporate performance. It may be hard to believe, but today some of the largest (not greatest) corporations in the world are gathering employees into small meetings to discuss "how acorns grow into large oaks" and the cycle of seasons. Feel good? So do we. Meanwhile, corporate performance declines perilously.

In developing a model of culture, we have looked so far at six characteristics of any culture and six forces that shape any culture. But culture, of course, has "outputs" or results. In our view, culture affects performance through *behavior* and *decisions*. These are the most important "outputs" of culture, whether it acts in harmony or disharmony with other organizational fundamentals such as technology and financial strength.

Behavior

Behavior has to do with how people interact—with everything from general demeanor to patterns of language. Culture guides and reinforces behavior through its system of values, beliefs, unwritten rules, norms, and rituals that everyone understands. Are employees competitive or cooperative? Is constructive dialogue possible or is mayhem more likely during fact-finding sessions? Do people respect others above and below them, or do they focus only on those above them?

An important manifestation of behavior is *passion*, a high level of enthusiasm and energy focused on the concerns of the organization. Do people care about their jobs, their careers, the organization as a whole? In organizations that provoke passion, employees (from housekeeping to top brass) feel a strong association with their roles in the organization. They care. The

---

Gyroscopic Behavior

The gyroscope in motion has a peculiar authority. Its smooth rotation and uncanny poise, its odd combination of motion with stillness, endow it with

Figure 6.3
Gyroscope

unique fascination. The spectacle of substantial energy controlled and directed is arresting. Let the gyroscope run down and it has no power to fascinate at all. It is inert. Not unlike people in all of these respects. The members of an organization are set in motion by its mission and culture. If the mission makes sense to them and the culture supports them, they too are fascinating to observe: They know what to do and how to do it, they know how to question, they know how to achieve. Like the gyroscope's rotation, their behavior is economical: no wasted motion, no extravagance, immense concentration. This is not an unattainable ideal. People in the best companies are like this.

length to which Marriott Hotel staff will go to make your stay special illustrates the point. You may have heard that a front desk clerk offered up his personal cuff links to a guest who'd forgotten his. And there is another story about the staff person who drove a hotel guest to the airport in his own car. These people are committed.

An important manifestation of behavior is *passion*.

Decisions, Decisiveness

Where a strong positive culture is lacking, indecision abounds. People are less than secure in their understanding of what is expected, how much is expected, and how often it's expected. When boldness overcomes the indecision of a weak culture, chaos typically ensues. Sports all-star contests are notorious in this respect. Not founded on a shared set of norms or style that bonds the team's actions, the play is nearly always unstructured and sloppy.

Although the connection is too little recognized, an organization's culture has a direct bearing on the decisions and decisiveness of managers and employees. Decisiveness is a very important behavioral characteristic: how decisions are taken, the time they require, who and how many people must be involved, and whether decisions are taken with or without fear—all these things have an immense influence on business processes and results. A hospitality example again comes to mind: If you stay at a Ritz-Carlton Hotel and call housekeeping to help you solve a problem, you may be surprised to find a housekeeper at the other end of the line who is authorized to spend up to $2,000 to satisfy your needs. No further authorization required. This is culture—a culture in which personal service to customers is a top priority. The Ritz-Carlton organization does not leave it to chance: Its training programs encourage initiative and decisiveness, its policies give employees the means.

Think of the number of decisions made each day in your organization. Thousands of decisions: how to serve a given customer; how to streamline your supply chain; how to treat a group of employees; how to develop new products and services. Thousands of decisions, each of which contributes toward organizational objectives—or not. Employees predict the probable outcomes of their decisions by referring, sometimes deliberately, sometimes by second nature, to their organization's culture. The sales function of one of our clients provides an example. Senior management has long endured bitterly adversarial relationships among the product managers of its various divisions. The culture reinforces the belief that "Anyone outside my division is the enemy." The culture consequently encourages a most extraordinary set of decisions. Managers will quite consciously sell a smaller volume or a less profitable mix from their own division instead of assisting a sister division to make a sale—and have even referred customers to competitors. This failure of trust is a crippling legacy from an era when external competitors were tame enough that management felt they had to fire up a competitive spirit by setting the left hand against the right hand.

A sense of comfort and psychological safety with peers, customers, subordinates, and superiors enables a person to take action decisively.

Trust is a critical force behind decisiveness and decision quality. And it has a far-reaching impact on productivity. A sense of comfort and psychological safety with peers, customers, subordinates, and superiors enables a person to take action decisively to further the organization's interests. Do people feel comfortable taking risks, speaking their minds, stating their needs? Does the walk match the talk? Do people agree publicly to one thing, but do something else later on?

Strength and Fit: What Makes a Culture Productive?

While many of the managers we interviewed acknowledge the importance of people, they tend to lean heavily on structural solutions to generate higher performance. Ghoshal and Bartlett get this just right in their *Harvard Business Review* article on the

Work Culture Development Process

The Queens Medical Center

After a major effort to reengineer several core processes, the management of The Queens Medical Center in Honolulu realized that shaping work culture entailed a very different approach than that of redesigning its processes. While the techniques of reengineering had rearranged work tasks and focused people on activities that make the patients' experience more efficient and comfortable, it did not truly directly address the organization's work culture. In an employee climate survey, employees had identified work culture as needing major change. There were perceptions that the organization was too bureaucratic—this being characterized as having too many "briefcase carriers," too many management meetings, cumbersome organizational silos, a lack of oneness, and other impediments to a team-oriented, focused organization. All were symbols or symptoms of a weakness in the work culture, but not necessarily causes.

In their discussions about work culture, the executives also recognized that elements of this same culture were responsible for fueling Queens' success! Queens has a rich heritage of patient care and service to the community, which dates back to 1859 when the hospital was founded by Hawaiian sovereignty of the time, Queen Emma and King Kamehameha IV. In fact, it was clearly evident in the climate survey that the employees were very proud of the Queens Medical Center. As part of the Work Culture change process, the survey results were shared in open forums and a presentation was made to the Board of Trustees of the Medical Center. The results were also published and mailed to all employees' homes.

Sharing the survey information also created an expectation that the Work Culture would indeed change. The executives of the Queens Medical Center spent several months seeking to understand the messages in the survey results and their implications. There was a lot of thoughtful dialogue about how a change in Work Culture should be pursued. The executives reached a number of conclusions. First, they concluded that shaping a new Work Culture entailed a process substantially different from the reengineering work under way at Queens. They began to see the task at hand as being much more complex than anyone had originally envisioned. It become evident that changing the Work Culture could also undermine what had contributed to the organization's success. It became clear how important and critical the Work Culture is. The executives also began to realize the importance of their leadership role in shaping the Work Culture and their obligations to the organization and its heritage.

To address these issues, the executives began meeting solely to discuss

Work Culture Development Process

The Queens Medical Center *(continued)*

their leadership role and how they could better support the organization and each other as a team. Additionally, a planning team consisting of several executives and representatives of senior management was established to develop a process of addressing the Work Culture issues with the senior management staff. A series of one-day retreats called the Leadership Forum was started. The management evaluation process was also changed and evolved to shape a management team focused around their Mission, Vision, and Core Values. The process of shaping a new culture was designed ultimately to involve the entire organization.

The Leadership at Queens realizes their institution is at the beginning of a long-term process. As they undertake a path of organizational transformation, they expect to achieve a Work Culture aligned around its Mission, Vision, and Core Values. While there will be growing pains and the normal setbacks associated with evolutionary growth, they also expect to achieve this goal of alignment because it is critical and an essential part of the organization's heritage and legacy.

---

changing role of senior managers in the more process-driven, people-oriented enterprises of today. They write:

> The structural element of the strategy-structure-systems doctrine that most managers rely on today is about allocating resources, assigning responsibilities, and controlling their effective management. The purpose-process-people doctrine of management rests on a different premise: that the organizing task [of today's managers] is to shape the behaviors of people and create an environment that enables them to take initiative, to cooperate, and to learn.[1]

One CEO recently told us, "We have the technology; we have the infrastructure; we have the financial strength. The only thing holding us back at this point is a decades-old culture—a mentality appropriate to the competitive environment

A strong culture can be an enormous advantage if it is in sync with the organization's strategies.

of 1970." He recognizes that culture is potent; it can block his company's strategy or catalyze it. What determine the impact of a culture are *strength* and *fit.* As Figure 6.4 illustrates, a strong culture can be an enormous advantage if it is in sync with the organization's strategies. On the other hand, if the fit is flawed, the strengths of a culture are likely to be among its greatest weaknesses: all of that tradition, all of those beliefs and norms propelling the company toward mediocrity or worse.

Figure 6.4
Cultures Fit with Strategy

Strong cultures can enable and reinforce strategy or can undermine it.

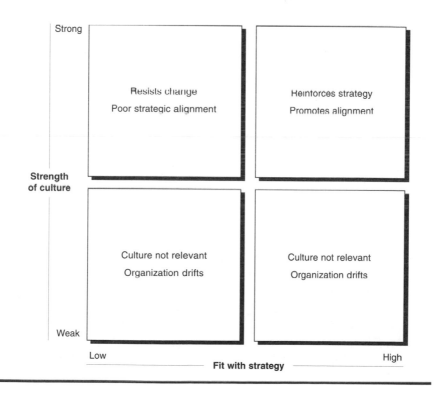

The Pragmatic Impact of Values Management

Developing an environment to forge new values does not just create a nice place to work. It's all about achieving bottom-line objectives. James Brian Quinn did about the best job we've seen in summarizing the practical importance of culture, which he analyzes in terms of values:[2]

- Consistent values will attract the kind of people who genuinely want to work for the company, and mutually held values create the trust needed for flexibility and effectiveness.
- Trust, created by common values, allows efficient delegation. People will work independently toward commonly held goals.
- People work harder to fulfill values they believe in, thus enhancing personal motivation and enterprise productivity.
- People who share common values will help each other, generating teamwork and adding value through shared solutions.

- Creative people can work efficiently on their own toward commonly held goals and can share the long time horizons needed for innovative success.
- Common values create group identity, improve morale, and eliminate needs for more detailed controls.
- High-morale organizations will band together, work intensively for short spurts to solve critical problems, and protect group secrets.
- People at distant points in the organization can be trusted to use their intuition to solve unique problems in ways consistent with organization purposes.
- Value-activated people will consciously seek new opportunities to fulfill these values and will not waste time on those that do not.
- Commonly held values tend to minimize squabbles, decrease internal friction, and reduce time needed to manage them.

Strong cultures with a good fit to strategy—and the business results or potential to prove it—attract the best people. Many organizations draw most of their strength and competitiveness from a single source: their people. The best people are attracted to organizations that actively support values such as integrity, quality, and care for the individual. This is not to suggest that the best people are attracted to organizations known to be "a nice place" to work. The men and women you want to attract are looking for something more like "a *good* place" to work—one with norms reflecting hard work, intelligence, and fierce competitiveness (focused externally). Hence the increasing attention given by leading companies such as Pepsi, Merck, and Microsoft to reinforcing their values—values that attract top people.

These companies have moved beyond the trite mantra that "people are our most important asset." They have come to recognize that:

1. People costs are the largest single element of operating costs.
2. The marginal revenue generated by switched-on people can make the difference between success and mediocrity.

These are not new insights. Acting on them is. In the chapter ahead, we will discuss the shaping of culture. In this, we will explore just how the best managers focus directly upon culture, and why they do so indirectly. In the meantime, see if you recognize any of the elements of your organization's culture in the following lists.

What are some illustrative values?

1. Product innovation.
2. Bright people (intelligence).
3. Collegiality.
4. High client-contact work.
5. Trading (any instrument, anywhere, anyway, anyhow).
6. Teamwork.
7. Balance of work and personal life.
8. Money; just money.
9. Big jobs for big clients.
10. Long hours, late nights, and weekends.

What are some illustrative organizational beliefs?

1. Our products are of the highest quality in the industry.
2. The quality of our people is our overriding source of differentiation.
3. Our industry is growing very slowly.
4. We are a beer company. *Period.*
5. Our customers want *services.* Product is secondary.
6. Creativity requires autonomy of the individual, division, and so on.
7. Traders make all the profit here.
8. We must attack ideas to test their mettle.
9. Quality comes from care: We have the time.
10. We know better; we dominate this industry.

Climate?

1. Managers have big offices (with many doors closed).
2. Almost nobody has an office.
3. People look grim walking down the hall.
4. Arrogance—everywhere.
5. Office hoteling.
6. Lots of noise and activity in the office.
7. The decor echoes the product.
8. Celebrations—birthdays, bridal, baby—nearly every week.
9. Casual dress.
10. Decor screams "Big money being made here!"

What about norms?

1. A marketing executive will be CEO.
2. People are at work by 8:00 AM here.
3. Big Decisions are never made in a meeting (always negotiated carefully and quietly in advance).

4. People work a lot of Saturday mornings here.
5. Commitment to work is measured in part by "face time."
6. We don't question the boss's decisions.
7. Secretaries are part of the project team.
8. You wait your turn here.
9. Until you've been here at least eight years, few will listen to you.
10. Debate; dispute, open contention; seemingly hostile deliberations.

Symbols?

1. Annual promotion ceremony
2. "Error embracing"
3. The CEO in the employee cafeteria
4. Individual rewards (vs. team rewards)
5. Type of furnishings (pictures, rugs, etc.) differs by level
6. Employee fitness center in the building
7. Customer service awards
8. Lots of staff "war rooms" fostering collaboration
9. An efficient global electronic network
10. Comprehensive employee support programs

And philosophies?

1. Ladies and Gentlemen serving ladies and gentlemen. (hotel chain)
2. . . . within an arm's length from desire. (food and beverage)
3. Any color you want it, as long as it's black. (Henry Ford)
4. Provide greater value (. . . and they will come). (retailer)
5. We try harder. (car rental)

6. Employee handbook: (retailer)

   Rule No. 1: The customer is always right.

   Rule No. 2: See Rule No. 1.

7. World-class professionals serving world-class clients.

8. Absolutely, positively overnight. (overnight package delivery)

9. Quality is Job 1. (automaker)

10. "All the news that's fit to print." (newspaper publisher)

Notes

1. Sumantra Ghoshal and Christopher Bartlett, "Changing the Role of Top Management," *Harvard Business Review,* January–February 1995, pp. 86–95.

2. James Brian Quinn, *The Intelligent Enterprise* (New York: The Free Press, 1992), p. 318.

Seven

Forging a New Culture

*One person with a belief is the social power equal
to ninety-nine who only have interests.*

John Stuart Mill

Creating a New Culture

In Chapter 6, we established the importance of culture and created a model for what it is and how it evolves. Well enough. Now on to the task of specifying how our organization's culture tomorrow is created out of the stuff of our organization today.

Our model for culture and techniques for reshaping culture come directly from our collective experience in working with organizations undergoing major change. The most unexpected insight we have gained is the core paradox of this chapter: In our experience, organizations that achieve real culture change *focus not on the culture but on those things that shape culture.* Successful transformations do not rely on lists of new, improved values and beliefs—that exercise is more likely to lead to cynicism than to valid cultural change. In fact, it gives cynics a better platform to deliver their message and do their mischief, because the wish list contrasts so dramatically with the current state of affairs. Cynics aren't slow to point out that "you can't get there from here" and to work against meaningful change. On the other hand, if you focus on the forces that shape culture, you avoid setting up a single target for potshots: There are many targets, and none of them has "culture change" written all over it. Each target focuses on a specific, practical concern that any loyal executive will regard as workable.

These are the steps we have found to be effective:

1. Create—and Communicate—the Right Competitive Context

Culture is, in part, a function of the organization's competitive context. While you may think of competitive context as an external beyond your control, think again. Competitive context is defined by the businesses you *believe* yourself to be in and by those you perceive as competitors. At Kodak, for example, managers often ask in a meeting, "Does this pass the Fuji test?" As we all know, Kodak produces a consumer product seen and recognized everywhere—film in those little yellow boxes. Fuji is Kodak's major competitor in that market. "Passing the Fuji test" means that the new product, service, or process is so potent that, were the people at Fuji to know about it, they would worry. This phrase, very much part of the culture, is a small but powerful signal among Kodak employees about who they are, who the competition is, and what their focus must be: winning in their core market.

Senior management can *create* a new competitive context. Consider AT&T. Robert Allen, that great company's CEO, could easily have accepted the traditional definition of his company: a wire-based utility whose monthly bill was as automatic as a dial tone. Instead, the senior executives of AT&T have transformed their competitive context by laying claim to a major share of the larger U.S. communications and information services market.

> **Competitive context is defined by the businesses you *believe* yourself to be in and by those you perceive as competitors.**

And they're still pressing ahead. Take a look at the cover of AT&T's 1994 annual report: a stark white jacket adorned with a single tiny goldfish. Bob Allen is communicating here a further redefinition of competitive context. Some people, at least in the past, could think of AT&T as a slow-moving behemoth. But in the global information, media, and communications market, AT&T is an unpretentious and fleet participant—a goldfish in a sea of opportunity. In our opinion, this masterstroke of context setting sends a powerful message to investors, employees, and customers. If we were competitors, we would be listening. Without doubt, this competitive positioning resonates with employees and is helping to shape a new culture.

Contrast AT&T with the many firms that did not alter the competitive context quickly enough. In 1975, did the Big Three automakers see themselves as part of a truly global market? In 1985, were Apple, Compaq, and Dell visible in the competitive context perceived by mainframe builders? Was Fox a rival to CBS in its sports broadcasting? To compete effectively, your people must share a deep-seated understanding of the competitive context. Working to shape your organization's competitive context *can* and *will* shape its culture.

2. Deliver a Concise, Well-articulated Strategy

Not all strategies drive culture. But good ones do—concise, well-articulated ones do. We have found that only when that overarching strategy is clear, concise, and well articulated will it be widely understood and deeply seeded into the psyche of your employees. Carefully crafted, your strategy can be a powerful way to shape culture, which in turn will drive behavior that supports that strategy.

At Southwest Airlines—an icon of success in a tough industry—a strong culture benefits greatly from a crystal-clear strategy that every flight operations manager, pilot, and baggage handler can recite: short hauls, low fares, on-time arrivals, no meals, no seat assignments, friendly service—and no energy wasted on trying to be anything else. The company's norms and values reflect this limited set of strategic priorities and thus gain amplitude. People at Southwest *live* the organization's vision and strategy; it shows in their behaviors and decisions.

Not every company is able to construct a unique strategy. In some industries, where the leaders share nearly identical strategies, there is an intriguing relationship between strategy and culture: *Quality of execution* becomes crucial, and a strong culture supports consistency in execution. Although a strategy may be industrywide, culture is always unique to an organization and differentiates it from others. When your company simply needs to be 2 percent better *everywhere* than the competition, the influence of culture can make that small, meaningful difference. Recognizing this, the savvy manager uses culture to differentiate. In a very real sense, culture *is* strategy.

Culture can be a key to differentiation.

The method you use to develop strategy helps to shape culture. Is your strategic plan the work of a brainy but isolated group at headquarters? Is it developed in a process remote from the "coal face" of your customer operations? Is it an enduring rite of fall, in which 10 percent of people's attention goes to strategy and 90 percent is focused on budgeting? The answers to these questions fall into that class of revealing details mentioned at the top of this chapter. The answers will say much about your organization's culture.

One of the best ways we know to move culture is to generate strategy through a process that taps the insights of employees on the firing line. This sends a powerful message: Things will be different. Our belief in your abilities and value extends beyond the perimeter of your job—it extends to your thoughts about where the company should go. We believe that you have a great deal to contribute to our future direction. The insights gathered in this way need to be filtered. But the source of such information must basically be the same: *your people.*

3. Be Visible; Be Genuine

Today's employees are all but indifferent to the blizzard of memos, newsletters, videos, and e-mail they receive. Only actions get serious notice—actions and symbols that effectively communicate senior management's priorities and commitments. Add courage and candor to those actions and you'll have people's undivided attention.

Becoming the CEO of Hewlett-Packard might not seem to require much courage. HP has provided the example of a right-thinking culture since it was first described by Peters and Waterman in *In Search of Excellence.* But even success can harden into mediocrity or worse if all things remain what they are while markets change. When Lewis Platt became CEO, he was determined to shake up the company so that it would not slide down the path so many other high-tech firms took. Because of HP's cultural and competitive strength, this course took courage. Platt responded by being visible in ways that mixed demanding leadership with personal modesty. In the Silicon Valley culture of perks and glamorous lifestyles, this chief executive was visible, indeed, in his Ford Taurus. On the job, he encouraged product development to take more risks—to be bold. He took a hard look at costs and encouraged executives to look outside of HP for supplies that others could better make.

Lewis Platt makes clear that the role of the leader has changed in step with changes in today's organizations and today's global competition. James Brian Quinn has effectively summarized the skills of the modern CEO in leading flatter, network-style organizations:

> In these new structures the relatively few who remain at top levels tend to need different skills from those that led to success in the past. At the very top, creating and driving a consistent vision of the company's or group's purpose is the primary skill that provides the glue for all its highly deseg-regated units. Second is the capacity to create the trust, sense of shared values, and consistent viewpoint that stimulate people in dispersed activities and locations to self-activate around the vision. The old stereotype—the self-centered, hard-nosed, political climbing executive—doesn't fit these roles well. Leadership and coordination, rather than order-giving, seem to predominate. . . .[1]

Yet management still needs to be tough and objective. For example, if cost reduction is a priority goal, management cannot spare itself or a favored department from the budget knife. Senior managers undermine their integrity and ability to lead if they cut budgets while preserving luxuries for the head office or protecting certain expenditures for political reasons unrelated to the welfare of the business. One CEO, new to his company, slashed headquarters costs and headcount over 70 percent, then moved the remnant to lovely Palm Beach, Florida. What signals did he send by these actions? Will employee behaviors be driven by a desire to pitch in and pinch out cost . . . or simply by fear? Cost objectives need to be reflected at the top.

No single individual can do more to reshape culture than the CEO. This person is an icon (unless invisible—in which case his or her absence is symbol enough). And the more the CEO emphasizes that positive "iconic" role, the more change will take place. It is an awesome responsibility, not to be taken as everyday management stuff. The point is made succinctly

A Developing Picture at Kodak—but It's No Instamatic

We do not mean to imply that the actions of a CEO, no matter how dramatic, will create a new culture overnight. That's why the best at the game work tirelessly. How many stores did Sam Walton visit each year? Hundreds. Jack Welch seems to be everywhere. This is tough going even for the most charismatic of leaders. Overcoming decades of obsolete beliefs, of long-held but unproductive values, is not easy. The following report from *The Wall Street Journal* couldn't be clearer about this:

> George Fisher, Eastman Kodak Co.'s chief executive, was recently asked about his personal life. "I have none," he blurted out. "But that's not important to me. This happens to be a time when all I care about is work."
>
> Mr. Fisher keeps 18-hour days, traversing the globe to call on employees and customers and [alliance partners such as Apple and Microsoft]. But for all his labors, the job at Kodak still isn't getting done as fast as he wants. And the 53-year-old Mr. Fisher, brought in from Motorola in December 1993 to shake up the stagnant company, is frustrated.
>
> "Kodak unfortunately has a very centralized, authority-conscious culture with people not comfortable going from the bottom to the top," he says. "The last years at Kodak have been so bad that it's a challenge to make people realize how good they really are."

After decades dominating the photography industry, Kodak, which is based in Rochester, NY, had lost ground to foreign competitors like Fuji Photo Film Co. and risks further losses to newer rivals in the fast-paced digital arena. In Mr. Fisher, Kodak's first outside CEO ever, the company was banking on a builder who could lead it into a new electronic age, meshing traditional photography with wireless communication.

This much he knew. Less obvious was the need for culture upheaval. No matter how many town meetings he holds or how much e-mail he personally answers, Kodak's plodding operating mentality remains tough to change. "I'm surprised I have the energy I do," he says. "The mind-sets here have to be worked on—but you can't change a culture just by decree."[2]

by Professor Ed Schein: "If one wishes to distinguish leadership from management or administration, one can argue that leaders create and change cultures, while managers and administrators live within them."

One final characteristic we have observed in CEOs who successfully lead culture change: courage. Courage is a powerful action *and* icon. Much of change management distills to managing courage: summoning courage in yourself and in those around you. As we observed a year ago in our book *Better Change,* we have discovered that a lack of courage is a major roadblock to change. Without courage, on your part and that of many others, you cannot expect to effect positive change. Acts of courage—such as accepting responsibility for setbacks—become lore and, over time, cultural icons. They establish courageous norms of behavior that favor extraordinary performance.

Acts of courage become lore and, over time, cultural icons.

4. Reshape (and Clarify) Your Performance Measures

A premise of our model of culture and its link to performance is that performance measures drive behavior. They also mirror important elements of an organization's culture—its values and norms, even its fundamental belief system. Reshaping your performance measures is still another way to achieve culture change without once mentioning that odd and mysterious goal, "culture change."

Measures and their associated goals have a direct impact on norms. What do we consider adequate growth for our business? What rate of growth do we deem heroic? What do we think is a proper return for our shareholders? How does this compare with the incentives provided to managers and employees when things go really well?

Properly focused and reported, measures draw a bead on what's important. But you have to work to make measures count. Success is not automatic. For example, all too often there are so *many* measures to which one *might* respond that their impact is diluted. One of our recurrent consulting assignments is helping clients reshape their measures. We start by helping them inventory current measures. By the time everyone stops counting, the number is usually in the high hundreds.

Inventory your measures. You'll find them everywhere. While there is often a tidy hierarchy of importance to all these measures, they may have no current relation to strategy, and their rationale may never have been sound. For example, a

Inventory your measures.

Fortune 100 manufacturing company was trying to rationalize its measures, which numbered in the thousands. The purchasing organization insisted on continuing to count the number of suppliers—a measure easily benchmarked and collected. However, it had little real meaning because multiple sourcing was not a strategic imperative for the company. The company dropped the measure.

Measures have a direct bearing on the organization's values. Do your measures drive people together? Or do they drive a wedge between them? A *Fortune* 50 manufacturing client wanted to line up the entire shop floor behind its effort to develop a low-cost, high-quality manufacturing operation. *Synchronous manufacturing* was adopted as an objective (and battle cry!) that employees could get behind. The objective was immediately embraced by both plant managers and manufacturing engineers, who had been lobbying for years for the company to move in that direction.

Managers brainstormed several measures that would detail whether the objective was being met. They decided to closely monitor the number of inventory turns, the percentage of capacity utilization, and the percentage of workers cross-trained in different shop-floor skills. Quality would be monitored by trends in product defects, and scheduling would be monitored by recording changes in plant hours scheduled. Each of these measures was discussed with employees and accepted, and a chart of performance against each measure was posted prominently in the shop so that employees could follow the progress of their march toward synchronous manufacturing.

Synchronous manufacturing and its subordinate goals became seared into the psyche of employees across the company. The result was a plant fully committed to the effort.

The best measures establish norms and support informal rules. They make operations efficient. As defined by Christopher Hart, "internal guarantees" can be used to put teeth into measures, help create rules, and generate a more positive culture:

> Simply put, an internal guarantee is a *promise* or commitment by one part of the organization to another to deliver its products or services in a specified way and *to the complete satisfaction of the internal customer* or incur a meaningful *penalty*, monetary or otherwise.[3]

As you can tell, he's not suggesting a casual promise. The penalties must be real. The goal is to replace the weak relationships that often exist between business functions with a candid, results-focused dialogue about effectiveness and continuous improvement.

5. Create "Working" Structures

Smart companies that want to create a culture of sharing and teamwork are beginning to think of their structure less as an office tower, more as a warehouse. A warehouse is horizontal with one focus—getting material out the door as quickly and efficiently as possible. There are few walls, and most of them can be moved around to suit present purposes. Changing the layout doesn't change the basic function of the warehouse. The structure responds flexibly to short-term variations in strategy and execution. In contrast, a vertical office block tends to be compartmentalized, with each space hard-wired for its inhabitant. To change the layout, you have to knock down walls, rip out wiring, take up the floor. Change is time-consuming, disruptive, and expensive.

In determining its optimal structure, a company needs to take culture into account as a key influence. The match between culture and functional structure should be as close as possible. Based on our interviews and experience, we recommend the following:

1. **Build structure from the customer back, to better support the organization's major processes.** More and more, organizations are dismissing the notion that a good structural design starts with the CEO and moves down the hierarchy, compartmentalizing staff until you reach the mail room and gardener. Instead, some management teams view structure as a mobile way to coordinate execution of processes. The structure should support the organization's ability to find raw materials, convert them into value-added output, sell and distribute the output, and receive payment. If any element of structure stands in the way of these key processes, that element needs review and change. An organization with the right attitude focuses first on actions and skills needed at the customer interface—and only then determines what else in the way of structure it needs.

2. **Widen spans of control and reduce management layers.** As the heavy cost of layer upon layer of management is being blown away, flatter structures are emerging. These new structures, while often driven by expense control, can have a very positive impact upon culture. Doug Sims, CEO at CoBank, removed layers at the bank in order to encourage greater decisiveness and greater ownership of issues and to make managers accountable. He knows that a flatter, wider organization requires managers to seek solutions more often than they consult the boss. Information exchange in these new structures forces managers to communicate horizontally, focusing them more upon customers and peers, not just up and down the hierarchy.

3. **Invest in your employees—all employees.** Superior customer service can only be achieved through knowledgeable, skilled, and empowered frontline employees. Employees need to master new skills, make much more rapid and complex decisions, coordinate action across multiple product lines and geographies, and interact with a host of rapidly forming and changing teams. These demands require skills not normally found in yesterday's organization.

Sowing these skills where it matters most—at the front line—is a key feature of the successful structures emerging today.

4. **Ensure the alignment of structure, performance, and rewards.** Structure is important. It defines roles, reporting relationships, and political power. It drives behavior. However, its power will be sapped if its key elements are not supported through meaningful personal performance objectives and substantial personal rewards. Examples of bad practice are everywhere today as managers "reorganize" into teams—but do not reshape their measures or rewards systems consistent with their objectives. Without alignment and reinforcement, a new structure can in fact confuse employees and undermine the change in culture you are seeking.

5. **Expect any structure to be temporary.** There is no such thing as a perfect structure. The test of excellence is "fit": How well does our current structure fit our current and future strategic challenges? If this question is uppermost in management's mind, structures will change as strategies change. Innovative companies recognize the need for this and design their structures to permit rapid change. They create some fuzziness in departmental missions, allow for overlap in team membership, and encourage multiple concurrent innovations in an attempt to find the most appropriate answer.

6. Create Supportive People Practices

The axiom here is "You are what you do—toward your people." What your organization does with and to its employees plays a major role in shaping their relationship to the organization and in shaping its culture. That relationship is built over the life of each individual's career with the company—beginning with the first details of the recruiting process and ending with termination or retirement and even postretirement. In this sector of organizational life, little things mean a lot if continuously reinforced. For decades the Christmas basket full of

Changing Culture by Changing Structure: Oakwood Homes

Oakwood manufactures, sells, finances, insures, distributes, and services manufactured housing. As part of an enterprisewide reengineering effort, management recently took a great deal of time to think through its goals, what capabilities it would need to reach its goals, and how to motivate its people to achieve those goals.

Management decided that the way to align performance with the newly reengineered processes was to make a structural shift away from a functional to a more process-based approach. The company's traditional configuration was functional: each major department separate and distinct from others, segmented by purpose. Executives at Oakwood believed that this structure was not working, that it was limiting their focus on the customer. They wanted to improve its customer rating for superior homes (82 percent) and customers' overall satisfaction with service (75 percent). Finally, Oakwood did not believe that it was doing enough to anticipate customer needs and develop new services. Were they to find a way to do these things effectively, they anticipated that they could add as much as 25 percent to revenue.

Management set up performance goals in all three areas—customer ratings, overall satisfaction with service, and the ratio of new products and services. While the organization's structure would no doubt have to

change, senior management emphasized one thing overall: Employees needed to learn to *think differently* about customers and about working together.

Oakwood managers began to sift through various structural alternatives. First, they looked at the possibility of a product-based organization, since this approach might better focus attention on the successful delivery of products and services. But they knew that a product orientation can degenerate into a turf battle as competing product groups vie for investment dollars, staff resources, and management attention. Further, it was unclear how product and service development would be improved with such a narrow focus on product line offerings versus customer needs.

Oakwood managers then considered a geographic orientation. They knew that customer needs vary by geography and that the company could easily divide itself by geography. But a geographic organization was likely to limit the sharing of ideas across boundaries.

Management finally decided on a hybrid organization with both process-based (horizontal) and functional (hierarchical) elements. The resulting structure is built on four main customer-focused processes:

1. Getting the customers.

2. Getting the product.

Changing Culture by Changing Structure: Oakwood Homes *(continued)*

3. Giving the product to the customer.
4. Keeping the customer.

In addition, two other key processes were prescribed:

1. Raising capital.
2. Managing the business.

The goal at Oakwood was a structure with fewer boundaries and more cohesiveness and, as well, a structure that concentrates key functional and management expertise at the core where it is most needed. Ultimately, the precise model adopted was not as important as the creative movement to make the organization more accountable to the customer. This new structure and its rollout reinforced the cultural norm at Oakwood of focusing on the customer while removing barriers to that behavior. The words and the actions are now in sync. In fact, the management and staff are now held accountable for their customer-oriented roles as reflected in the new organizational titles and the performance and reward systems that support them. The structure and culture are mutually reinforcing. With their hybrid model, senior managers now stand ready to reap the benefits of both functional excellence and cross-functional teaming.

---

products Procter & Gamble gives each employee has strengthened that company's sense of community. Likewise, we find that an employee's first day on the job—the welcome received,

Strong, positive cultures result when rewards are strictly linked to performance against objective criteria.

the orientation provided—is taken as a harbinger of many, many things to come. The foundations of culture need to be established immediately and constantly buttressed to achieve real change.

Consider employee rewards. Smart companies do not allow rewards to be handed out haphazardly. A strong, positive culture results when rewards are strictly linked to performance against objective criteria. It is reinforced when the company routinely seeks out managers and employees who consistently achieve beyond their job descriptions. This is a way of showcasing values—of giving a very individual face to the desired culture, behavior, and decision making. When Kerm Campbell took over as CEO of Herman Miller, he set out several goals for the company. Reflecting these goals, the 1994 annual report is written around corporate heroes who have made the right things happen. Each hero is showcased with pictures and quotes, as in the feature stories of a magazine. We should add that the psychic rewards are backed up with financial rewards, and this is as it should be.

7. Drive Culture from the Top Down and from the Bottom Up

So far, we have been recommending ways to drive culture change from the top. But you can and must work to create change from the bottom up as well. Organizational change won't happen without personal change. We all wish that this weren't so, but it is. Recognizing this, you need to provide your people with the coaching and tools necessary to make the changes they must. Many companies are finding a "360 degree feedback" program—in which employees evaluate each other anonymously through a third party—helpful, but only when backed up by personal counseling and follow-up. It is not enough to show someone his or her weaknesses. The managers we interviewed emphasize the need to work with people both to make clear how they can improve and, with a light hand, to make clear when necessary that the desired improvements have not yet been made.

You may also need to use middle managers more effectively. Early in your culture change program, help middle managers learn the key points of the new value system, and then brainstorm how these values can be lived—and transmitted to one and all. Although many have been pushed out, the remaining middle managers are at the center of organizational transformation. They are often in a position to make or break it. As important transmitters of new values and emerging

Organizational change won't happen without personal change.

Figure 7.1
Drive Culture Top Down and Bottom Up

The campaign to reshape a culture must be strong, multidimensional,
and as penetrating as the culture itself.

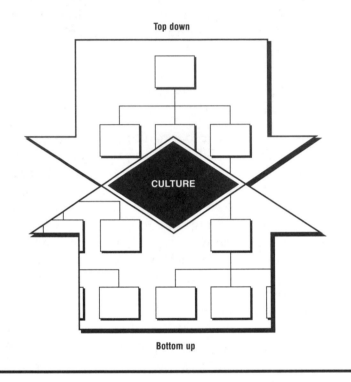

strategies, they have to be rewarded for their participation in
structured, distinct ways, and they must learn how to reward
those reporting to them.

Conclusion

The importance of culture will only increase as organizations
continue to transform toward flatter, looser, networklike structures. We have attempted to draw a bead on the issues surrounding culture and the core paradox that one needs to focus

The importance of culture will only increase as organizations continue to transform toward flatter, looser, networklike structures.

on things other than culture to create a new culture. Offering an experience-tested model, we hope to have provided a tangible set of issues to work on in order to create positive change, and more than a little, in your organization's culture.

It is our hope that you will find this chapter to be one of the most valuable in this book. Culture is central. With few exceptions, it is misunderstood and underutilized. Become an exception. Successful work on culture change offers a way to be exceptional in more ways than one.

Notes

1. James Brian Quinn, *The Intelligent Enterprise* (New York: The Free Press, 1992), p. 375.
2. Wendy Bounds, "Kodak under Fisher: Upheaval in Slow Motion," *The Wall Street Journal,* December 27, 1994, Sec. B., p. 1.
3. Christopher W. L. Hart, "The Power of Internal Guarantees," *Harvard Business Review,* January–February 1995, p. 64.

PART FIVE

THE FOURTH PARADOX PRINCIPLE:

True Empowerment Requires Forceful Leadership

Whatever does not spring from a man's free choice, or is only the result of instruction and guidance, does not enter into his very being, but still remains alien to his true nature; he does not perform it with truly human energies, but merely with mechanical exactness.

**Karl Wilhelm von Humboldt,
German statesman, philologist**

Eight

Empowering through Leadership

The final test of a leader is that he leaves behind him in other men the conviction and the will to carry on.

Walter Lippmann, U.S. journalist

W e visited the topic of empowerment in a chapter of our first book, *Better Change*. To our surprise, we launched a dialogue with executives across the country. Many are working hard to involve their people more actively in all aspects of the business: managing, planning, employee development, recruiting—everything. However, it became clear that none of them finds this easy. None feels intuitively able to know just how much rope to give their people, to understand when to withdraw, when to step in and lead. There was veiled tension in their reports and reflections. They were dealing, we came to see, with a paradox:

•••••

True empowerment requires forceful leadership.

•••••

The managers with whom we spoke want it both ways. They want to draw upon the best characteristics of the newly democratized workforce. They want to capture the spirit of initiative in their people. They want to use the social skills of their employees to succeed in an environment that demands personalized service. On the other hand, these managers do not wish to rely solely on employee initiative. They are reluctant to just "let it happen." And for good reason. Leadership—a new form of leadership—has never been so important.

Power must be used effectively in order to successfully surrender that power to others.

To understand this paradox, we need to explore the characteristics of leadership and empowerment. As with the other paradoxes of this book, workable and powerful answers are not found at one extreme or the other. Synthesis of seeming opposites is the key. To solve this management enigma, power must be used effectively in order to successfully surrender that power to others.

A New Perspective on Leadership

A new generation of corporate managers is beginning to understand and live a new, interactive model of leadership.

Their leadership relies more on the power of *influence* than of command and control to motivate. While they may not have all the right answers all the time—in our complex world, who does?—they move the organization in the right direction through vision and strategy. Their leadership is based on mutual respect and reinforced by effective communication skills. They understand the importance of clearly defining decision rights at all levels of the enterprise. And they cultivate decisiveness and commitment—but only after drawing on the creativity of vigorous debate.

A leader is, above all, responsible for achieving the organization's goals.

Leadership is not the same as management and control. A leader is, above all, responsible for achieving the organization's goals. The buck stops there. *Someone* has to be fully responsible for the organization's long-term success. This responsibility sets the leader apart and confers on him or her both the right and the duty to intervene, to take charge when necessary.

The role of the leader

- Establishing and communicating a vision and strategy
- Setting objectives
- Motivating people
- Creating a productive culture
- Developing the organization
- Initiating transformation

Many corporate leaders are practicing this kind of leadership. Take the example of Ken Coleman, senior vice president of Silicon Graphics. Coleman doesn't talk about empowerment. But he believes that "people have the ability to perform at much higher levels than we generally believe they can." One of Coleman's favorite stories is about a hotel owner in the United Kingdom who did a survey of hotel employees to see if they could remember more than 50 names at any one time. Given proper incentives, the hotel owner found that the employees could remember up to 200 names. The point Coleman takes away from this: At almost any one point, a manager can say, "My people have greater potential."

Coleman has helped create an environment that balances the demands of leadership and a new sense of empowerment. At Silicon Graphics, people can achieve their potential, and they, in turn, believe in and commit considerable energy and enthusiasm to the company. While average turnover in Silicon Valley is 25 percent, Silicon Graphics' has been 7 percent.

To allow employees to achieve their potential, Coleman nurtures people's skills and values, which, in turn, creates a passion for what they are doing and a new level of commitment to the company. "Passion can be your most powerful weapon. You won't believe what is possible." When passion is unleashed, "your people will do the best for you, because they know they are doing the best they can for themselves."

At the same time, the organization has a right to expect a new level of commitment from employees. As Coleman puts it, "You have to create an organization where commitments are real, and where employees know that it is *not OK* to not be committed." Business objectives are important: "This is a business enterprise, not a university." And commitments are real.

To balance organizational and individual commitments, Silicon Graphics has set in place a vision around the importance of visual computing; it is a vision in which everyone at the company can believe. Further, individuals are given latitude in achieving that vision. As Coleman says, "You must have a high tolerance for people who use a different method than you would to achieve the vision."

Harry Moulson, managing director in charge of the most profitable division of British Gas—the pipeline and gas storage division—understands the need for leadership just as Coleman does, but he exercises it in a completely different way to achieve equally good results. He has moved his office from a serene riverside suite in London to a corner desk in a room as busy as it is noisy: an open-plan office in Solihull near Birmingham, in the north of the United Kingdom. This is not a public relations exercise. Moulson understood that he needed to get rid of the vestiges of hierarchy that had stymied British Gas in the past. The decision to give up a private office sent a powerful message through his organization: The barriers are coming down.

Just three years ago, British Gas was a stable—some would say stuffy—utility with a bureaucratic mentality. Thirteen management and supervisory levels separated the chief executive and, in Moulson's words, "the guy who digs holes in the street." Facing tough competitive challenges, British Gas began a restructuring project aimed at regaining its competitiveness. It reorganized into five national business units from 12 regional units and created a process-based organization.

But the real story is the style of leadership Moulson has used to make this division the most profitable in the company. He understands that balancing the leadership/empowerment paradox requires an in-the-trenches, "I'm no better than you" style of leadership. He's in the field with his people—*leading* in order to empower. He's willing to confront upper management, and his courage is not lost on the frontline employees. Such actions communicate that the people of his division can create a high-performance environment driven by their ideals and ideas.

Empowerment

Exercising this style of leadership allows these new corporate leaders and their organizations to reap the benefits of a philosophy and programs centered around empowerment. Coleman and Moulson understand the importance of empowerment with a clarity that may escape others. Empowerment can appear to be a luxury we can't afford at a time when speed and decisiveness are crucial. But it is no hollow indulgence. There are few things more powerful than switched-on workers who believe themselves to be valued for more than their necks down. We have found that empowerment can revitalize an organization, but only when it is genuinely, forcefully implemented.

> **There are few things more powerful than switched-on workers who believe themselves to be valued for more than their necks down.**

Empowerment is a milepost in the evolution of work. But there is no clear consensus on its meaning. In our experience, the most thoughtful managers boil it down to the following:

- **Improving Decisions**—Creating a distinct architecture of decision rights to clarify responsibilities and promote decisiveness, speed, flexibility, and responsiveness, particularly to customer needs.
- **Battling Complexity**—Managing the enormous complexity in today's business environment by breaking it up and pushing it *out*.
- **Gaining Flexibility**—Using the flexibility and resourcefulness of employees to respond to continuous change.
- **Creating Passion**—Capitalizing on the full potential of the human spirit by creating a highly charged, high-initiative workforce, motivated to overcome big odds in order to achieve the organization's objectives.

The managers we interviewed are not a group of wild-eyed radicals preaching the gospel of empowerment as if *it* alone can save the company. They see it not so much as a cure-all as a natural and potent way to motivate people, gain versatility, and deal with complexity by distributing it. They point to a need for flexibility in serving customers, and they know from experience that well-trained employees can provide this flexibility. Many confess that they are surprised by the fountain of new ideas that flow from increased employee involvement. The majority say that they could, should, and will do more along these lines.

> **Empowerment is a natural and potent way to deal with complexity by distributing it, motivating people, and gaining versatility.**

Employees welcome empowerment for many reasons beyond their instincts for freedom and latitude. The restructuring and downsizing over more than a decade have permanently dispelled any illusion they might have about the permanence

The Internet: A Metaphor for Empowerment

To understand the potential and the challenges of empowerment, consider the organization of the Internet. By pushing complexity *out,* the Internet gains enormous flexibility and capacity. The massive workload and communications trafficking taking place minute by minute on the Internet is divided up and widely distributed. Each network node is powerful enough to do its part. There is no reliance on "the center" for command and control. Cut out a node, truncate some linkages, the work proceeds. The overall architecture and underlying standards integrate the whole of the network into something much larger than the sum of its parts.

Like the Internet, empowerment pushes complexity out to individuals and groups capable of grappling with it. Management at the center of the company no longer shoulders responsibility for the bulk of the workload. Instead, that workload is broken down into more manageable pieces and shouldered by those who understand their piece best. Empowerment signals that everyone in the organization is accountable for his or her actions. In a truly empowered world, the buck will float around, stopping where it must but never pausing too long in one spot. At times, things get messy and look somewhat out of control. But in the end, like the Internet, the whole of the company becomes much larger than the sum of its parts.

The development of the Internet would have been impossible without certain software, operating systems, and telecommunications standards. Without standards, the Internet could never have been woven together. Empowerment also relies on certain standards to make things efficient *enough.* Standards in this case apply to issues such as decision rights, cultural norms relating to communications patterns, decisiveness, inclusion or exclusion, and organizational structure.

of *any* institution, let alone the one for which they work. Smart managers and employees (the ones you need) don't want to sit back and oversee their own demise. The people we interviewed say in effect that if the captain cannot be wholly trusted to complete this voyage, *they want a hand on the tiller.* Thus, many employees seek the opportunities empowerment provides to take more initiative, to be more decisive, to make better decisions. They want influence.

The leadership/empowerment paradox is indeed centered around the *sources of influence.* To feel that they have influence, employees must be able to affect decision making in their areas of responsibility. This, in turn, requires them to be genuinely involved in the business. And our experience shows that genuine involvement comes about only when leaders lead, that is, when they not only invite but at times *force* real participation in pivotal decisions.

Empowering employees requires long-term commitment and provides lasting rewards in return. Every company where we interviewed is engaged in some form of organizational change involving new strategies, new structures, new cultural characteristics, new technology, new processes. Managers seem to be convinced that these solutions will be durable only if they empower employees. We also encountered signs of the key paradox: Where leadership was clearly in evidence, the benefits of empowerment are being achieved and embedded in the culture.

Balancing Leadership with Employee Involvement: The Heart of the Matter

Solving this paradox requires a balance of leadership and employee involvement. Those of us who lead teams and manage people need to get this balance right daily. In a hundred situations a month, each of us must decide: How much leadership? How much "involvement"? Or, as one of our clients put it, "I struggle each day with this question: When do I push the *leadership* button and when do I push the *involvement* button? I know I need to push *both* on most issues; but when, and how much of each?" No manager or executive can escape this issue. Gill Amelio, CEO of National Semiconductor, was recently quoted: "Empowerment is hell. And, not because it isn't working, but because of the uncertainty of nonintervention . . . All of us are action oriented . . . And learning to recognize that sometimes [intervening] is not the right thing to do—that you might actually suboptimize the performance of the organization—knowing when to intervene and when not to intervene are new skills."[1]

Two Examples—One Bad, One Good

Decision rights must be explicit and carefully mapped against the real needs of the business. Too often, however, they aren't.

Recently, a large multinational instituted a process-based approach aimed at better customer service. Unfortunately, management failed to think about the impact of this change on its European subsidiaries. By switching from a geographic structure organized around a group of powerful country managers to a structure based on line of business with power residing in the United States, the company put each U.S. product line and associated management team in control of all aspects of that particular business from suppliers through sales. European operations became an extension of sales and distribution in the United States.

Intended to empower those with the best potential to serve customers, the new structure is failing in Europe. While in theory the managing director for Europe was to be given the leadership necessary to make the transition, in practice he has been given little influence over decisions in his market. The country managers now report to several different U.S.-based product-line managers but continue to run their operations as fiefdoms. Competing for inventory that is monitored only on a Europe-wide basis, they must manipulate the system to meet their needs. The results? Productivity has declined, inventory is scarce, and the European customers the process

system was designed to benefit are going elsewhere.

In contrast, a major oil company is starting a process orientation by taking into account the need to empower managers at several different levels, that is, confer on them broader responsibilities together with explicit decision rights. The company is reorganizing around its most important business processes, which include the management of strategy and business performance, research and development, manufacturing, and distribution, marketing, and selling. These core processes will, in turn be supported by a network of services grouped around finance and administration and IT infrastructure. The plan calls for the company to outsource many core operations such as the search for new reserves, refining, and product and service development. Other internal processes, such as human resources management, will also be outsourced.

Management has precisely outlined the new responsibilities of middle and lower-level management. These managers know that they are free to make decisions to control and coordinate outsourced functions. They will also be expected to manage the key internal support teams. Managers in charge of shared services will be empowered to take real action to ensure they function smoothly. The result is something quite new and potent: nearly a virtual oil company—with employees empowered to make it work.

Figure 8.1

Image of Balance Scale: Leadership versus Involvement

Walking the balance beam of leadership and initiative on the
one hand and empowered involvement on the other is a
constant challenge to all managers.

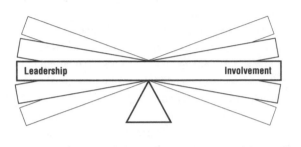

One of the most vital tensions of this paradox is the need
to foster open, freewheeling debate—and the need, therefore,
to gain unqualified commitment by all parties once the decision is made. High-performing organizations manage to have
it both ways: healthy, creative conflict in generating ideas and
exploring alternatives, decisiveness and commitment to initiatives once they're blessed.

Smart managers do want both. They recognize that most
people wish to be a part of things—that they've had a say in
things. If you want their full energies, they expect to be included at some level in the discussion of ideas and the development of solutions. They want to be informed and consulted
on issues that affect their work.

Unless decision rights are clearly defined, these deliberations can become hostile and the discussions prolonged. Debate can degenerate into rancor. Nothing gets done. Managers
become frustrated because they see no forward movement.
Employees become frustrated because they've been told they
are empowered but their solutions are not always adopted,
and they may even have a "losing streak" during which the

boss's ideas prevail again and again. Involvement is messy but necessary. Manage without involving your people—but don't expect much from them. Involve them, and things get complicated fast.

Because of this complication, clear thinking about what decisions are most important and who ought to make them is essential as you push toward higher levels of employee involvement. Managers who succeed in this exercise are explicit about decision rights. They lay out the architecture for decision making in their organization. They answer the question, "Who decides who decides?" At each level of the organization, they know, those who are responsible know, and everybody else knows.

> **Smart managers answer the question, "Who decides who decides?"**

Teachings of the Gyroscope: Empowerment

Suspend a spinning gyroscope in a loop made by doubling its pull string. The gyroscope will maintain any angle above or below the horizontal at the bottom of the loop. It magically resists gravity. Its internally generated forces allow it to perform this feat.

Not unlike empowered employees. Energized by new responsibilities and matching decision rights, and properly prepared for their new roles, employees can perform daring acrobatic feats within their spheres of influence. Nothing is too much—no process puzzle, no strategy search, no demand for sheer time on the job if conditions require it—when they are certain of their ownership and reasonably sure that a triple somersault in midair will be noticed—and in its proper time rewarded.

Figure 8.2
Gyroscope Image

The Tale of a Flightless Bird

The case of Kiwi Air Lines provides a perfect example of empowerment that tends to anarchy without limits and strong leadership. Kiwi started as a good idea. When Eastern Airlines went out of business, former Eastern pilots decided to set up their own company. Given the implosion of Eastern Airlines over labor-management issues, it was only natural for this new employee-owned carrier to opt for labor-management peace through employee empowerment.

At first, employee involvement seemed to be working well. The employees performed their duties enthusiastically, service and dependability were judged positively, and passenger traffic picked up. The airline grew steadily from 1992, and within a short time had increased the number of miles flown by 200 percent.

Gradually, however, involvement turned to contention and then to anarchy. The employee-owners perceived no limits to their empowerment. Although the pilots had hired managers to run things, they did not respond to management suggestions because they were, after all, *owners*. Flight attendants began to disregard certain management requests, such as offering products in flight. Pilots refused to fly charters or meet with travel agents. Meetings became nightmares because everyone wanted to be part of each decision. "For the sake of solidarity," unpopular decisions were *not* made. The situation soon escalated into a hate-mail campaign against the chairman, Robert Iverson. Pilots began to reject all of his suggestions—including his proposals on the leasing of planes and ways to get new investors on board. When he was summarily terminated, his parting comment was, "One of the stupidest things I ever did was call everybody owners."[2]

This is not to suggest that Iverson was right and the employees wrong. It *is* to suggest that empowerment needs boundaries, and leaders willing and able to impose them.

What You Can Do as a Leader

As a leader who wishes to make dramatic improvements in your organization's performance, begin by recognizing that even an empowered workforce wants and needs a strong leader. This recognition takes courage in a society that has become sensitive to the rights of diverse groups, many of which are crying out for greater "voice." But we know of no shining case of empowerment that doesn't involve the participation of a strong corporate leader.

The Courage to Empower

Courage is often the result of a personal turning point or revelation that lifts an individual to a new level of understanding. This understanding becomes a firm part of "the courage of one's convictions." Consider the example of Wayne O. Smith, executive vice-president with the BFGoodrich Chemical Company and chief operating officer of BFGoodrich Specialty Chemicals.

Smith's perspective is truly extraordinary in every sense of the term: He was a prisoner of war in Vietnam. Smith describes the unique source of his own courage—his turning point—as happening early in his five-plus years as a POW. For many weeks after ejecting from his F-4 Phantom and being captured, he was isolated and subjected to an extraordinary level of abuse. Then one day he was able to exchange a few words with another POW on the way to a washroom. The other POW conveyed the tap code used by others to communicate in the "Hanoi Hilton," despite being locked in a small, windowless cell. Smith describes the effect: "That moment probably changed my life for the years I would be interned in North Vietnam, but even today I'm sure it has affected my thinking and my actions. It snapped me out of my depression and misery . . . everyone supported each other in remarkable ways . . . Without such a lifeline of support from the others I'm really not sure that I could have mustered enough inner strength alone to have continued the will to live. When I reflect on the greatest value from my experience (as a POW), it is the appreciation of the benefits we can derive from each other: our families, our neighbors, our co-workers."

Smith has put this lesson to good use at the specialty chemicals operation of BFGoodrich. The company is well along in a dramatic transformation from a tire manufacturer to an aerospace and specialty chemicals company. Specialty Chemicals' strategy is to leverage its technical expertise, flexible production capabilities, and market presence in the chemical industry to provide essential products to its customers.

The challenges Smith faced when he arrived last year were clear. Since over 80 percent of the shareholders were new in the last few years, it was imperative to show that the new BFGoodrich could produce consistent long-term results. BFGoodrich needed to become the highly respected performer it had been in its previous 125 years and attract a loyal investor following. Smith had to develop a plan for Specialty Chemicals to do its part and motivate its management and employees to make it happen.

Smith began by establishing the Segment Executive Team (SET), a group of six top managers and himself. This group met three times each month to develop the strategy they would follow in the business units. They agreed on a strategy that focused on certain

The Courage to Empower *(continued)*

core products and capabilities while divesting others. Once he had the agreement of the SET, a larger management group was convened, called the All Chemical Team (ACT). This group was asked for input about how best to implement the strategy and asked, as well, to shoulder important roles in carrying it out.

These teams helped get many managers involved, but Smith truly wanted *everyone* to be involved and empowered. So he went further, using the SET and ACT teams and his own energy to get the message out. He made videos, appeared on the shop floor, and repeated key messages over and over. Finally, he surveyed all employees to assess the culture and created what he called Value Added Teams (VAT) to address specific concerns raised by the survey. The VATS began their work with initiatives to:

1. Eliminate bureaucracy.
2. Align reward and incentive systems with strategy.
3. Improve the effectiveness of communication programs.
4. Manage talent and technical skills of employees and management.
5. Globalize the business segments (Europe and Asia).

In addition, Smith set up four ongoing councils that deal with issues in manufacturing; human resources; health, safety, and environmental; and purchasing.

As you might expect with his life experience, Wayne Smith is no ordinary leader. And with his charismatic style he might have set himself up and run things like General Patton. On the contrary, Smith has had the courage to lead forcefully and then get out of the way—letting the people of BFGoodrich do the rest.

Built on the example of senior managers like Wayne Smith, what follows are insights about how best to lead an organization toward greater levels of truly effective   empowerment.

1. Connect the Dots, Then Establish and Communicate Vision and Strategy

Readers of our book *Better Change* find that the notion of connecting the dots strikes a responsive chord. Connecting the dots means analyzing the coherence of management and employee ideas and making sure that they result in a whole greater than the sum of the parts. Our work with companies and research continue to support this notion. Connecting the dots applies to the entire corporation.

There are questions to be answered that only leaders of independent mind and courage can answer. What is the relevance of the various initiatives? What value is added by each and by the sum of them all? How do they reinforce one another? What are the optimizing economics? Are any of the "dots" extraneous? Should they be moved—or just plain erased? Having drawn the picture and made, if necessary, some tough decisions, top leaders bring the workforce on board. They actively communicate to employees what the picture they've drawn means.

If the picture you draw is honest, coherent, and engaging, employees will naturally want to get involved.

That leaders must develop and communicate a vision is conventional wisdom. That they must do so in a way that includes employees is not conventional wisdom. If the picture you draw is honest, coherent, and engaging, employees will naturally want to get involved. They will line up to be a part of it. If the vision has little to do with anything other than increasing shareholder wealth, they will not line up—and you will have lost a major opportunity both to lead and to empower.

2. Focus Directly on Decision Making

If you tackle the leadership/empowerment paradox head-on, you have to create a decision rights architecture. In the command-and-control model of the past, decision rights were clear to everyone. This is not so today. Decision rights are a combination of authority and responsibility with awareness of where the real limits lie—and today all this must again be spelled out and communicated clearly. High-performing organizations understand the importance of the question, "Who decides?" and of that key related question: "Who decides who decides?"

The way decisions are made must be clear and reinforced. At each level, the goal is to ensure that decisions are the best possible, made swiftly and based on real data and credible assumptions. Reality looks different from different levels. Only those with the relevant data and the right perspective can make realistic, timely decisions. A strong rationale for empowering frontline employees is that empowerment puts the decision in the hands of those with the data and with reality (the customer!) looking them square in the face.

Assigning decision rights includes deciding which are the most difficult and important decisions faced by the organization, and who should make them. The answers are not as obvious as they sound. The managers we interviewed have taken the time to identify various types of decisions and to get management to agree on who decides what, where, and how.

Decision making in the context of ongoing operations is one thing. Dealing with crises is a different matter, and must often be approached differently. Smart companies set up specific mechanisms for crisis management—often involving temporary teams of the type discussed in our chapter on the individual and the team. In one client organization, for example, ad hoc teams are put together to handle seasonal crises. These temporary teams are put in place only to make certain crucial decisions. Once the issues are resolved, the team is dissolved— until it is again needed.

Senior managers in empowered organizations put in a good deal of time thinking about how to delineate responsibilities. In the pattern of accountabilities and responsibilities throughout the organization, they need to gauge where the views of employees deviate from their own. They make a point, often, of stating clearly where responsibilities begin and where they end.

3. Reignite Middle Management

For years now, it has been fashionable to bash middle managers. Weren't they the ones blocking change? Weren't they the laggards who filled non-value-adding coordinator roles?

Weren't they the ones being wiped out in streamlined, flattened, networked organizations? In the older, bureaucratic notion of the corporation, their role in the middle was to "pass on" decisions made at the top to those implementing them at the bottom. Business reengineers could discover no value in this role.

The move to flatter organizations has taken out layers, and many so-called middle managers took the hit. Companies responded to cost pressures by getting rid of people with only coordinating roles. But plenty of middle managers survived, and some of the best executives we know are looking at them from a new perspective. They see, not hapless pencil pushers, but rather a value-adding resource at that unique place, the middle, which offers a 360 degree perspective. Middle managers are in the best spot to integrate the corporation because they can translate strategy into execution.

Middle managers are in the best spot to integrate the corporation because they can translate strategy into execution.

Tomorrow's horizontal organizations will never work without managers serving as structural linchpins. As our organizations become flatter, these individuals will operate where hierarchy and horizontality meet. The larger and more complex the organization, the more process-based you seek to become, the more critical become these individuals.

Midlevel managers now have the opportunity—and the need—to develop new skills, such as coaching and facilitation, and to contribute directly to customer satisfaction. Leading UK retailers such as Sainsbury's (food) and WH Smith (stationery and office supplies) have headed in this direction.

Midlevel managers will need encouragement to make this transition, and even then it may not be easy. They are often the most cynical about the potential benefits of change, since they've "seen it all before." This attitude can be addressed; it is not beyond hope of change. One insurance company focused

Figure 8.3

Tomorrow's Midlevel Managers

Tomorrow's midlevel managers will be the linchpins at the nexus
of hierarchy and horizontalness.

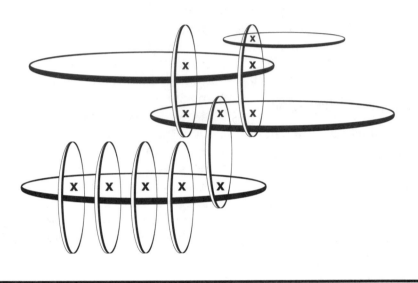

executive-level training and incentives on its middle managers—an extraordinary show of interest, respect, and expectation. An aircraft manufacturer focused its culture change
program squarely on middle managers, who soon perceived
in this an opportunity to shape the future of the organization
and thus became partners in achieving success. In a particularly astute move, this organization made some of the most
resistant middle managers personally responsible for delivering certain aspects of the program. While this approach required much senior management oversight, it succeeded in
turning around many of the midlevel managers.

Because they have borne the brunt of past de-layering programs, middle managers are often the first to give up and
leave. Of course, the best go first. It is in your organization's

interest to keep the best—but you'll be able to do so only by reigniting their sense of mission and confirming their value to the organization. An effective approach used by a number of our clients has been to communicate early and often to these individuals—always backing up words with actions—regarding their new value to the organization.

Contrary to conventional wisdom, your remaining middle managers may be essential to your organization's success. Developed and deployed properly, they can be a prime agent in the empowered organization. Their task? To turn strategy and vision into reality. And if you are moving toward becoming a "virtual company" by outsourcing a high percentage of activities and investing a high level of trust in your network of alliances, these men and women may just be the key to success.

4. Transform Creative Conflict into Commitment

Talk it up. Decide. Commit. Employees want to be involved in the business. Engaging them in decisions and forging consensus is now much more important. On the other hand, speed, initiative, and responsiveness have never been needed more. You want both. You need both. (See box on p. 154.)

Talk it up. Decide. Commit.

Dangerous notions: forging a culture around creative conflict, expecting complete buy-in from those whose views are not reflected in the decision. Dangerous and potentially transforming. Quaker's reengineering team saw this as a way to shake up an industry like ready-to-eat cereals that is long on tradition, long on brands that have been part of the American way of life since anyone can remember, and short on vibrant opportunity unless the organization springs to life. Renewal cannot be achieved without decisive actions that make sense to the entire company, not just to the folks at the top. People will commit when they see a great organization worthy of their commitment. And their commitment increases the greatness of the organization.

"Creative Tension," Says the CEO

The Quaker Oats Company has made a serious effort to transform its approach to the cereal business. Driven by a team, under the leadership of President John S. Breuer, Quaker Oats is empowering and involving its people at all levels throughout the organization. The new approach involved a horizontal, process-oriented organization coexisting with what's left of the vertically oriented, functional organization that preceded it. The innovation was to understand and value the possibility of keeping both styles in play. This coexistence produces *creative tension* if you get it right and all-out war if you don't. The traditional Quaker culture avoided conflict. The new Quaker values getting conflict out in the open and resolving it. The basis for resolving conflict between vertical, department goals and horizontal, process-driven needs is first who owns the customer and second strategy.

The goal has been a flatter, more dynamic Quaker with accountability and decision making pushed down. Accountability for specific goals is clearer. Team members are co-located, and designated process owners are given specific responsibilities. Further, the team has changed the reward system so that people will be paid on the basis of specific skills and value added to the organization. Managers and executives are to have the flexibility to move around the organization in new patterns of mobility. The result is a recharged workforce committed to making certain that Quaker attains a new leadership position in its industry. The old culture is changing, with the new one taking its place.

5. *Learn to Lead Horizontally*

Leaders who want successful lateral and vertical collaboration, cross-functional team efforts, and core process effectiveness need enough interpersonal dexterity to share power and responsibility. You will need to inspire and motivate those above you and beside you as well as those below you. You will need to manage through influence and by exercising political savvy in ways that will almost certainly be new.

Surprisingly enough, you can be most valuable as a model of decisiveness and initiative in contexts where you have limited direct authority. Giving others a role model of *sharing* power will be of much greater value than being decisive when

---

Figure 8.4

Horizontal Leadership

Tomorrow's leaders will have to draw upon a host of new skills; leading through the power of influence, not simply authority.

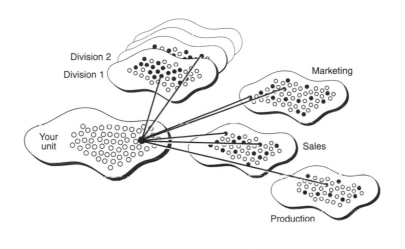

---

there is really no one in a position to oppose you. Acting as a role model is an effective means of leading and empowering concurrently.

Take the initiative even when you don't control all the marbles. Invest in your peers. Influence your peers. Promote the inclusion, not the exclusion, of others. Build consensus out of conflict. Get to decisions, and take action. All of this is what it means to be a role model today and lead in a more horizontal organization.

People have to feel that you're serious about this kind of leadership, and actions will always speak louder than words. Putting out the message in town meetings is important, but your interactions with others will do that much more. Think of Harry Moulson at British Gas, sitting at a desk in a busy office far from the elegance of London's executive world, shoulder to shoulder with his people.

Exercise your horizontal leadership muscles.

Exercise your horizontal leadership muscles. Join the local United Way board or some other governing board in which you must lead but have no power base. It will challenge you. You'll do some good. And you'll develop this new form of leadership.

6. Nurture Diversity

Empowerment is not easily achieved, even with the traditional white male workforce. And new problems will be posed by a more diverse workforce with more women. Enabling and fully empowering women and minorities presents unique challenges—challenges we must face, and face now. There will be fascinating paradoxes that need to be resolved. For example, as one executive told us, "Part-time work is a full-time job." Now what does *that* mean? You must already suspect that he has managed to state one of the key paradoxes in the employee experience of steady part-time work.

Bold leadership will be needed to enable and empower this new workforce, to nurture diversity, to *force* inclusion of those who add to the diversity of our thinking but need our help (and vigorous leadership) to bring them into the mainstream. Bold leadership will take many forms. It will certainly exercise a strong hand to establish enabling programs (such as part time, flex time, telecommuting, day care, etc.). And it won't ignore the need to reinforce cultural beliefs, norms, and celebrations that encourage others to accept diversity in the workplace.

7. Create Empowerment Zones

Reaping the benefits of empowered employees need not take years. Few dynamic leaders have the patience for that. Yet the term *empowerment* is often used in a sweeping, universal sense, referring to the full empowerment of an entire workforce. While a worthy objective, this would depend on wholesale cultural transformation, which would indeed take years. A great deal can be accomplished in short order by focusing one's efforts. "Empowerment zones" can be established in almost any structural, functional, or team setting. By carefully defining the targeted employee population, you can quickly give selected employees new authority, new responsibilities, and new latitude in serving their customers.

The logic for segmenting employee groups can be developed out of the original stakeholder analysis that underlies any serious change program (see our book *Better Change* on stakeholder issues). It is almost always true that different stakeholder groups move up the change curve at different paces. Some get with the program quickly, others lag. Whether they sprint or jog, stakeholder groups provide the most logical targets for empowerment zones. Each group will have a different agenda, different decision rights, and a different pace in receiving broadened powers. Using this approach, you "zone" employees according to their resistance to change— and this is likely to match their aptitude for greater latitude and accountabilities. We should add that this approach usually provides for earlier gains. By segmenting the employee population carefully, those ready for new responsibilities can move ahead quickly. They will also provide a role model for others.

Conclusion

One of the managers we interviewed—an individual known for his skill in managing people—perhaps said it best. When asked why he was so successful, he said simply, "I show them how. Then I mostly let them run. But I'm not reluctant to jump in when need be." There is real leadership in this attitude. Staff line up to work for this fellow. They want plenty of latitude. And plenty of leadership.

Notes

1. Gill Amelio, "An Interview with Eric Nee," *Upside*, February 1994, p. 12.
2. Adam Bryant, "One Big Happy Family No More; At Kiwi Air Lines, Hazards of Employee Ownership," *The New York Times*, March 22, 1995, Sec. D., p. 1.

Nine

Of Carrots and Sticks— and Technology Management

We are never betrayed, we betray ourselves. The world wants to be betrayed. Wisdom is found only in truth.

Johann Wolfgang von Goethe

L eaders managing those who manage major risk have a special charge. Empowering the men and women whose job it is to stick their necks out requires an uncommon understanding of projects and their risks, people and their motivations, and the interplay between organizational threats and incentives. We are thinking particularly of large-scale information technology (IT) ventures. Very real risk is shouldered by those who seek to provide their organizations with world-class IT infrastructure or who develop products for tomorrow's high-tech markets. Savvy leaders understand risk and the psychology of those who manage it. Through enlightened and forceful leadership, they empower their managers to act boldly yet always with intelligence. Those who cannot empower in this way will find the powers of emerging technologies to be just beyond their grasp. You do *not* want to put your organization at this disadvantage.

Endless Opportunities

The possibilities brought about by advances in information technology are truly astonishing. Since the advent of computers in the 1960s, technologies that help produce and distribute information have grown in sophistication at breakneck pace. Information technology is in fact one of few fields in which hype and predictions come close to what actually happens. Breathtaking advances in miniaturization and fabrication techniques have given us power in a palmtop computer comparable to that of a system the size of your garage just 30 years ago. And, astonishingly, computing has become cheap. Cost/ performance ratios have dropped to the point that a computer is now thought to be an appliance everyone should have, at work and at home.

This growing affordability spreads technology to a wider base of users. What was once the realm of highly trained MIS personnel is now common to most managers and employees. Moreover, the use of pen-based software and mobile digital communications allows the technology to spread to field professionals such as police officers, nurses, insurance claims estimators, and all manner of sales, delivery, and repair personnel. Increased bandwidth and global access to communications are making it much easier for individuals and businesses to share information.

Today, we have enough computing and communications power to make possible a new generation of applications that can increase productivity dramatically. While the central focus in the first decades of business computing was to automate tasks, in the future it will be to integrate work and capture and communicate knowledge. The opportunity to use technology to transform our organizations has led some companies to look for ways to create the "wired" organization, less dependent on traditional departmental structure and physical proximity. Wired companies can restructure the way business is done by encouraging workers in different locations and functions to collaborate in real time.

Endless Challenges

While the potential of technology seems infinite, the road to infinity is rocky. The continuous turmoil in technology markets presents a serious challenge to managers. An ever-changing array of vendors makes it more and more difficult to select the right technology. Determining which vendors will survive is a critical question for managers obliged to bet millions on their wares. Sorting out which partnerships will endure and which will develop market-leading standards and products is nearly impossible. Product cycle times are continuing to collapse, challenging all of us as the pace quickens.

While the potential of technology seems infinite, the road to infinity is rocky.

This anarchy brings with it unpredicted and unwanted side effects. The liberating force of the personal computer has unleashed innovation and creativity but also given rise to anarchy, redundancy, and waste. Used wisely, information technology enables inspired solutions. Developed carefully, those solutions can be very cost-effective. But wisdom and care are all too often missing in action.

Companies today spend millions of dollars—sometimes tens and hundreds of millions—on information systems projects, only to be plagued by late deliveries, cost overruns, unacceptable performance, missing functionality, and unstable operation. Despite the promise of information technology, few organizations have mastered the ability to develop systems that work. As a result, IT project failure is an issue of great concern to senior management. One telecommunications official admitted to us early in 1995 that his company had not successfully introduced a new system in 10 years! Sadly, such a track record is the norm rather than the exception. Some surveys have indicated that as much as 75 percent of the money spent on new systems is expended on applications that either never make it into production or fail to meet the objectives that justified investment in the first place.

This presents a fascinating and most important dilemma for senior managers. They want their project people to have a can-do attitude, to push through barriers, to believe in themselves, to do the impossible. But they also need them to be realistic. They need to know when their developers are in trouble, when they're not going to make delivery dates. After all, top management is making promises too—to customers, to employees, to the board, to shareholders.

Senior managers responsible for those developing large-scale IT solutions need to deal with the paradox at the intersection of human nature and large-scale project management. The paradox begins to open out when you consider Maslow's hierarchy of human needs: safety at the bottom, self-actualization at the top. Your task as senior manager is to provide that sense of safety. Their task as leaders of a demanding project is to "actualize" the project successfully—and thereby contribute to their organization's success at the same time as they confirm and deepen their self-recognition as able professionals.

You will need to understand the conflicting demands being placed on your project team. Are you asking them to perform a miracle? Yes, today, we ask a great deal of people—even a minor miracle, occasionally. But while asking for that, you must simultaneously provide a safety net for the developer in trouble. You need to make it *okay* to raise a red flag—and at the same time you need to increase the incentive to "make it happen." You will need to lessen the threat of failure, at least to the point that your people won't self-destruct because they feel compelled to ignore real problems. And you will need to reinforce their willingness to "break glass" to get it done. At this point of tension resides the paradox of this chapter:

> **When asking for a minor miracle, you must simultaneously provide a safety net for the project manager in trouble.**

• • • • •

*When you manage those who manage large projects . . .
emphasize the carrot, not the stick.*

• • • • •

*When you listen to those who propose major IT projects . . .
emphasize the stick, not the carrot.*

• • • • •

To understand and work with this paradox, senior executives (particularly those without much of a technology background) need to look into the reasons why projects fail. Once you understand typical failures, you will be better able to help IT project teams avoid them. And you don't need technical knowledge to manage expertly in this context.

Escalating Rewards, Escalating Risks

Senior executives now rely more than ever on information technology to transform their organizations. Thus, the impact of failure in the development of large systems is greater even than a few years ago. Ten years ago, it was a disappointment but no crisis when the EDP department was eight months late delivering a less than perfect accounts payable system. After all, the company had operated just fine for 50 years without that system. A decade ago, it was disturbing but no big deal when a systems investment of several hundred thousand dollars was lost because the intended application blew up somewhere along the line.

Times have changed. Systems are now so critical to operations that they are allocated a larger and larger slice of the long-term investment pie. The hurdle rate applied to such investments has tended to rise, as has the penalty for failure. In many organizations today, IT is a key part of "24 × 7" operations, that is, operations around the clock. Naturally, there are back-up procedures to get through down times. But a company's ability to do business degrades immediately when systems needed to conduct business are not on-line.

The investment needed to create new systems can be enormous. Recognizing that their information systems are outdated and hinder their ability to compete, many companies are overhauling them. Corporations becoming "global" need global information systems. Their goal is to integrate applications at all stages of the value chain and worldwide. Increasingly ambitious goals mean increases in costs. Five years ago, a "big" system project had a seven-digit price tag. Today, eight- and even nine-digit price tags are not unusual.

Balancing Forces

Figure 9.1
Gyroscope

Place a spinning gyroscope on end. Now gently try to push it over with one finger.

Surprise! The gyroscope doesn't fall over. Nor does it push back. Instead, it moves away from your finger, and the central shaft begins to revolve slowly in a circular motion called *precession*.

A perfect balance of forces has been restored—through an unexpected, counterintuitive move.

People are like gyroscopes!

Today's software makes possible greater communication across the organization, helps develop a process-based organization, and increases the positive impact of functions on one another. But this level of integration can make problems bigger. Like the electronic systems of a modern car, in which the malfunction of a single part can shut down everything, the entire operation risks shutdown when a problem crops up in a tightly integrated large-scale system.

Today's large-scale systems cost so much because they're so sophisticated and can be used for so many purposes. Fifteen years ago, systems developers would move and merge data from one set of files to another in a sequenced pattern of mainframe COBOL logic. Today, developers are being asked to create synchronous applications with data distributed to machines all over the world. The character-mode ASCII video screens of the past are being replaced with refined graphical user interfaces. In times past, a single vendor's field engineers arrived, pulled "the computer" out of a box, and plugged it in. Today, systems engineers hook together as many as 50 hardware and software components from 50 different vendors.

Unfortunately, the technical tools and management arts needed for systems development have not kept pace with our increasingly ambitious goals. The hardware cost/performance ratio has been doubling every two to three years. Software development productivity improves by an order of magnitude more slowly.

The consequences of failure have increased, as well, because systems play such a large role in achieving today's business goals. The promise of those new applications is so great that companies want to implement them as soon as possible. Few take into account the long lead times needed to develop the system and train employees how to use it. These realities significantly increase the size of the investment and the level of risk.

All of this has changed the atmosphere around IT projects. The transformation is startling. Large-scale information systems are now developed in an atmosphere of unrelenting pressure. Leading the development of large systems has

The longevity of today's CIO is about 30 months.

become a perilous activity, right up there with alligator farming and bungee cord research. In the United States, the longevity of today's CIO is about 30 months. Very few senior IT officials receive that 25-year pin. And how many senior executives boast about their systems development staff?

The tension surrounding large development projects requires senior IT developers, with their reputations and careers on the line, to find a just balance between openness and discretion. Under conditions of anxious effort toward a difficult goal along a risky path, there is a natural temptation to cover up delays, hide mistakes, and put off the inevitable truth-telling session. Project leaders ask themselves, how much "can-do" attitude should I adopt? All projects have problems. Given our problems, when do I need to come forward and tell the CEO that we're not going to make it? When do I tell the CFO I need more money to finish?

Why Projects Fail

Why do projects fail? As a manager, what can you do about it? Conventional wisdom maintains that the cause of most failures is the technology itself. Wrong. Information technology project failures are rarely caused by technical problems. Failures result from one of two causes: (1) the project was unrealistic from the beginning, or (2) management's approach to the inevitable problems that arise turned glitches into disaster. Executives spend too much time fussing with technology, not enough time *managing it.*

We want to press here a counterintuitive explanation for IT project failure, which we believe to be the correct explanation of most failures. *Large systems development project failures almost always stem from misconceived or pathological combinations of incentives and threats.* Neither the threat nor the incentive is properly conceived, appropriately communicated, or accurately perceived. And their timing is typically way off.

The Unrealistic Project

Unrealistic project expectations often arise from head-on collisions between the aspirations of IT professionals and their managers' needs to keep costs down and get things done quickly. Start with this caution: IT careers depend on getting projects approved. Approvals are most forthcoming for projects that promise lots of benefits, low costs, and speedy implementations. There is enormous pressure to lowball estimates in the face of management's natural desire to keep a lid on costs. Likewise, the pressure to overestimate benefits can be overwhelming. Today's "lie" pushes the day of reckoning out two years.

Information technology project failures are rarely caused by technical problems.

Are IT managers dishonest? No, but they *are* human. And humans have an uncanny ability to rationalize self-interested behavior. Moreover, the more competent managers are more likely to convince themselves that they can "handle it." In short, first they fool themselves, then they communicate foolishness to management.

Unrealistic project estimates often start out with a careful appraisal of the effort to develop software, but then seriously underestimate the effort required to make that software work in the new environment. The typical software project has four fundamental components:

1. Developing the new software application
2. Developing the interfaces to other existing applications
3. Converting and loading of data into the new application
4. Rollout—that is, establishing the operating environment, installation, training, etc.

People tend to focus on how long it will take to develop the software, and their estimates are generally credible. However, estimates for data conversion, interface development, and rollout are often crude and hopelessly optimistic. Evidence shows that software development comprises less than one-half of the typical systems project—but it is usually estimated at 70 to 80 percent and receives a like amount of estimating effort.

To grasp how these estimates can go so far off the mark, consider the myriad complexities of conversions. The great architect Ludwig Mies van der Rohe said, "God is in the details." Clearly, he wasn't an IT person. As far as IT is concerned, the devil is in the details—especially the details of data conversion. Data converted from multiple systems almost always requires significant cleanup. Sources doesn't correlate properly. Content values differ. Account numbers don't match. On the front end, it can appear simple: just find the data, map it, and code up a couple of conversion programs. However, experience always belies this simplicity. It is not uncommon to find that as much as 10 percent of the data cannot be converted by any automated method. As a result, literally hundreds of thousands of records need to be converted manually. There goes your estimate.

Most IT professionals know about these potential difficulties. But the individual doing the estimate almost always wants dearly to make the sale to top management. And the senior managers who have the power to review and pass on such estimates don't often have the technical know-how to question the numbers. At this point in the process, the incentives to estimate low are great, and the threats of doing so are minimal.

At the outset of most projects, the desire to get the project approved is fueled by legitimate initiative and enthusiasm. These things can overwhelm good judgment. As the proposal climbs the ranks for approval, the first really dispassionate official to examine the estimates is too senior to know what's going on. You can see why many IT projects are doomed before they begin.

Once systems development is under way, managers tend to stick with the original estimates well beyond the point where it becomes obvious that they are unrealistic. A classic "accordion effect" ensues. The project plan is revised weekly. Early

milestones are missed, but the end date holds firm. Consequently, all dates in the middle are squeezed ever closer together—like an accordion bellows.
Reality is ignored. Milestones turn
into millstones.

Reality is ignored.
Milestones turn into
millstones.

The care shown in planning and
development should match in size a
project's promised benefits. The estimates for both must be more realis-
tic. Sophisticated managers have learned this, and they have
begun to run critical estimates by independent "red teams" for
review. Such teams have no stake in the outcome. They focus
a realistic eye not only on the size of potential benefits but also
on the degree of anticipated difficulty.

Turning a Glitch into a Disaster

Once the project has been planned and approved, pulling the
plug is very difficult. As the project moves along, a number
of strange phenomena typically occur. In the first place, the
bevy of incentives that launched the project is replaced by a
swarm of threats. In other words, management's attitude
changes radically. Second, few managers have the courage to
cry "time-out" when they see a potential problem. Yet this is
precisely when leadership is so crucial.

These are not the only undesirable phenomena. Based on
our participation in thousands of systems implementations,
we have developed a comprehensive list of the problems
systems projects encounter. There is surprising predictability:
We haven't had to revise our list in five years, although we
would have been happy to do so. While new technology can
cause problems to differ in detail, none of the problems is
fundamentally new. But the old ones die hard. Sources of
trouble include scope control, estimating, project management,
and more. These problems will not "crater" a project without
management's help, but they do give management its opportunity to do just that.

By understanding the potential sources of trouble, you can
better estimate the cost of a project and, just as important,

know what to look out for as the project progresses. The most common problem is scope. Without crisp boundaries, the process known as "scope creep" sets in. To keep proposed investment costs down, project scope is often defined as narrowly as possible. Once the project is under way, however, and its potential becomes better understood throughout the organization, little things are added by management request or by the developers acting on their own. While features may be added, no one wants to add hours, dollars, or months to the project plan. The foolishness begins as those responsible tell themselves they will compensate at a later stage for the additional time and money required right now. Anyone who has hired a contractor to build a house will understand how unrealistic this is. You didn't anticipate that you and your spouse would suddenly hanker for a bay window looking west. That's fine, and maintaining enough flexibility to modify a design is not a bad thing. Scope creep is something different: It is a change in specs accompanied by failure to exercise honesty and common sense. The only way to avoid its negative consequences is to add time and money to the plan when adding features and functions.

Few companies subject their project estimates to a searching reality check. While few homeowners would sell their homes without having an appraiser compare their asking price to actual sales of similar homes, amazingly few companies do as much for systems projects. Another common problem is a mismatch between estimates and schedules. You not only have to review the amount of work, you have to verify whether you have allowed enough real calendar months to get all of this done. Too often, developers assume they can sharply increase the number of people on a project. They forget the learning curve necessary for people to become really productive. The result is what we term "cumulative optimism": a little optimism here, a little there—and suddenly you're a fool. The mystery is that few managers realize they do this to themselves because, after all, they were *only a little* optimistic—here and there and, well, a little bit there, too.

Little thought is commonly given to how much project success depends on parties and parts of the project outside the project manager's direct control. Organizations today are flatter, but project developers cannot realistically count on much help from across functional boundaries. In most companies, there are still too few incentives for cross-fertilization. The plan must take into account the time required to work (coordinate, negotiate, etc.) across borders.

Both senior and project managers should be realistic about their familiarity with the technology involved. Familiarity born of real experience will help them to know whether they understand both the potential and limits of a technology. If not, they must allow for experimentation. Unfortunately, most IT project managers are too confident of their technical abilities to admit that they don't understand something. Conversely, senior management is too confident of its "people judging" capabilities to admit that it doesn't have full confidence in the IT manager.

The Recipe for Failure

Here's the recipe for failure: Start with a project of real promise, one with lots of enthusiasm focused on its outcome. Then add a glitch. Next, add some very unpleasant consequences if the project leader faces up to the glitch here and now. Finally, throw in a pinch of the human tendency to rationalize and postpone. Allow the situation to simmer for several months. Presto—you've got yourself a mess!

> **Start with lots of enthusiasm. Add a glitch, some unpleasant consequences, and a teaspoon of rationalization. Presto! A mess.**

In extreme cases, we have seen behavior that can only be called pathological. The pressure can get so bad that IT project managers on occasion seem more than a little like an animal willing to chew off a leg to get out of a trap. The situation can become that painful, that destructive. A little problem develops. The project manager sees it for what it is—but the penalty for confessing even a minor problem is huge. In the face of this threat, the project manager rationalizes the problem away and

An All Too Familiar Tale

When a problem is first encountered, you can bet the ranch that the project team knows about it. Yet all too often the problem is left to fester until it becomes so bad that it can no longer be ignored. Several years ago, a major state agency undertook a large systems project using a systems integrator. Project staff decided to replace COBOL with a new programming language that promised significantly reduced development times, thus lower costs.

The work was meticulously planned. The new technology was subjected to the intense due diligence a $6-million investment demanded. Phase I software modules were programmed—representing about 15 percent of the system. The new programming language was working well.

At that point, the client authorized the project team to take the project to the next phase, which involved bringing Phase I on-line for a large number of computer terminals. As the team started moving in this direction, system performance plummeted. The new programming language was not

adequate for this phase of the project. The project manager calculated that the cost of switching back to COBOL— including reprogramming Phase I— would be $300,000. Fearing the impact on his career of recommending such a course of action, especially in light of certain performance-linked incentives offered by his superiors, the project manager chose not to inform senior management. Instead, he went to the software vendor with his dilemma. In typical fashion, the vendor said, "No problem—we'll be fixing the deficiencies you've come up against in the next release of the software."

The entire system was then programmed using the new language. And it failed miserably. Agency operations were severely affected. Senior managers from the systems integrator finally stepped in to reprogram the system to COBOL. What would have cost $300,000 to fix when the problem was first uncovered cost $3 million.

Facing up to the problem today always involves doing something unpleasant today. Putting the problem off always makes it worse.

---

doesn't disclose it. Months go by. No miracle occurs. The hole just gets deeper and deeper. At that point the manager goes off the deep end. Arguing. Picking fights with management. Calling in sick for days at a time. Anything to get out of the situation, to escape the problem.

What Can You Do?

Senior managers have begun to understand that they create the psychological pressures that are the behavioral backdrop of IT projects. All too often, these pressures give managers the incentive to push for approval of marginal projects and penalize managers who surface problems. The good news is that risk/reward systems can be devised to encourage effective behavior.

1. Best Paradox

As we have already argued, when managing those who manage large-scale projects you are well advised to remove threats and reinforce incentives. On the other hand, when managing those whose job it is to *propose* large projects, you should minimize the incentives and increase the threats! To our minds,

---

Figure 9.2
Threats and Incentives

As projects are proposed, you must manage the often overzealous incentive to make them happen — as this leads to faulty estimates, unrealistic cost/benefit projections, and other hazards. Once under way, however, you should work to limit the threats that inhibit an honest confrontation of the real issues, while reinforcing the need to stretch and reach new levels of achievement.

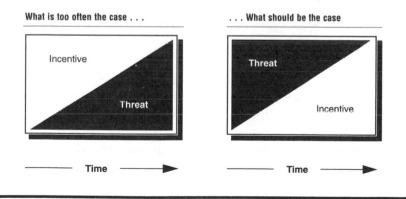

this situation is subtle enough to deserve an award for Best Paradox.

Penetrating the paradox begins by recognizing that high-initiative managers naturally tend to overstate project benefits during the proposal stage—while simultaneously underestimating anticipated costs. Your objective should be to force them to take a more independent, arm's-length view of the project. You want those who submit investment proposals to feel a real burden of responsibility to propose only worthy ventures. You want them to feel a threat, albeit a mild one. Further, you want to minimize the pressure they feel to get projects approved.

Conveying the threat is easier than limiting the incentive. Not long ago, a CEO gave an object lesson in the art of the threat. His major sports franchise was not making money at the time a project manager proposed a new systems effort to clean up and integrate some existing applications. In response to the project proposal, the CEO asked sternly, "Will it increase ticket sales? Will we win more ball games?" The next time the manager came around, he had a rock-solid business proposal to offer the CEO. The threat had been nothing personal; it was a simple statement of business objectives. But it worked.

Minimizing undue incentive to get projects approved is another matter. As you address the issue, you will be dealing with IT managers (the developers) and the line executives who typically sponsor such projects. For the developers, it is best to assure them that there are important initiatives to be undertaken and that they will play a role in them. However, they should not be encouraged to feel that any specific project proposal is must have, must do, at all costs. For the line executives, perhaps the best approach is to be very demanding in terms of return on investment and accountability. While line managers may be tempted to pass accountability down to the developers, make it clear that in most cases you simply won't buy that. If a system flops, you will hold the sponsoring line executives responsible. It is up to them to make the solution work.

2. Protect the Project People from the Consequences of Truth-telling

How many times has a senior executive said, in so many words, "We never penalize anybody for telling the truth." Would the project staff in your organization believe this? Trust is critical to truth-telling. At every stage of the project, people must feel that they can tell the truth without fear.

You have to build amnesty into your project efforts. Often, you will need to be very specific about amnesty. Do not assume that your people will understand that they can own up to mistakes or problems without fear of consequences. In our experience, this degree of candor is hard to achieve. We have seen that

Build amnesty into your project efforts.

candor appear most forcefully, and beneficially, in the context of a special effort to "lay everything on the table." Get out of the office into a relaxed setting and work toward a constructive dialogue. Without trust as a backdrop, it will be difficult. Paradoxically, when you need truth-telling the most it is sometimes hardest to get. For this reason, work hard to maintain that important covenant. A helpful step is to assign an independent—and powerful—executive to review projects. Part of this executive's charter must be to protect staff who surface unpleasant truths.

3. Estimate Wisely

A good estimate helps enormously. Procedurally, it helps to set up a process whereby independent parties validate estimates (both benefits and cost/time estimates) and revalidate them at key intervals during the project. For this to work, however, the officials validating the estimates must be in a position to protect project people from the consequences of truth-telling.

It is important to benchmark detailed project estimates against at least one similar project done elsewhere. Don't listen to those who say the project is unique. Of course it's unique—

Bringing Systems Thinking into the Process

The intricacies of creating and implementing an effective application system are anything but linear. The complexity of today's applications, the dynamic interactions of evolving user perspectives, shifting priorities, and an ever-changing business environment make the development of software an enormous challenge. Systems thinking can help.

We would encourage the reader to check out the models and system archetypes Peter Senge explored in *The Fifth Discipline.* Managers responsible for those who develop large IT systems will find special relevance in a systems archetype that Senge calls "Shifting the Burden." His definition follows:

> An underlying problem generates symptoms that demand attention. But the underlying problem is difficult for people to address, either because it is obscure or costly to confront. So people "shift the burden" of their problem to other solutions—well-intentioned, easy fixes which seem extremely

efficient. Unfortunately, the easier "solutions" only ameliorate the symptoms; they leave the underlying problem unaltered. The underlying problem grows worse, unnoticed because the symptoms apparently clear up, and the system loses whatever abilities it had to solve the underlying problem.[1]

This pattern can be seen in many a systems development failure. A short-term "quick fix" is made. It provides temporary "relief" but masks an underlying obstacle that gets worse with each new expedient. In the end, the real issues result in missed deadlines, budget overruns, and failed objectives.

A systems thinking approach provides those within and above the project a structured approach to think about issues. It also fosters dialogue and encourages you to push just a little harder to confront reality, to face those issues we often know at a gut level but allow the pressures of the day to obliterate—until they reassert themselves with magnum force.

---

they all are. However, intelligent comparisons will be informative and valuable. Even in cases where the technology is fairly new, it is always possible to find another project with similar attributes.

Benefits estimates must be scrutinized. Senior management should never be shy about questioning the benefits of the

Protect the project people from the consequences of truth-telling.

technology. A good rule of thumb is to listen to the proposed benefits, then discount by 20 to 30 percent. If the project still looks worthwhile after applying the discount, all to the good. If not, rethink the project.

4. Replace Sticks with Carrots

The key imperative is to eliminate penalties for facing up to issues early—without eliminating the incentive to succeed. This amounts to replacing sticks with carrots.

As the bumper sticker says, "S—— happens." Anticipate it by means of a contingency budget. You may need to reframe the psychology and penalty/reward system surrounding the use of that budget. Typically, when a project team draws from a contingency budget, the team is viewed as performing less capably. Undoing this psychology is the first step. The second step is to convert the stick into a carrot.

The contingency budget, in our experience, should equal about 20 percent of project cost. Promise the project team a bonus based upon the amount of contingency funds that go unused—provided, of course, that the software works. The stick is now a carrot. We have found such a contingency bonus much more effective than the usual threat of a penalty if the project is not finished "on time."

5. If You're Going to Fail, Do It Early

Failing early is a whole lot less expensive than failing late. Consider what mechanisms you can put in place to force a failure early, if one is to occur. Use prototyping to ferret out glitches. Use pilots to fail early with limited impact. At an early stage, develop a slice—make it a thick slice—of the system and try it. Do benchmark tests. Stress-test the software as soon as possible. Create some interfaces as soon as possible to discover how difficult that exercise will be. Convert 5 percent of the data in the first month. Some of this may be tricky to pull off—but failing early, if fail you must, will save you a bundle.

Communications

Technology's Invisible Hand

New information technology is often installed to open up communication— to "wire" or "network" an organization so that functional silos can be dismantled and customer-focused process teams can be built. Yet new IT has a dramatic, often overlooked impact on one of the most critical processes in an organization: when and how people communicate. Communication defines people's interactions and, ultimately, how they work together to accomplish business objectives.

In addition to the host of behavioral factors that affect the success of any new IT implementation, there is another layer of postimplementation behavioral implications to consider. Sociologists Lee Sproull and Sara Kiesler argue that understanding how technology will interact with routine practices and policies, and imagining the ways in which technology will lead to long-term changes in how people communicate and work together, is best brought to light by a "two-level" perspective on technology change:

A two-level perspective emphasizes that technologies can have both efficiency effects and social system effects. Most inventors and early adopters of technology think primarily about efficiency effects, or first-level effects, of that technology. We argue that second-level system effects are often likely to be more important for organizations . . . New technology can cause people to think and behave in qualitatively different ways. The consequences are more profound and the measurement is much harder than when measuring immediate changes in efficiency.

First-level effects of communication technology are the anticipated technical ones—the planned efficiency gains or productivity gains that justify an investment in new technology.

Second-level effects from communication technologies come about primarily because new communication technology leads people to pay attention to different things, have contact with different people, and depend on one another differently. Change in attention means change in how people spend their time and in what they think is important. Change in social contact patterns means change in who people know and how they feel about them. Change in interdependence means change in what people do with and for each other and how these coupled functions are organized in norms, roles, procedures, jobs, and department.[2]

Communications

Technology's Invisible Hand *(continued)*

Start preparing your organization for this invisible impact of new information technology. From the moment the project is approved, raise the incentive for the project manager to incorporate these "second-level" effects into the work plan. Develop strategies to manage them effectively and ensure better business results from the new system investment.

---

6. Take All the Obvious Measures to Protect Your Investment

Give yourself every chance by using the common approaches to good project management.

- **Invest only if the business case is compelling.** This may seem obvious, but the size of today's average IT investment and our national fascination with the potential of technology make it imperative that your business case be compelling. When this is so, the project will move more efficiently through the obstacles and problems—organizational and other—that always develop. Your business case must have broad support to carry the weight of today's sizable investments.

- **Plan as if it were the D-day invasion.** We can't overemphasize the importance of meticulous planning. Each piece of the work should be well defined, using benchmarks if possible. Each task should have a definable output and result. Benefits should be quantified, stated in clear, precise terms, and connected with performance measurements. It is important to quantify how much knowledge workers need at each stage.

    Make a realistic appraisal of the abilities of your IT people, and on that basis plan for the learning curve. Plan also for turnover and frustration, and allow for letting off steam. How wide is the project manager's span of control? Can it be widened? All stakeholders who will affect the implementation process should be identified and the group of sponsors who will get their buy-in outlined.

- **Pick the best project manager available.** We have seen the best-planned projects undone by managers who weren't genuinely able to lead the effort. Conversely, the right manager can sometimes make up for a project with a somewhat flawed plan. The best project managers provide the best reality checks. Most important, perhaps, they will know whether the team in place has the expertise to carry out the project, and they will know when personnel changes are necessary.

Conclusion

The hope that information technology enables organizations to reshape their business model to become efficient, effective, and competitive has been with us for several decades. There can be no doubt about the efficiencies gained through the intelligent application of computers and telecommunications networks. On the other hand, only a few companies have leveraged IT to its fullest extent. Their stories, oft told, are known to most managers: American Airlines' SABRE reservations system, American Hospital Supply's use of terminals at customers' sites. And there are others.

In the coming decade, we believe it will no longer be true that only a few companies will have truly mastered the uses of information technology. There will be obvious gains in the escalating potential of information technology and the competitive need to use it effectively. As its potential continues to grow, the pressure on all of us to use it wisely can only increase.

This combination of potential and competitive pressure will place a higher price than ever on missing deadlines, missing budgets, and missing functions in the development of information systems. Systems development will begin to move into the set of core competencies your organization must develop— or must outsource. There will be no other choices. The decades-old *hope* will soon become a mandate. Those companies that learn how to create and implement systems effectively will dominate markets in the decades ahead. Those managers who understand the nuances of motivation and fear that have such impact on project teams will help their companies win.

Be one of them.

Notes

1. Peter Senge, *The Fifth Discipline* (New York: Doubleday, 1990), p. 104.
2. L. Sproull and S. Kiesler, *Connections: New Ways of Working in the Networked Organization* (Cambridge, MA: The MIT Press, 1993), pp. 1–5.

PART SIX

THE FIFTH
PARADOX PRINCIPLE:

In Order to Build, You Must Tear Down

Less is more.

Ludwig Mies van der Rohe

Ten

Crafting Strategy in the New Environment

If you are planning for one year, grow rice.
If you are planning for 20 years, grow trees.
If you are planning for centuries, grow men.

Chinese proverb

When General Norman Schwarzkopf said, "No battle plan ever survived contact with the enemy," it seems he had it right. Executives are beginning to understand just how right. Yet all agree that strategic planning is essential. The general had a plan for Desert Storm, and planning hadn't been left to deskbound soldiers in Washington. The wisdom of his advice goes beyond a simple caution that no plan can hope to take into account all the vagaries of battle. What he left unsaid but surely intended is that you had better prepare your ground commanders to develop and execute "real-time" strategy and tactics. Without leadership of that caliber on the ground, victory will be elusive.

This lesson is becoming clear to companies poised to be the market leaders of the next decade. Strategic planning is being forced out of a back room at headquarters and pushed into the line. For years, strategic plans have been developed largely off-line, away from operations. Plans were often innovative but created in an abstract zone distant from the market. For this reason, they took into account few if any nuances that customers use to select among what they perceive as competitive alternatives. They also ignored or underestimated the ability of the competitive environment to change suddenly through new competitors or products and services "coming out of nowhere." In the worst of circumstances, plans were developed by brainy staff with little battlefield experience. Analysts with reams of data and a handful of "killer charts" were dispatched by headquarters to *inform* managers in the field. Many of these plans failed. They were out of touch; they won only lukewarm commitment from line managers.

The line managers we interviewed will have nothing more to do with plans that overlook market realities, which are now *global* realities for many managers. For this reason, planning is more difficult yet, if anything, more important than before. The irony—we would even say the paradox—is that in many organizations, strategic planning is becoming less relevant and more important at the same time. The aim of sound planning is more necessary than ever, but the decades-old planning process is heavily flawed for today's purposes.

In many cases the planning process has become a costly annual ritual in which a formal, wordy document is created with high purpose but little impact. This traditional approach to strategic planning (mechanical, top-down, and centralized) has failed. In client after client we have seen expansive plans that receive dutiful notice but little buy-in. One problem is the number of organizational layers that must be penetrated to translate the plan into action. Another is the sheer lack of connection between planners and line staff. Disbelief in the plan, and in the planners, causes line managers to resist even the valuable ideas in the plan. Neglect of a plan leaves you with no plan.

> **In many organizations, strategic planning is becoming less relevant and more important at the same time.**

When strategic planning is disconnected from operations, problems arise. Next thing you know, consultants appear on the doorstep clutching their favorite management theologies (experience curves, growth share matrices, value chains, etc.)—each touted as the key to your future. After weeks of expensive consulting work, the report is dropped on your desk. One manager with whom we spoke, a survivor of several such episodes, calls this the "seagull" approach to strategy consulting. Each time, consultants deposited their report and flew off to the next client.

When disappointment with the process peaks, all real strategic planning is put aside. One frustrated senior executive at a U.S.-based *Fortune* 50 manufacturing firm told us, "[Our CEO] simply doesn't believe in a centralized planning staff. So he got rid of it. But nothing has been created at the divisions in its place. Our plans are almost exclusively 'bottom-up.' We just add up the numbers!"

Good strategic planning is built on objectivity, analytical and creative skills, and a broad base of experience. Good strategic planners can be the source of creative and objective insights. However, the best companies now recognize that sound planning also has to involve those running the business and those closest to the market. Fusing these skills and experience is not easy. Smart companies now recognize, paradoxically, that . . .

•••••

The best strategic planning departments don't exist.

•••••

Great planning exists: Look at companies like Chrysler, Disney, Marriott, and General Electric. Great execution exists. McDonald's, Microsoft, and Federal Express are examples of world-class execution. But as with the other paradoxes explored in this book, the best managers now understand the need for synthesis and balance: synthesis of strategy and execution, integration of planning and operations, balance between thinking about the future and being clear about conditions today. Their objective is not a plan; it is *strategic change.*

This paradox of strategic planning ran through our interview with the CEO of a major bank. In the midst of a major organizational change and on the heels of a merger, he was outspoken in his disdain for detached strategic planning staffs. His model—which we see emerging in many forward-thinking organizations—is to bring together a cross-section of stakeholders, including major customers, for in-depth dialogues around the organization's vision, purpose, and strategy. In this case, an outsider was used to facilitate the process and provide an independent view. But the essence of the process involved developing a *collective* vision and strategy that won commitment from the entire group.

This should not be confused with the traditional "strategic planning off-site meeting," in which an orchestrated program of discussion reaches conclusions developed by staff and CEO *prior* to the meeting. Far from it. The bank's process engages all participants and draws out discord and debate to create a plan around which all can rally. This approach requires a careful blend of leadership and involvement, as discussed in Part 5 of this book.

The CEO leads this effort, but he insists on the working involvement of his managers. For example, decisions are hammered out *in* meetings whenever possible, not just discussed and set aside, only to show up in a directive from headquarters a month later. This means that the CEO must allow for—indeed demand—genuine dialogue about strategic issues before decisions are made. In-line planning staff can help frame the issues and potential solutions. They can bring facts and objectivity to the process. But the decisions lie with the line managers. All too often, we have seen a CEO put forth a strategic alternative, followed by a restrained discussion by managers who simply echo the idea. The process must encourage the participation of the entire group to reach the best solutions and to ensure their best efforts in implementing the new strategies.

In one organization, genuine dialogue started when the CEO asked the head of finance to present the strategic issues and proposed plan of marketing, asked marketing to present production's ideas, and asked production to present the finance plan. This merry-go-round fostered some of the best and most candid insights we've ever heard in a strategy meeting. Generating real dialogue—open, candid, and sometimes bare-knuckled discussion—is the leader's responsibility. So too is building commitment and accountabilities, once decisions are made. Real dialogue lays the groundwork for better teamwork and brings everyone on board: No one has been left out of the discussion, and it is far less likely that an influential manager will be left alone holding a piece of the puzzle that he or she feels the others are unwilling to recognize.

Good strategic thinking is seldom born of a quiet birth. In the best companies, the debate can be raucous. Many good leaders accept this. Some relish it. One CEO complained, "We're just too polite!" In fact, the absence of visible tension and dissension is a sign of decay. Throughout the early and mid-1980s, Ford and Chrysler were in turmoil. But when both companies faced genuine threats, they were able to cast off the past and make real changes in strategy. Lots of debate, discord, and disharmony. But by 1990, they had done the hard work of reorienting their companies' strategies; others were less far along.

A new breed of managers is emerging in this mold, and they're impressive. Consider Bob Lutz, president and COO of

Chrysler. Lutz was a staff engineer at BMW and Ford who constantly saw his ideas for innovations killed by corporate finance departments that subjected the ideas to departmental budgets and other obstacles. When he went to Chrysler, he set out to change that pattern. He came up with the notion of platform teams—cross-functional product design teams that would not have to subject their strategic ideas for new cars to any discipline other than activity-based costing (ABC), which he saw as the only accounting system that would appropriately value them. In fact, Lutz connected this cost system not only to product design but to all functions throughout Chrysler. The result is a corporate revolution that is making Chrysler more responsive both to the customer and to its best design ideas. Once upon a time, Bob Lutz was a highly motivated, highly frustrated line manager. At Chrysler, he seized his opportunity to put his market savvy into action.

"I'm not saying I want my planners to get their hands dirty. I'm saying I want those with dirty hands to do the planning."

This new breed of manager is not likely to be a staff planner recently transferred to headquarters from the field. Senior management may have a small planning staff close at hand to assist with planning. But line managers must own and lead the process. As one senior executive told us: "I'm not saying I want my planners to get their hands dirty. I'm saying I want those with dirty hands to do the planning."

Off-line staff planners—even those who *were* in the field—tend to lose a sense of the marketplace as well as the culture of the organization as it exists "at the coal face." Doing even the right kind of thinking about the future, they lose sight of present market realities. An executive at a Wall Street broker/dealer complained to us about several very significant—and in his opinion unfortunate—strategic decisions that could only have been made by people on the sidelines of his organization. Citing an example, he said, "That decision could not have been made by someone who is sensitive to our culture. *We are traders. Period.*" Successful strategic planning requires planning and analytical skills blended with real knowledge of operations and a feel for customers.

Communications

Strategic Plan for the Common Man

There was a time when strategic plans were the stuff of clandestine binders full of top secret findings and stratagems thought to be barely intelligible to the middle manager, much less the employee at large. Strategy was something to be conceived by brainy staff and top executives, and only then visited upon the company. It was often never spelled out to those who had to make it work in the real world.

Oh, how far we have come. Today, most CEOs go to great lengths to communicate company strategy—to the point that it becomes virtually a mantra to managers and employees.

A terrific model is found in GE's 1994 Annual Report. A decade ago, the report might have been a dry recital about the company and its year. This report is an inspiring portrait of GE's overarching strategies, woven into very nearly a primer on managing a global corporation today. In their opening letter to share owners, Jack Welch and Paolo Fresco outline their philosophy and strategies for all to see. They discuss issues such as simplification, speed, and operating without boundaries. Their words are anything but pedestrian. For example, they distinguish "stretch"—a cultural underpinning at GE—from being "fixated on a meaningless, internally derived, annual budget number." Instead, they suggest that performance is to be "measured against the world as it turned out to be: how well a business anticipated change and dealt with it."[1]

Jack Welch may be the master communicator among CEOs today. Sharing his thoughts effectively, he infuses GE with the level of strategic thinking that fuels the company's success.

It is not uncommon to hear someone characterize a manager as being "a good operations guy" or "good at execution." Similarly, you could probably name several "strategic thinkers" in your organization. Many today conclude that this division no longer works; the luxury of having planners over here and managers over there no longer exists. In effect, they must be one. As with the paradoxes discussed throughout this book, the future lies in between, through a careful blend of what at first seem to be unrelated opposites. The speed of change, widening spans of control, the increased importance of customer service, and even micro-marketing have all conspired to make strategic *thinking* a prerequisite to success for many managers who are "good at execution."

To compete in the world ahead, you'll need to have it both ways. Your managers must be both highly skilled at operations and able to think and act strategically on the battlefield. The speed of change alone means you'll have to rely more on line managers for strategy. The basis of competition and underlying market conditions change more rapidly than ever before. They could make those plans drawn up last year obsolete, maybe dangerous. Like field commanders, your line managers are the only ones who can know what's going on in a marketplace that changes so rapidly. You have to rely on them to size up the risks and seize fleeting opportunities in the face of competitive advantages that can quickly slip away. Yet day-to-day pressures often lead line managers to think short term and postpone strategic thinking for another day as they fight "today's alligators." That strategic thinking is exactly what's needed today, despite the alligators.

Strategic *thinking* has become a prerequisite to success for many managers.

A strong analogy to the failings of many traditional strategic planning efforts is found in the areas of product planning and production. For years, product planners and production schedulers have struggled to refine their forecasting methods. All manner of techniques have been used to better predict demand in order to build the right products and order the right components and materials in the right quantity. In some instances, costly forecasting departments have been created to organize legions of analysts to crank out product demand forecasts.

Alas, despite all the efforts made to refine demand forecasting, it often remains today an unfulfilled objective. Like that specimen just beyond the reach of a child's first attempts with a butterfly net, the changing markets always foil our best predictive attempts. Refinements in our techniques seem always to fall just short of the extent of change in markets, competitors, and products. Forecasts have been mostly misleading, results mostly disappointing—and inventories mostly filled warehouses.

Better Guidance

The gyroscope is at the heart of some very sophisticated navigational systems. In spatial navigation systems based on inertial guidance, internal gyroscopes are used to detect changes in the position and direction of a rocket and react accordingly. Things get interesting as soon as you realize that the gyroscope provides guidance only when subject to the same forces and conditions as the rocket itself. It reacts to those forces in real time and, in the overall context of the guidance system, responds to maintain the desired orientation and flight path.

Line managers in the thick of things can provide valuable feedback to give your organization a proper orientation and keep you on the track to success.

Figure 10.1

Gyroscope

As a result, production planners today rely less on forecasting. They are moving, instead, to what some call "demand-pull" production. The focus shifts from the accuracy of forecasting to the speed of production and distribution. Gone are the predictions of "off-line" analysts. Now energy is committed to creating efficient methods of production and distribution—processes that respond to *actual* demand in a timely manner while cutting inventory levels.

The parallels with strategic planning should be clear. The disconnected, long-term planning function is gone. Firms are relying more on the ability of operations to adjust to demand and market conditions in real time. Where this approach is being used, line managers at all levels are very different from their counterparts of the past who simply put their heads down and cranked out widgets, once they were given a production schedule. These managers are developing a broader perspective, sharper analytical skills, and fine-tuned sensitivity to market action.

The Environment Mandates In-line Strategy

The frustration of managers with traditional strategic planning is internal—all of that goes on behind closed doors. But there are external factors that add to the need for change in strategic planning. As well, the current passage from restructuring to learning to operate in the new structures is influencing the theory and practice of strategic planning.

A New Breed of Customer

Perhaps the most important environmental shift is the new customer—a more independent, informed customer; more selective; aware of many alternatives. Consumer products companies have discovered that you can no longer count on brand loyalty. Consumers will go elsewhere quickly. Because they were pleased with what you did last month doesn't mean they will be pleased next month. This new independence is frustrating to many managers, and it comes close on the heels of a greater understanding of the lifetime value of repeat customers. A loyal car buyer, for example, can be worth hundreds of thousands of dollars to his or her chosen manufacturer over a lifetime. Smart managers are doing all they can to avoid customer churn, in light of the long-term value of loyal customers and the increasingly high cost of finding new customers. It costs much more to obtain a new customer than it does to serve existing ones.

> **It costs much more to obtain a new customer than it does to serve existing ones.**

These new realities push responsibility from headquarters into the field. Line managers who have direct contact with customers can report back on issues that may soon make the company's strategy impotent. Customer retention requires more than being "close" to customers. It requires that you understand the *evidence* they use to purchase and that you *anticipate* shifts in these buying attributes before they occur.

Even though companies cannot count on loyalty, many have found that they *can* develop lasting and profitable relationships with customers. These relationships are built on more than brand name. When companies make the effort, they

Figure 10.2

A New Breed of Customer

A new breed of customer is challenging managers today. They are more demanding and less loyal; expect absolute quality as the norm and—through wanting simplicity in their products and services—are driving complexity into your business operations.

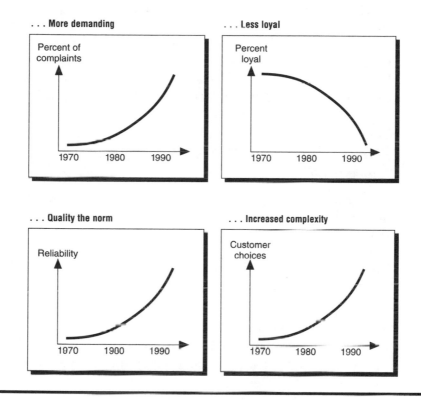

discover that customers actually want long-term relationships, and that the heart of such relationships is trust. Companies learn not to break that trust. They also learn to develop relationships that go beyond isolated transactions. The whole world was witness when Intel nearly breached its implied contract with many devoted, long-term users of its microchips. Intel righted its course of action in time to maintain these ties by deciding to replace any chips that might exhibit the now famous calculation error. But customer relationships go beyond crisis management. UPS, for example, ask its drivers to spend more time just socializing and building relationships with the customer.

When Chrysler decided to redesign its market-leading minivan, the company counted on the loyalty of the many customers with whom it had built relationships. At the same time, management knew that the company had to *go beyond* what customers said they wanted. Before its market share began to slip, Chrysler took steps to *anticipate* what customers would ask for in the future. Cross-functional platform development teams received input from a broad spectrum of stakeholders—line managers, designers, engineers, marketers, cost experts, as well as past and target customers—to come up with a new strategy for the minivan market, and then a new design.

Market Complexity Is Driving Planning into the Mainstream

Trying to understand its place in its markets has always been at the heart of a firm's strategic planning. Today's trend toward micromarketing and the resulting product proliferation require a greater level of in-line, real-time planning—planning hot-wired into the market. There is a new need for information, distinct from traditional market research.

Traditional research often yielded general information and some hints about market direction, but little information about the precise qualities or product values the market wanted and demanded. The research was too general to provide a sound foundation for strategic planning, and in many cases proved dangerous to the health of the corporation. Remember New Coke? Moreover, this research did not build on the knowledge of line managers, knowledge that can help the company understand which creative ideas will work and that profits from knowing how the market is changing now.

The best senior-level managers know that they need research on customer needs. They also know that customers are not very good at revealing what they *really* want versus what they would like to have. A major failing of much market research has been that questions can be asked of customers in ways that yield positively misleading answers. But the best line managers pass market information through a lens of intuition and experience. They distinguish between usable market information and a buzz of data that leads everywhere and nowhere.

The Basis of Competition Continues to Change

In the classic approach to strategic planning developed in the late 1970s and early 1980s, companies and their consultants would analyze their industry to learn how to compete in that industry. They would then figure out how to distinguish themselves from the competition, how to block new entrants, and how to protect market share. In this static view of strategic performance, the company could win in a carefully targeted market segment through lower costs, superior execution, and/or the perceived uniqueness of its product or service. The approach, largely divorced from operations, focused little on the need to create strategic change or deal with volatile market conditions.

Unfortunately, the world has never been static, and in the last decade the speed of change has rendered many strategies obsolete. The basis of competition has evolved from factor costs to experience and scale, to operating globally, to managing time, and now to technology. It appears that nothing provides a company with a sustainable competitive edge. We have all witnessed the fortunes of companies that cling to an outdated competitive formula and see their markets erode.

The most sophisticated companies are beginning to *ignore* the competition.

Moreover, the most sophisticated companies are beginning to *ignore* the competition because they recognize that they must be ahead of it rather than react to it. An old hand at retail strategy told us that, as little as 10 years ago, a retailer could duplicate on the local level the strategy of a market leader and be confident of success. As he put it, "Anyone opening up a discount department store in the late 1970s basically had a license to print money." Now, however, imitation guarantees little in retailing or any other industry. Companies can set themselves apart today by asking their field managers to fine-tune their strategy. When these managers then align all processes and systems to support the strategy, operational excellence becomes a powerful competitive advantage.

One CEO told us that he began to ignore the competition when he received reports that two of his major competitors were waiting to see what he would do. A pipe dream of his, he said, was to get together with the CEOs of the top five companies in his industry and ask each to write down the essence of his strategy. He would take each statement, edit for style, and have them typed on uniform cards. Then he would shuffle the deck and hand each of his major competitors a strategy. "None of them," he said, "would be able to tell his strategy from the others." This CEO understands that, for his industry, the most important feature of strategy is how well it is implemented and refined lower in the organization.

An End to the Reengineering Era?

Despite what's happening in the environment, thinking strategically hasn't come easy to many managers. Perhaps the most vivid proof of this is reengineering. In many companies over the last five years, strategy has been replaced, or at least overwhelmed, by a preoccupation with reengineering and process redesign. Some of the leading consulting organizations have increasingly focused on reengineering. Many corporate giants worldwide have been swept into a fury of reengineering. The pressure on profits is real everywhere. Managers have had to respond. How have most of them responded? Reengineering.

The results have not been all bad. On the contrary, much good work has been accomplished under the banner of reengineering. But these efforts have rarely been balanced. Our survey research confirms that the vast majority of reengineering has had cost cutting as its chief objective. That has certainly been the major result. When the pressure to increase profits heated up in the last decade, most managers naturally responded by cutting costs. Cost cutting is a lot easier than pushing up sales and seeking new sources of revenue. You can see costs. You can control them. Cost cutting produces improvements and short-term results. In short, cost cutting is the easy response—but not necessarily the strategic response.

In a recent survey of companies undertaking reengineering projects, we found that managers are generally pleased with the results. Fully 65 percent of *Fortune* 500 companies surveyed reported meeting or exceeding expectations. We found, however, that this satisfaction applied mostly to the cost side of reengineering. Streamlining business processes, increasing productivity, cutting costs, reducing headcounts, and eliminating low-value work—these are the things that reengineering has done.

When it comes to revenues, however, the results are not so good: only about a third of the surveyed companies reported that reengineering had helped them either bring new products or services to market more quickly or grow their markets. This is no surprise. Very few managers have been truly strategic in developing their reengineering goals. In fact, they have often had exactly the opposite long-term effect. We have seen management groups insist on cutting costs to produce short-term benefits—thereby heightening the risk of business failure in the longer term. We have seen core competencies destroyed. We have seen crucial market opportunities missed because management was spellbound by reengineering for cost reduction.

Only about a third of the surveyed companies reported that reengineering had helped.

Objectives in a reengineering effort are generally set out in terms of cost, quality, and speed. But these dimensions do not capture what we have come to think of as the most important objective of all: reengineering for revenue. In the first big wave of reengineering efforts, had as much attention been placed on "reengineering for revenue" as on cost cutting, we can only imagine the benefits. This focus forces a greater level of strategic thinking and analysis on the responsible managers. You will detect that we have just returned to the core theme of this chapter.

A New Era: Reengineering for Revenue

Managers are telling us that they want to *reengineer for revenue*—and want to use the effort to change their approach to strategic planning. Increasingly, our clients want to look at both sides of the profit equation, cost *and* revenue, and it is clear to them that this requires strategic thinking. It requires looking at the future to decide where best to invest corporate resources. It also calls for some tough decisions. A company in the automotive industry asked us to do a worldwide benchmarking survey as the basis for reengineering targeted to cost reduction. Working together, we determined that cost reduction was far from the whole answer. To spend only 75 cents on a product line with a limited future was certainly preferable to spending a whole dollar—but perhaps it was time to spend neither 75 cents nor a dollar but to reconsider lines of business and focus resources where the potential return on investment was excellent over the long term. What was reengineered in this instance was as much the minds of the managers as anything else—by which we mean, what was reengineered was strategy.

We often counsel managers to better "connect the dots"—to build connections into their business model, their management initiatives, and their customer value proposition. To think strategically in the decade ahead, the manager will actually have to take this metaphor one step further: Connect the dots, yes, but keep in mind that changing conditions may make it wise periodically to reconnect them *differently*. This is what creative strategic thinking is all about! In the normal approach to a puzzle book, the dutiful child connects the dots according to a numbered sequence. He or she draws the picture that is meant to be drawn. But there is always one creative tot who won't connect the dots by the numbers. She draws a line from, say, 1 to 5; he draws a line from 2, around 9, and back to 3. They add a few dots along the way!

When children of this caliber sense that the picture isn't forming to their satisfaction, they don't mind assembling the dots into a different picture. Sometimes the result is a mess. At other times, the result is an entirely new picture, surprising and spectacular. Hire that child!

When line managers learn to connect the dots differently, what they get is a strategy out of the ordinary—one that will perhaps provide the next great revenue stream for the company. Yet this is just what operating managers find most difficult to do.

Reading this, you may be reminded of that fellow on one of your project teams—the guy with such extensive line management and industry experience. When someone suggested a different way to connect the dots—a different way of looking at the business—this individual dug in his heels. "You just can't do things that way in this business." Only when his assumption was challenged did the team really start to think differently, even strategically. Winning companies are often the ones where managers proved able to think strategically and redefine the business—before the market passed them by.

Managers will have to be given the time and opportunity to develop this new way of thinking and new perspectives on what the company should be doing and when. As they move along this path, they will learn an important fundamental of strategic planning—nothing less than fusing intuition and analysis, right brain and left brain. The best strategies result from a careful synthesis of fact and intuition.

Balancing Creative Vision and Core Purpose

Smart executives formulate broad strategic outlines that set the boundaries for and channel strategic thinking but do not become straitjackets hampering management action. Much has been written about the need for senior management to establish the outlines of a broad vision for its company's future. In making planning more of an in-line function, however, this need becomes even more important. The vision has to be broad enough to allow latitude for action, but sharp enough to provide the kind of ideological convergence that line managers need to guide their actions. Consider carefully its application under different scenarios. Think about how it should change as the scenarios change.

It's not easy to balance latitude and convergence. When the focus is too narrow, good opportunities are lost. Insufficient focus, on the other hand, issues a carte blanche to the unbridled creativity of high-initiative managers. For example, several years ago a major insurance client sought joint venture partners to help underwrite the cost of information technology investments it needed to remain competitive. This effort was very successful—in fact, so successful that the head of the joint venture decided to expand into a wide range of technology services. Unfortunately, these services had nothing to do with the organization's strategy and diverted attention and resources from the real priorities. Finally, as the venture wandered still farther into the wilderness of possibility, the insurance CEO called its leader to order and removed him from his post. This individual's initiatives were creative. They were also undermining the parent enterprise.

Build Change and Stability into Your Vision

Decompose your strategy into what must remain stable and what must evolve with the market. The broad outlines of your vision, mission, purpose, and strategy should take into account the reality of shorter and shorter product life cycles in many industries. Being number one or two in the industry doesn't necessarily last. To keep pace, strategies must change quickly as markets change. Because the basis of competition can change, a company can misperceive the new terms of competition unless its senior managers and line managers keep striving to deepen their understanding. Responsibility for this degree of strategic awareness rests with senior executives for the broader, longer-range view and with line managers for the specific perspective on which to base the next step.

Since line managers will provide much of the basis for this deeper, real-time perspective, the company must provide a forum in which line managers can honestly report what they see and experience in the field. Creating this forum is not as easy as it sounds. To do so requires removing the barriers to communication between corporate layers. The phenomenon of "shooting the messenger" is alive and well in business today. It takes real courage for middle managers to force senior managers to confront the realities of today's fickle markets. Smart companies, however, have seen or directly felt the damage that blinders can do. They make an effort to learn from the customer sense and overall feedback of their frontline managers. Such managers can help the company see market changes and, on that basis, preempt the competition by means of what Henry Mintzberg has termed "emergent" strategies.[2] These often modest strategic ideas, piloted by managers at the customer interface, can combine over time into powerful new strategies of far greater dimension.

> The phenomenon of "shooting the messenger" is alive and well in business today.

Strategic thinking requires continually introducing new blood (or at least new ideas) into the organization. When an organization has a static strategy, you can be almost sure that it is also inbred. We recently completed an assignment for a client badly in need of change. The problems stemmed from an inbred philosophy. The culture had for decades shown a strong belief that there was no need to look elsewhere for new ideas. One senior official—a long-term employee, like most in this organization—admitted to us that in her 20 years with the company she had *never* had an in-depth conversation with "an outsider" (her term) about business practices. It was no surprise, then, to find some very unusual practices in place, practices that looked absurd to her after benchmarking them against similar organizations.

Develop the Organization with the Flex to Support Evolving Strategy

One CEO believed that his company's renewed success had been achieved, against considerable odds, by building an adaptable organization with the flex to take advantage of its best opportunities. The company had a long history of success, but at the point we take up its story it had fallen on hard times because its key market was in a major downturn. The CEO helped to rescue the organization from near collapse and re-built around the concept of no longer tying the company's fortunes to a single market. The company reorganized into nine strategic business units, functioning as a portfolio of diverse investments—a hedging system, if you will, that allowed management to move deftly among its nine businesses as markets flourished or retreated. A point of importance: The strategy relied on field managers with a keen sense of the market and the means to communicate with core management frequently, frankly, and without fear.

Make Sure You Know the Answer to "What Business Are We In?"

This is, as you must already know, the soundest of questions. Consider, for example, that some observers predict that the laptop computer market will soon evolve into a fashion business. In the view of these prophets, laptop technology will continue to evolve, but the factors that drive buying decisions will come to resemble and then entirely mimic those of the fashion industry. Parallels to this phenomenon are everywhere. Retailing, for example, is taking on characteristics of the entertainment industry, with Disney and Warner Bros. leading the trend.

Is a major publishing company in the publishing business? Would it be better off viewing itself as a distributor of information? Information is becoming homogenized, instantaneous, delivered through multiple channels. Or should a major publisher view itself as something more like a manufacturer assembling innovative products for consumers? Whatever the answer, asking the question helps companies determine their vision of the future and the core competencies they hold most sacred.

Set Up a Sophisticated Measurement and Feedback System. Gather the Right Information

Strategic flexibility cannot be achieved without the right market information systems. The best companies divide such systems into two types: information gathering on the one hand, performance measurement on the other. Effective information gathering depends on gaining friendly access and asking the right questions in a structured manner—not as easy as it sounds. The company has to learn how to inquire rather than impose. Customers are being bombarded with surveys and questionnaires, so much so that they rarely take them seriously. In the 1960s, survey researchers could count on most questionnaires being returned. By the 1980s, return rates of 30 percent were considered remarkable.

The best companies are creating new ways to engage customers, and they share the resulting information broadly throughout the company. For example, Bose, the U.S. manufacturer of high-quality stereo equipment, is doing an impressive job of bringing its major customers and suppliers directly into the product design process. United Airlines is doing no less with its high-mileage fliers. Customers can react in real time to product and service ideas, share their feedback, and help to work out problems. Trusting relationships develop. The market information—invaluable—serves both the company and the customer because both reach closer to the product or service ideals they have shared.

Market information of this value needs to circulate in the company; it should not be too closely held. It can help to shape how the company is organized and operates, how functions interact to serve customers. A feedback system that allows market information to circulate throughout the company, and a culture that highly values acting on such information, are competitive advantages that can't easily be matched.

Many companies will also need to reconfigure their performance measurement system to monitor strategic effectiveness.

Consider just four fundamental questions the typical CEO ponders each day:

1. What's happening in our markets?
2. Are these markets changing?
3. Are we on strategy?
4. Is our strategy working?

Few companies have information systems that even attempt to answer any questions other than: Are we performing against expectations?

Few companies have information systems that even attempt to answer any but the last question, which asks, in effect, Are we performing against expectations? But aren't the first three questions even more important? We suggest that in the long run they are. The folks at headquarters can come up with the answer to question four because that answer is nothing more than a report on history. On the other hand, field managers need all the intelligence, experience, and technology support they can possibly get to dig out answers to the first three questions and to react to those answers strategically and creatively.

Work Relentlessly to Develop Line Managers Who Are Strategic Thinkers (the Key to the Paradox)

Line managers are analytic by nature. They understand the market and industry. People who set strategy, however, must have strong vision and the drive to create something new. Achieving balance and close interaction between people with these two quite different profiles is the key to the paradox of this chapter.

Companies need to make efforts to value and encourage managers who understand their markets. Similarly, they need to provide periodic opportunities for high-quality training and retraining in this area. Provide new kinds of training annually, not the same old programs. Send managers to trade shows and encourage them to travel to different markets. Never skimp on the travel budget when it supports the development of market wisdom. Consider the best thinking about the present as the foundation for your future.

Conclusion

When we used earlier the metaphor of connecting the dots, we referred to the child who connects the dots in a new, imaginative way. Other children march through the puzzle as instructed. This one stays partly within bounds but strays out to the edges of the possible, redefining the game. Look for this quality in some of your managers. Cultivate those rare ones. Yes, teach them to recognize where all the dots are. But occasion in them the skills and flexibility to craft a product/service mix perfect for today's market—and tomorrow's.

No organization can afford too many nonconformists who challenge everything. Yet no strategically alive organization can afford not to have one or two such individuals. Successful companies in the decade ahead will possess managers who are willing to challenge traditional thinking and norms, who can conceive and deliver creative solutions, yet stay within the bounds of mission and strategy.

Connect those dots in fresh ways before the market—your competitors and your most demanding, valued customers—does it without you. Let your managers create preemptive strikes—not just routine plans promising routine results, but true strategic change.

Notes

1. *General Electric 1994 Annual Report* (U.S.A.: General Electric Company, 1995), p. 4.
2. As discussed by Henry Mintzberg, *The Rise and Fall of Strategic Planning* (New York: Free Press and Prentice International, 1994).

Eleven

The Fall and Rise of Human Resources Management

If my boss calls in, be sure to get his name.

A network executive in *Fortune*, April 14, 1986

An historic change is occurring in the way human resources are developed and managed: the birth of a much
more genuine desire to use human potential to the
fullest. Is it only an irony of the times, or does it follow some
law of paradox that this awakening has begun during the
downsizings of the 1980s and 1990s? Be that as it may, the
result has been that firms are rethinking and experimenting
with how human resources are managed, how jobs are
designed, and how to motivate employees. Managers are more
attuned than ever before to the relationship between competitive success and how people are employed. They are aware
of the immense productivity gains that can be freely given (or
not) by today's workforce. And they sense that their organization's business results are at stake.

The emerging paradigm for managing people will end a
century of flawed thinking. Through most of the century,
employees have been regarded as little more than "neck-down"
workers, hired for their brawn, not their brains. Knowledge
workers, largely a post–World War II phenomenon, have been
shackled by control systems and concepts of specialization
devised a generation earlier for the factory. Now, however,
high-performance organizations are
giving employees the freedom and
power to take action and experiment.
In the coming decades, those organizations that can capitalize on their
human potential will outperform the
rest. Business executives joined long
ago the debate over what exactly motivates human beings.
Traditional approaches have been the bank account (pay for
performance), employee pride (job enrichment), or involvement in decision making (job fulfillment and responsibility).
Picking from this menu, companies have created systems to
track development, make promotions routine, make pay more
equitable, and so on. They have created virtual corporate
universities to train employees. And they routinely, if at times
gratuitously, declared the importance of human resources in
phrases such as, "People are our most important asset."

The emerging paradigm for managing people will end a century of flawed thinking.

Today companies need to remotivate the employees left
after downsizing, need to reenergize these "most important

assets." A troubling number of employees are less motivated, less loyal, and less committed to their organizations than they were before. Worried about their futures, working longer hours, aware that the deal has changed, employees are under stress.

To complicate matters, the New Economy is creating a voracious need for hot skills in information technology, telecommunications, biotechnology, and other knowledge-intensive fields. Employers can be held hostage as they struggle to build specialized intellectual resources. Salary demands in these disciplines are escalating, while employees in less critical functions may feel left behind. Communications has made today's labor market much less imperfect than in even the near past. People with key skills have better information about job openings, have more life and career options, and are more mobile and adaptable in changing jobs or careers.

Like most administrative disciplines, human resources management has been treated as a science, just as strategic planning, marketing, and manufacturing have been. The goal has been to be as precisely right as possible. Unfortunately, experience shows that we have too often been precisely wrong. Managers who balance the paradoxes in job design and the management of people leaven their scientific and procedural expertise with a healthy dose of intuition. These managers place high value on flexibility, not just on policy manuals that define employee rights and obligations.

The central paradox of this chapter is a genuine puzzle. In an era, long overdue, when the focus has become the productivity and effectiveness of people; at a time when senior executives have finally awakened to the importance of leveraging the unique skills of the individual; and at a moment when business leaders have come to rely on teams, the human resources professional seems to be all but invisible. Thus, the paradox:

• • • • •

Now that the importance of people is recognized by all,
where's the HR function?

• • • • •

You may think this a harsh judgment. But in our experience most of the innovation in people management is happening "on-line," in the midst of operations. It is being imagined and carried out by managers and their employee teams, often without much involvement or leadership from human resources professionals. And most of these changes are being made "on the fly."

Some HR professionals have seen their organizations advance and retreat around them while they hold the low ground, that is, low-value-added administrative activities. Others have created a *virtual* HR function, vesting administration and leadership in line managers and giving little more than implementation support.

In this chapter, we observe and draw conclusions from changes that have been evolving for some time in the relationships among employees, managers, and HR professionals. We argue for a new human resources agenda and for tearing down the old. We offer ideas on job design, on expanding the role of the manager, and on better managing project-based work methods. This is the matrix in which the new is appearing: a new inventory of issues surrounding the management of people, a new distribution of responsibilities to the players in this drama—the employee, his or her manager, and the HR professional.

Something of a road map is already emerging, even if the destination remains blurred.

Sweeping Changes in How We Work

Job design is rapidly evolving. The traditional obsession with measuring employee fit is giving way to a focus on employee growth. The once stable, well-defined jobs of years past are now continually evolving, with the overall purpose of making the organization more adaptable in changing markets. Creativity, resourcefulness, flexibility, innovation, and adaptability are becoming much more important than the ability to perform a precisely specified job.

In some organizations, titles and categories are changing. For example, the term "employee" is giving way to associate,

Figure 11.1

A New Human Resources Agenda

In the decade ahead, we will see a new management agenda of human resources responsibilities distributed to the employee, his or her manager, and the new HR professional.

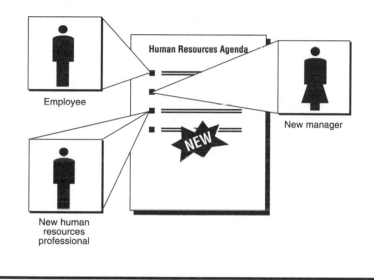

and "manager" is giving way to coach and facilitator. Where there is substance behind these title changes, firms are also recognizing that they might see further gains in performance by changing the very basis of the traditional employer-employee (master-servant) relationship and all it has sponsored in the way people have been treated.

Many of the managers we interviewed show real commitment to searching out smarter ways of putting the full capabilities of the human resource to use. They know that this will require new ways of thinking about jobs. Consider, for example, succession planning. The value of succession planning for specific jobs is being overshadowed today by the need to develop pools of adaptable talent. The incentive to plan who will run the U.S. Division three years from now approaches zero when no one can predict how the company will be organized in three years. Better to spend time developing a pool of men and women who might lead any number of future organizational forms. Competence in a given job is becoming less important than a manager's *core* competencies and overall characteristics. These trends reflect a move toward flexibility and the need to be broadly right rather than precisely wrong in a more hurried world undergoing radical change.

We can see a move toward flexibility and the need to be broadly right rather than precisely wrong.

However, there is a paradox in this shift from tightly defined jobs to broadly defined roles. People need to be more flexible, but many key processes are being more tightly defined than ever before. TQM and related quality programs drive greater precision into our processes as we seek to perfect products and service delivery. Procter & Gamble, for example, used to speak of attaining an "$x\%$" service level in delivering goods on time. Now its objectives are more demanding. Management is focused on what some call perfect orders— orders for which every contact with the customer is as it should be, with no rework or delays.

As work processes become more precisely defined while jobs transform from narrow functional roles into flexible, multiskill zones, many a manager is sure to be confounded— at least initially. We believe that understanding the nature of this change will go a long way toward learning to manage it practically.

One of the guiding principles of world-class process reengineers is to see to it that workers become multiskilled. The evidence has shown time and time again that this can lead both to superior quality and to a more satisfied workforce. We lived for some two centuries with Adam Smith's view of the strict division of labor. However, three factors argue against continuing this pattern. First, division and specialization reinforce inertia, and inertia is unacceptable when firms need adaptability rather than constancy to compete. Second, composite skills and flexibility are required to support a shift from mass production to production of customized goods for micromarkets. Third, the process reengineering efforts under way in many organizations don't divide labor so much as integrate it.

Project work is moving to center stage in our organizations. Our employee surveys indicate a marked increase in the amount of time managers and the workforce are spending in projects away from their "normal" jobs. The increase in project work is due in large measure to the need for broad-based change, which is typically planned and implemented by multiskilled project teams. The effect is dramatic: Many employees are being asked to double up—get the normal work done and contribute, as well, to several project efforts.

In the decade ahead, your ability to keep pace with evolving markets and competitors will depend on your ability to carry out projects successfully. Traditionally, *operations* has produced goods for and delivered services to customers. Efficient operations will continue to be important and represents a core competency for many companies. But this is no longer enough: You cannot afford to be a 10 in operations and a 4 in project work. Many companies today are no better than a 4 when it comes to project-by-project management of transformation.

> **You cannot afford to be a 10 in operations and a 4 in project work.**

Sweeping Changes In the Role of the Manager

At the center of the strange blend of chaos and inertia in human resources management is the fast-changing role of the manager. All of us with managerial experience were raised on a steady diet of hierarchical control. We adopted a vertical perspective (giving most of our attention to our sphere of responsibility and our boss) with only a nod to colleagues and peers. We were evaluated by those above us, just as we counseled those below us. Our power and influence flowed from the position we held. In the most extreme expression of this hierarchical view, the position defined the person—no one dared to exhibit the characteristics of a CEO until he or she was made one.

The emerging process (or horizontal) perspective is changing this. The role of the manager is becoming more lateral, with much more focus on customers and processes. This concept of horizontal process flows and internal customers/suppliers, encouraged by the swell of reengineering efforts, is becoming entrenched. Service and support functions are more aware that they must expand their service role and limit the onerous consequences of their agenda of control.

Structures are also becoming more hybrid. Some organizations have overlaid process responsibilities onto functional structures. Others are experimenting with multiple concurrent roles for managers and self-managed work teams. While developments of this type are often driven by need and rooted in genuine interest and commitment, some hybrid structures represent cosmetic rather than substantive change—the silo structure, the functional focus, continue to determine behavior and decisions.

We used to give direction. Today, we are more likely to offer help, to coach. This does not signal softening of the brain—it's simply a recognition that responsibility, initiative, and skill are spread widely in a process-oriented, empowered organization. Spans of influence and responsibility are widening, but they are no longer viewed as zones of exclusive control. The concept of the manager as coach is taking hold after a period in which the training department was largely responsible for developing individual capability. Is coaching the *central* role of the manager today? Some ambitious, take-no-prisoners, well-managed organizations are beginning to think and act as if this is so.

However, for many managers today the burdens of administration and day-to-day firefighting leave little time for effective coaching. Making matters worse is that restructurings have cut layers out of corporate management. Wider spans have enlarged the charges of those managers that remain. Structural change is, in many cases, now playing catch-up with the consequences of this cost cutting. Managers are struggling to fit it all into their day.

Some organizations are finding an answer by dividing the manager's roles. A real premium is being placed on coaching: setting and agreeing on performance standards, reviewing the delivery of customer service and other performance goals, locating the reasons for underperformance, and initiating performance improvements. Administration is being eliminated or delegated. Under this model, a manager can sustain a span of influence of 20 to 25 people rather than one-third or one-half of that number. Dividing tasks and delegating some of them cuts management overhead. It also focuses managers on helping and supporting their people.

All of the project work referred to above, spawned by a desire to manage change, has given new importance to the disciplines of project management. The effect upon managers is profound. All of a manager's time sometimes and some of a manager's time always is now siphoned off to lead or contribute to projects. Yet because most managers have operations backgrounds and scant project experience, their efforts often have more to do with scrambling up the learning curve than decisively helping the company turn a corner.

A bleak picture emerges when one considers the importance and volume of project work today and in the decade ahead. Projects wither from ineffective sponsorship. Many also proceed without a sound cost/benefit case to support investment in them. Project planning and budgeting are weak. Projects are run by committees that are effective only at insulating all involved from accountability. Scope is regularly changed, so that victory is difficult to declare or deny. As a result, too little performance improvement or organizational learning takes place in light of the investment.

Many managers do not easily accept their new role. They are asked to give up power and do different things in order to be more effective leaders of the organization, but many believe they will become *less* effective because they have less power. Moreover, the things that motivated them—the prestige, control, and the trappings of power—are now less valuable. This can unleash a host of problems, and the psychological ramifications are only now being understood. As Harry Levinson has observed:

> Executives are men and women of high aspiration. As a rule, they are very ambitious, seeking power, prestige and money, and nearly always are competing intensely against other executives. . . . They have extremely high ego ideals that revolve around power. They have deep-seated, unconscious pressures for attainment; their conscious goals are merely the tip of the iceberg.[1]

While Levinson's comments are aimed at senior executives, they are equally well suited to managers in general. The psychological difficulties of *middle* managers, who want power but have not yet attained it, are sometimes just as marked and complex as those of senior managers who can no longer move upward. When managers at both levels are required to operate more through influence, less through control, they need to draw on different skills—which they may or may not have.

The manager's role in performance appraisal is also changing radically. The manager's traditional power and influence are now increasingly balanced by formal accountability to others—peers and subordinates. Many organizations are supplementing traditional downward appraisal systems with upward feedback or 360 degree feedback (not circular but spherical: down, up, and across to peers). The perfunctory appraisals of the past are being transformed by more thoughtful and thorough counseling. In a few organizations (British Petroleum comes to mind), the annual pay review has been turned on its head; now, a portion of pay is based on assessments of managers *by their subordinates*. Managers are being asked to show their worth in a more democratized workplace—worth valued in terms of effectiveness in creating conditions in which people can deliver the best results.

Sweeping Changes in the HR Function

Under these changing conditions, the human resource function is polarizing. The polarization divides HR professionals who have withdrawn to administration from those who are seeking to redefine the role of HR in a way that adds value. Despite a small but growing number of exceptions, HR is still widely seen as reactionary. The exceptional HR professionals today are not driven by the 1980s interest in strategic human resources management. That movement was primarily about HR trying to secure a place in the boardroom by demonstrating relevance to strategic business goals. The current interest is in adding measurable value to the business.

The increased complexity of our environment is transforming HR by overturning the traditional view of how to motivate employees. This view mandates that all HR efforts be directed toward increasing performance, including investment in training and career development. The premise is that if we coordinate the levers of employee motivation and performance with a well-defined set of performance outcomes, we will get the highest level of motivation and performance. The employee's incentive to reach defined goals is pay—in part individual, in part focused on the team, in part linked to organizational performance.

The next element in this approach is to invest training dollars where they will improve performance. Career development is focused on building the managerial competence that leads to outstanding individual and corporate results. Communications are designed to reinforce individual, work group, and corporate goals. Performance appraisals assess against objectives defined in the last period and set objectives for the next period. Recruitment of new staff and promotion of existing staff are based on norms and standards we link with effectiveness—and so on. All parts of the system are aligned vertically and laterally, and are mutually reinforcing.

The trouble is, things change continuously. Goals and objectives change. Incentive programs, notoriously clumsy, at the end of the day typically pay the lazy little less than the industrious. Training never quite connects with results. Performance appraisal falls into ritual or disrepute. On and on. In a more complex environment, it's hard to keep this kind of system aligned with changing circumstances. In more fluid and hybrid organizations (part hierarchical, part horizontal), it is impossible to systematize in this way the blend of skills, objectives, and incentives that characterizes each job. The system becomes too complex in design, too cumbersome to manage and, when implemented, too diffuse in impact. Some of the strongest senior managers do everything they can to undo HR systems that miss because they are too complex. Jack Welch of GE has been dismantling his company's complex pay systems for almost ten years now.

This flawed approach to HR management is giving way to a new focus on the relationship between the employee or team and the immediate manager/coach. At the place where coach meets employee, complexity can be simplified, goals adjusted in real time, and the performance of the individual maximized. By carefully examining this relationship between supervision and work, firms can fashion a new human resources agenda.

At the place where coach meets employee, complexity can be simplified.

The human resources agenda is already changing radically at high-performing companies. They are aware of motivation and job design issues, and that awareness is speeding up the slow transition from Payroll to Human Resources. The genie is out of the bottle—and already well away from the confines of the traditional HR department.

Examples of change run the gamut of traditional HR responsibilities. Simpler, leaner structures and the shift away from tightly prescribed jobs to broader roles make designing and administering pay structures easier. Even before the research can be applied, the speed of change outdates research on the connection between employee competence and improved performance. The old methodologies of HR management, such as job classification, are perceived to add little value to the business. They are being tossed out in favor of simplified, commonsense procedures. Extensions in the role of the manager, such as reacquiring responsibility for recruiting and training their people, relegate the HR function to a narrower policy and support role. Erosion of the power of unions, at least for now, and decentralized bargaining have weakened another cornerstone of HR's traditional power base.

All of these changes mandate that the HR function be carried out in a different way, on a different scale, with different goals, doing different things. The choice for HR is to become a marginal support function or to embrace new opportunities and a more mainstream agenda.

The New Agenda

What's a manager to do? What are smart companies doing? The answers lie in distributing the new HR agenda among the HR professional, the manager, and the object of all this—the employee.

> **The answers lie in distributing the new HR agenda among the HR professional, the manager—and the employee.**

This will take time and will require the organization to take a different view of work. But the three-way balancing act will lighten many of the burdens of work design and employee motivation and free up the manager to do what he or she ought to do best—motivate people, inspire, coach, nurture, push.

Workable ideas emerge from all this. Here they are.

1. Establish and Implement That New Agenda for HR

The HR control function (payroll, labor negotiations, legal procedure governing employment) is no longer the heart of the matter. All the rest is what's important, and it revolves around service delivery: helping managers hire the best people, retain them, train them effectively, compensate them fairly, consult and communicate with them, accommodate them, discipline and fire them, manage their absenteeism, and the like. In a few—far too few—organizations, HR professionals are stepping up to this role with initiative, a sense of urgency, and an understanding of what adds value to the business.

More thought has to be given to which activities should be performed *inside* the business and which should be contracted out. Innovative HR managers are showing that they can deliver defined and customized services faster and cheaper than any external service provider. Naturally, this makes the decision to outsource a difficult one. The smart HR managers are improving service, cost, and quality by means of *internal* service contracts that have teeth in them. In this way, they establish themselves as a fully accountable service provider with "skin in the game."

> **Make HR professionals true business *partners* as fully accountable service providers with "skin in the game."**

Make HR professionals true business *partners*. Ask the tough questions. Have you defined the HR group's products and services? Can you define service quality standards? Are these nice to have or imperative? What do they cost per unit? What are the costs of different levels of service? Can the needed services be reliably provided? Are alternative suppliers available? Can productivity and costs be improved?

A few companies have begun to find qualitative ways to measure the effectiveness of human resources. In service companies, where productivity measurement has been so vague that it evokes comment in every article on the service economy, some companies have begun to figure out how to measure and reward properly. They define service and quality in their profession, and then set standards. From there, it's a simple step to measure performance against the standard and, as well, to measure the cost of achieving the standard. Companies that frame internal relationships in terms of customer and supplier can develop a contract that serves as a powerful incentive and a yardstick for accountability and measurement.

Probe for the rationale of your HR function as it is and as it might be. Many questions come to mind. Have you made sure that the size and scope of HR reflect the new roles you believe it can and should play? Have you cut out non-value-added functions like job classification? Have you considered contracting out processing activities like payroll to better focus resources on building core capability? Can you redirect the resources that addressed collective bargaining toward improved internal communication and involvement?

Will your senior HR executives for the next decade be more numerate, more commercial, more focused on business results? Will they understand how to measure HR service delivery? Will they be able to show genuine leadership on how the business will make the most of its human potential? Seeking answers to these questions will improve your thinking on the issues.

2. Give HR Professionals a Pivotal Role in Supporting and Facilitating Change

In fact, insist the HR professionals take a pivotal role in supporting and facilitating change. At Rover and National Power in the U.K., HR professionals have helped orchestrate change. They developed and executed the communication process; helped to build change assets (i.e., change agents and skills across the organization); helped to manage the people consequences of change (e.g., the speed and cost of severance programs); provided advice and support regarding the change process; and helped guide management interactions. They helped assimilate technology as well by helping people use it to work efficiently with minimal delay and wasted motion.

Someone in the organization needs to offer these skills in support of the change process. Some HR groups have seen the light. They are making their bid. Others have stuck to their knitting. It is unraveling before their eyes.

3. Rehabilitate Learning with Less Classroom Training, More In-line Coaching

To criticize training is heretical. However, much of the corporate training investment is squandered. It has too little impact on bottom-line performance. Billions are spent annually on training, yet few companies know how to measure the effectiveness of their investments. While some companies spend prodigally, others provide no training whatever. In a recent U.K. survey of 176 companies employing more than a thousand people, more than 50 percent had no budget at all for training, while among those with training programs only 13

Communications

Make HR "User Friendly"

HR groups need to communicate with employees about more benefit programs than in the past, programs that offer a greater number of options. HR groups that do this smoothly go a long way toward convincing employees and managers that they are part of the solution.

New technologies can streamline HR's relationship not only with employees and management but with the outside vendors of the insurance and savings programs, child and elder care, and emergency services in their charge. E-mail, telephone voice response systems, computer networks, even kiosks can be integrated to communicate personalized information and, where appropriate, automate functions previously handled by HR staffers.

This technology can be used for benefit program education and enrollment, form distribution, benefit election changes and confirmation, claims filing and status, and retirement plan investment status. Bank of America, Visa International, General Motors, Merck, Apple Computers, and Sears manage extensive benefit programs, covering thousands of employees, in just this way. The information is more accurate, and operating costs can be reduced.

Employees win by gaining immediate, 24-hour access to timely, trustworthy information. In the office, at home, or on the road they can look after all of their personal HR needs by means of a telephone and a desktop computer. The company wins because employees have greater confidence in the HR function and spend far less time chasing facts and figures, more time where it counts the most. The HR function wins by bringing ease and certainty to one of the more anxiety-provoking, complex features of internal management today.

---

percent believed they could determine whether the programs had been effective.[2]

Training professionals have been notoriously slow to assess the changing needs of corporate clients. Here is a painful example. Managers in the United States today have a credible selection of training alternatives designed to guide them on the delicate issues involved in firing employees. Wonderful—but why did most of this guidance become available only after more than 10 million U.S. employees had been fired in the period 1990–94 *or* –95?

Ten days of training per year is giving way to the concept of "every day as a development experience." The centrally driven, classroom approach is being replaced with the legitimate demand to learn by doing and to learn from coaching on the job. High-performance companies are finding that classroom training away from the workplace (especially among groups that do not and will not soon interact with one another) is of limited benefit if the aim is to acquire functional skills. There is little new or startling in this notion—none of us learned to ride a bike in a classroom—yet training continues to be something we assume occurs *away from* the workplace.

> **Ten days of training per year is giving way to the concept of "every day as a development experience."**

Familiar problems persist. Managers are not prompted to (or particularly interested in) creating a receptive environment to support returning trainees. Compartmentalized training fails to take into account job-to-job interdependencies. Classroom training separates concepts and laboratory practice from their application in the workplace.

There is and always will be a place for classroom training. But high-performance companies will question and revise that place—led by their senior HR managers who understand that the new business model does not detour around HR, it drives right through and urgently needs them to get on board.

Innovative companies have not abandoned training—but they *have* begun to make their training programs more effective. They are broadening the concept of training: It occurs more frequently on the job, it includes everyone in the company. They no longer emphasize off-site training, except for management education and in circumstances where large groups need to be sensitized to common issues. In-line training for individuals and work groups tends to be more cost-effective, relevant, and needs-driven. However, because this approach to training is so closely tied to what people normally do and where they normally do it, it can be undermanaged as if it is not "real" training but only an improvised workshop. The ad hoc, sincere efforts of well-meaning managers are generally not enough to create an effective learning situation. You will need to support this form of training through an infrastructure and professional advice, and you will need to work with your line managers/coaches to help them become effective practitioners.

Some do it better. At Chiat/Day, for example, training is not a discrete event broken out from daily work but an ongoing, real-time apprenticeship in which each employee learns from a more experienced team member. About teaching such intangible skills as creative development, worldwide creative director Lee Clow comments, "We don't teach batting—players learn from watching others swing." However, this type of learning organization places more responsibility on the employees because there is no HR department to watch out for them. Says Clow, "People must step up to the plate and be able to identify their own contributions and other positions they want to learn to play."

Research being carried out by The Learning Center at the MIT Sloan School of Management is shedding new light on the metaphor of *practice* in the business environment. In sports, the military, and the performing arts, practice is the foundation of excellence: batting practice, war games, endless hours at the keyboard laboriously practicing pieces that will one day dazzle an audience. These professions use practice to build skills, stamina, and intuition. They each employ *practice fields*—real and relevant representations of the work they do, differing only in that the penalties for mistakes are minimal.

An innovative program at Bell Labs, the Productivity Enhancement Program, is a useful example. The company asked a number of its star engineers to develop an expert model. The result was a set of nine prioritized work strategies the engineers believed other employees could master. Training sessions to pass on these strategies occur in the normal workday. Productivity increases in both star and average performers have been striking. According to their self-evaluations, for

The Power of Context

Imagine yourself sitting in a classroom behind a desk in row three. The instructor at the blackboard is drawing

Figure 11.2

Gyroscope

his rendition of the gyroscope with arrows pointing this way and that to show the forces at play in its action. He hopes to teach you the secrets of the gyroscope's mysterious powers and intriguing behaviors.

You would learn, sure enough.

Now imagine yourself aboard a ship at sea, pitching and tossing. The chief navigator escorts you to the source of the ship's guidance systems, to the brains behind its stabilizers: the mighty gyroscope. He explains its behaviors, its characteristics, its value in context. You observe the forces acting on it and its reactions to those forces in real time.

You would learn a lot more.

example, participants typically report a 10 percent increase in productivity immediately after the sessions end, growing to 20 percent after six months and 25 percent after a full year. This steady upward curve is totally atypical. For most training programs, effectiveness is greatest on the last day of the program and falls to zero after a year.[3] Motorola has reported that productivity gains from similar training can be as high as 30 to 1.[4]

We don't hesitate to repeat that in this shift to on-the-job training, the manager becomes coach and mentor. The line manager passes along his or her skills and in the process becomes more attuned to what the employee needs to learn. Just as quality control in manufacturing has been shifted from the back end of the production line onto the line itself, training has begun to be tied to the job—and captures that *teachable moment* with the manager as coach. Rather than maintain large training centers, companies are using their own star performers, as Bell Labs does, to create a new culture that emphasizes learning instead of training.

Squeeze training for results. Press those responsible for training with the same tough questions you put to line employees. Ask them to justify training investments. Ask if the defined employee competencies reflect the competitive strategy of your business. Ask what coaching takes place every day for every employee. Ask if its incidence and quality are being measured. Ask whether your managers have the skills to coach. And do they encourage employees to take responsibility for their future employability? Answers to these questions will drive results.

4. Redefine Jobs and the Way Work Is Done

If your organization has been successfully reengineering core processes, you are off to a good start at redefining jobs and the way work is done. The principles of reengineering, properly applied, are consistent with many of the ideas about work put forward here. Intelligent reengineering is broad-minded and multidimensional. It emphasizes giving workers multiple skills. It seeks to link the efforts of people across the enterprise in order to increase the value added by each. It takes into account the whole individual, including work-family concerns. It puts many more employees in touch with customers, or at least attunes them to the real needs of customers. It relies on information technology wherever it's cost-effective and reserves for the workforce those decisions and actions that require judgment and the human touch. Waste is minimized. Learning is built into the processes and people as work is reengineered.

All this sounds very promising. And it is, when reengineering is properly applied and resolutely adhered to. This is too seldom the case. We recommend that you *not* move on to "bigger and better things" until current reengineering efforts are not only complete but meet high standards. Assess your organization's real progress in reengineering the work of your employees. Does the result stack up positively against the work characteristics outlined in the paragraph above? Was there initially, and is there still, a clear mandate for the reengineering effort, measured in terms of the resulting cost, quality, and speed of core processes? Have the objectives been met? If the answer is no to one or more of these questions, you probably know where to resume and intensify the effort of work redesign.

5. Redefine the Manager's Job

Are your managers overseeing the smooth operation of core processes? Are they in the right places in the organization? Do your managers spend most of their time on (a) setting performance goals, (b) reviewing performance against goals, and (c) coaching and supporting to improve performance? Are managers helping to solve problems or are their actions disrupting work flows?

Are managers focused on serving internal or external customers? How many managers without an internal or external customer can your organization afford? Do you have the means to measure a manager's performance? Are those means unambiguous? (We find ambiguity in even the best measurement schemes. Chapter 12, on the paradox around performance measurement, may help.) Do measures reward inputs to a job? Or are they linked to processes and to customer outputs? A switch to outputs may be warranted.

Ask yourself whether your managers are generally giving direction or giving help to employees. Can you afford the former if your competitors have found a way for employees to do this for themselves and each other? Are your managers psychologically equipped to become coaches and helpers? Consider the opportunities for involving your managers in problem-solving or change-initiating project teams. Do they have spare capacity? Could they generate some spare capacity? Do they have the skills needed to staff project teams? Can you afford to fund change programs? By working out answers to questions like these, the new role of managers in your organization will emerge.

6. Reshape Evaluation and Appraisal Mechanisms

You've probably heard the many excuses for avoiding what we believe is a worthwhile shift to 360 degree feedback. "Our workers just aren't qualified to make such judgments." "Our senior executives are not ready for this." "People won't be candid in giving advice to the boss." All of these excuses ignore two important issues: (1) the folks in the best position to comment on your management skills include those you manage; and (2) 360 degree feedback (*properly done*—for example, without attribution or fear of retribution) is one of the few ways to expose managers to the *reality* of their behavior.

One of the managers we interviewed wanted to establish a mentoring program for the staff. While he wanted the mentorships to evolve naturally and spontaneously, that wasn't happening. Convinced that he needed a more formal program, he wasn't sure that genuine relationships would develop if he assigned mentors. On the other hand, if he allowed the staff to select their mentors, he was concerned that a handful of his managers would be selected by many, and another handful would be humiliated because few or non selected them. After wrestling with the problem, he set up a program that guaranteed each staff member none of three mentors that he or she listed.

The results were as expected, maybe worse. Three "key" managers went without a single nomination. Each of them was shocked. Incredulous, one went so far as to call several times to suggest what amounted to a recount of ballots—the program in his mind was a general election. He could not accept this evidence of the staff's feeling for him as a potential friend and mentor.

The lesson to be drawn is that very few of us understand how others perceive us. We receive almost no raw, unfiltered feedback. Even traditional counseling from above is seldom as effective as it needs to be. If the organizational superior has not already sugarcoated what he or she has to say, the individual being counseled is more than likely to rework the message to suit personal needs and perceptions.

Deutsche Bank 360 Degree Employee Feedback Survey

As part of a continuous improvement initiative over the past two years, Deutsche Bank, N.A., the North American subsidiary of the German-based international bank, has administered a 360 degree Employee Feedback Survey. The survey gives staff the opportunity to better understand how they are seen by their co-workers at all levels, and serves as a reminder that co-workers are internal customers whose opinions count.

Deutsche Bank's 500 New York employees and 40 Chicago employees each receive a questionnaire that lists every employee at that office from assistant vice-president up to and including the CEO. Employees use the questionnaire to evaluate those whom they feel they know well enough to rate. Numeric ratings are provided for six strategic competency areas and overall performance:

- Professional competence
- Customer skills
- Management skills
- Productivity
- Teamwork
- Leadership
- Overall assessment

In addition to providing numeric performance ratings, respondents select adjectives to describe the individual from a list of 28 possibilities, ranging from decisive, knowledgeable, visionary, and hardworking to arrogant, self-serving, unmotivated, and mediocre. Respondents also specify the frequency of their interaction with each employee they rate (daily, weekly, monthly, or occasionally).

The survey data are analyzed for EEO (Equal Employment Opportunity) purposes to confirm that there is no bias in survey ratings due to gender, race, or age. Employees receive confidential personal reports at their homes detailing average ratings and the number of people who rated them. The average ratings for peer employees (i.e., those with a similar position or job title) are also presented for comparison, along with the quartile ranking of their rating for their peer group. The report also shows the same information using the percentage of ratings that are highly positive (i.e., a rating of 6 or 7 on a seven-point scale). Finally, the report provides a tabulation of the adjectives chosen to describe the employee, in order of their frequency of mention.

The process goes a long toward informing individuals about how they can better work together—top down, bottom up, and laterally.

Figure 11.3

Requisite Influence of Tomorrow's Managers

A new form of project management is becoming critical. To be
effective, managers will need to invest in their peers and learn
to influence their peers.

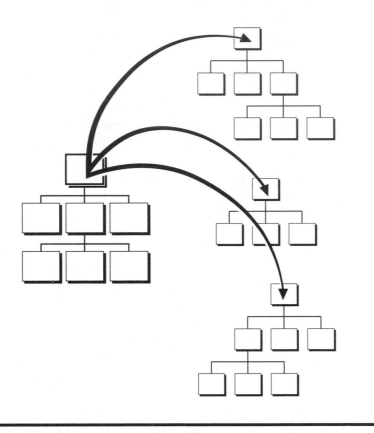

7. Institutionalize Project Management and Project Work Skills

Project skills must be made an important learning objective,
but few organizations are responding vigorously to this challenge. The "technology" of managing a mobile workforce and
deploying people flexibly on projects has yet to catch up with
the business reality. Both project management and project work
skills need strengthening. Neither should be confused with

Project skills must be made an important learning objective.

---

some of the woolly-headed team training taking place today. Good project skills training focuses on hard-nosed task planning, estimating, project budgeting, and issue resolution. It teaches project management skills in project teams drawn from throughout the organization and therefore subject to competing priorities.

Leverage learning by means of real business initiatives. Real projects, as opposed to classroom-bound ones, are now seen by high-performing companies as the best vehicle for learning. They provide the opportunity to stretch and challenge an individual or team in a situation that also delivers a genuine business payback. HR professionals can play an important role as brokers by matching individual employees with a defined training need and project sponsors who need people to carry out their mission. Challenging project work is an effective crucible of learning. Target specific learning objectives. Overstaff; sprinkle in some rookies to do staff work and learn work methods as they do.

Conclusion

On the uplifting side of things, we see many fertile opportunities for line managers to select, develop, train, review, and promote employees with little need for intervention from a traditional human resources department. The manager as coach and mentor is a powerful concept—and more powerful still when implemented. To locate training on the job yet create "practice fields" where mistakes can be made without penalty is a powerful concept. To think in terms of multiskilled employees and managers capable of moving knowledgeably into and out of project teams creates an entirely new vision of the organization and its people.

On the other hand, traditional HR departments often prove to be a drag on the way toward that vision. We have been deliberately tough in our observations, but not merely for the pleasure: We believe that resilient, innovative HR groups can lead toward this vision. We hope that the recommendations

We have been operating in the context of our traditional hierarchies for most of the current century. We need to rethink our approach as we enter the next.

in this chapter will stimulate the thinking of senior executives and HR leaders about work, job design, supervision, project effectiveness, and the management of people.

Our moment in business history is a fascinating one. We have been managing organizations through traditional hierarchies for most of this century. We need to rethink our approach as we enter the next.

Notes

1. Harry Levinson. "On Executive Suicide," *Harvard Business Review*, July–August 1975, p. 119.
2. *Control of Industrial Relations in Large Companies*, Industrial Relations Research Unit (Coventry: University of Warwick, 1993).
3. Robert Kelley and Janet Chaplain, "How Bell Labs Creates Star Performers," *Harvard Business Review*, July–August 1993, p. 134.
4. Thomas A. Stewart, "Fixing the Economy. US Productivity: First but Fading," *Fortune*, October 19, 1992, p. 56.

Twelve

Measuring Up

"Gratiano speaks an infinite deal of nothing . . . His reasons are as two grains of wheat hid in two bushels of chaff: you shall seek all day ere you find them, and when you have them they are not worth the search."

Bassanio, in William Shakespeare's
The Merchant of Venice

No book on managing paradox and tension in today's multinational organizations would be complete without a chapter on measurements. Measurements—not data—are the foundation of management practice. Properly designed and used, measures can articulate strategy, drive change, shape behavior, focus action, and align management around activities that lead to success. Without sensible, balanced measurements, *most* of your organization's energy and actions are of no value to customers, to shareholders, or to employees. The worst measures (there are many) destroy value.

Measurements provide a visible beacon in dealing with paradox. Correctly designed, they support decisiveness and balanced judgments. But measurements themselves are subject to paradox. Managing the modern corporation is not a neat, linear, well-ordered equation in which variables relate in a predictable way. Just as soon as things seem to be going well, someone discovers that your latest silicon chip creates an error at the eighth decimal point—or that a random criminal act has compromised your hallowed brand name.

Measurements are the foundation of management practice.

Many organizations have *just begun* to overhaul their key measurements despite the sea changes discussed throughout this book. When these objectives are conceived simply in terms of cost, quality, and speed, one might think that the science of performance measurement would be getting simpler. It isn't so.

Simplicity might have been possible in a more static environment. We might have been able to craft new measures in response to the increased attention to quality, the need to get products developed faster, and the heightened importance of customer service. But the world keeps changing. For those organizations stepping up to a genuine overhaul of their measures, their experience is like changing a tire at 50 miles per hour.

Flotsam, Jetsam, and Old Measures

What gets measured gets done. Right? Not always—not when performance measures conflict with one another. This is just what occurs when there are too many. Most companies today are awash in measures. Like so much flotsam and jetsam, they linger on, even in the face of new strategies and structures, new markets and new products. Measures still in place that were developed to support strategies long since discarded result in inefficiency and waste because yesterday's measurements influence today's managers.

> **Most companies today are awash in measures.**

The changes over the last decade require you to thoroughly reevaluate your measurements. For example, reengineering has put great stress on traditional measurements. Done correctly, reengineering results in a process view of work, in greater focus on the "horizontal" flow of activities across functional and organizational boundaries. Clearly, new measurements are needed to propel and sustain this view of the organization's work. But in nearly every company we visit in the post-reengineering era, old measures linger on, creating bottlenecks, driving bad (parochial) behavior, creating waste. You can literally "feel" the tension this creates, the contradiction and inconsistency between the newly reengineered business model and obsolete measures that persist like a hangover.

Measures tuned to the performance of cross-functional teams are consistent with today's focus on efficient processes. Yet we have found that many companies still have many measures in place that undermine this strategy. At one company where we analyzed selected reports sent to senior executives, we were able to identify *600* different measures. That wasn't every measure—we just stopped counting! You have to wonder how the company's managers or employees could tell what was important. Measurement overload is counterstrategy, no matter what the vision and strategy. Measurement overload is also at the heart of this chapter's paradox:

• • • • •

Develop really effective measures. Get rid of a lot of them.

• • • • •

Killing measures isn't easy. Old measures die hard. Managers use measures to ratify and endorse their success. Existing measures explain the rules of the game. Managers are adept at protecting them, especially if they have contributed to the individual's success. This being so, you cannot expect managers to give up old measures easily. All manner of rationale will be brought forward to protect the status quo. And the longer a measure has been used, the more securely moored it becomes until it becomes a cultural norm. At one company, profit "by unit"—a measure abandoned some seven years ago—is *still* being calculated with bootleg spreadsheets, using dubious allocations, and reported in various management forums.

We all develop a level of comfort in our ability to control or manage by the existing measures. We even begin to believe that to some degree we can "manage" the results themselves. New measures threaten to undermine our mastery.

Many staff members owe their existence to obsolete measures. In one client company, an individual carefully compiled and analyzed the cost of premium freight. He believed that his very existence depended on this measurement. When the premium freight measure was replaced by "percentage of on-time shipment," he just kept reporting the old data. That was his job! "Besides," you hear people say, "we may be asked for this information. What will we do if it's no longer available?" And they may be right. Someone *might* ask about the cost of premium freight—and this would guarantee the survival of that measure, even if it has long since lost its usefulness.

High-level users of this information may preserve it out of simple courtesy and team spirit. Roger Noall, senior executive vice-president of KeyCorp, stated as much to us: "I get all of these reports that I really don't read, but I just assume someone else needs them. I would be glad to have them disappear, but they must be important to one of our managers." Everyone feels the same way. They assume that the report *must* be important to someone, otherwise it wouldn't exist. "I don't read the report, but so-and-so probably does." Tearing down obsolete measures takes work. It requires forceful leadership.

Measurements: The Cornerstone of Strategy

Performance measures are a primary strategy deployment tool. Establishing them is one of the foremost responsibilities of management. As organizations transform themselves and as change becomes a way of life for most companies, intelligent measurements only gain in importance. Managers in greater numbers are beginning to reshape their measurements as their markets change and their strategies evolve. Few traditional measures provide the tools executives need to manage their now flatter organizations, in which giving help has replaced giving directions. And for those bold enough to attempt any form of "virtual corporation," the traditional measures are mostly bankrupt.

Killing measures isn't easy. They die hard.

Some managers and management gurus promote a simpler, more linear view of operations. Forget that view. Complexity is with us. So too is tension:

Long Term	**Short Term**
"Our measures must take a long-term view."	"But, no, the Wall Street analysts want results this quarter."
Customer Orientation	**Budget Orientation**
"Customers come first."	"Hey, I have to make budget or my department head will have mine!"
Cost Focus	**Revenue Focus**
"You'll have to do without it. We need to cut costs."	"How am I going to hit my new revenue targets without it!"
Hierarchical View	**Horizontal View**
"We spend $20 million *in* purchasing."	"We spend $75 million *on* purchasing."

ROI can be improved by reducing inventory. True . . . well
. . . maybe. But not when reducing inventory causes out-of-
stock conditions and lost sales, events that seldom boost ROI.
The mathematics are correct, the left-brain thinking is wrong.
Corporate life is just more complex than the equation indicates.
Fortunately, executives know this.

Measurements: Organizational Glue

Historically, large companies became successful by careful
division of duties. They concentrated capital and people on
simplified tasks in order to obtain
economies of scale. Every once in a

**Tearing down obsolete
measures requires forceful
leadership.**

while, they brought out a new product or they geared their marketing
efforts to improve product prices. But
for the most part they retained the
industrial model that originated in
the first half of this century:
Taylorism—efficiency through division of duties and through
carefully separated functional cells hierarchically arranged.

Economy of scale remains important. But most companies
now compete on the basis of innovative products, differentiated services, low-cost provider status, or customer-targeted
marketing. So the old measures designed to monitor the old
company are no longer relevant. They must be replaced by
measures consistent with today's competitive needs, and even
these new measures need to evolve as business conditions
change.

Rubbermaid and 3M have done just this. Both companies
have stated that new products—those less than five years
old—must represent a large proportion of their sales. This is
a fully measurable goal. Companies following such a growth
strategy keep track of the number of new products, product
development lead time, the target cost of new products, the
number of patents, the percentage of drawings electronically
produced, and product life cycle. These product tracking
measurements receive as much attention as budgets.

Never before has "the right structure" been less clear. As organizations become more fluid, those carefully drawn lines on the organizational chart seldom depict the day-to-day workings of a company. No structure operates as cleanly as the chart suggests. Corporate life today is just too complex. The *real* organization continuously changes. Customers, investors, and regulators make it so. Hierarchy is under pressure from cross-functional teams. Some companies reorganize around critical business processes. Others feel that such a step is not needed as long as teams can address cross-business issues. But, independent of their formal structure, most organizations are trying to become "more horizontal."

Despite these new, more fluid, less formal organizations, there must be enough "structure" to ensure that strategies are carried out and objectives met. This is precisely what measurements do. A good performance measurement system cuts across organizational boundaries and measures what is important, independent of company organization. The measurements report how well objectives are being achieved.

The Need for Balanced Judgment

The internal cohesion of an organization makes balanced judgment necessary. Figure 12.1 illustrates the interrelatedness of several common manufacturing performance measurements. Bringing to market a wide variety of products might improve overall market share—but the cost of manufacturing complexity will soar and show up as higher unit cost on the plant's measurement chart. Maintaining several different vendors for the same part may improve negotiating leverage—but the company will need more purchasing staff to maintain these relationships, and this will push cost up. Reducing inventories can improve cash flow—but less inventory could also affect customer service.

Management's challenge is to monitor *all* the levers of success simultaneously and to adjust one or more in the event of a problem. Managers need to understand how shrinking inventory affects not just customer satisfaction but all other

Figure 12.1
Measurement Linkages

It is the interrelatedness of our organizations that drives the need for judgment and the need for balance in selecting and using measures.

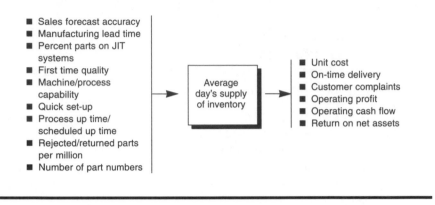

- Sales forecast accuracy
- Manufacturing lead time
- Percent parts on JIT systems
- First time quality
- Machine/process capability
- Quick set-up
- Process up time/ scheduled up time
- Rejected/returned parts per million
- Number of part numbers

Average day's supply of inventory

- Unit cost
- On-time delivery
- Customer complaints
- Operating profit
- Operating cash flow
- Return on net assets

organizational success measures. There can be no quick fixes, just relentless, small changes toward the goal. While the term "continuous improvement" has fallen, mortally wounded by the mighty notion of "reengineering," the day-to-day workings of a company should strive for small gains, even after process reengineering completes its chore.

Management's challenge is to monitor *all* the levers of success simultaneously.

Figure 12.1 shows the measurements of an actual company. Focusing on "day's supply of inventory" will probably improve cash flow. But to reduce inventory levels in a meaningful manner, an organization must also:

- Reduce its manufacturing lead time
- Put its parts on a just-in-time system
- Make items right the first time
- Invest in highly capable machine tools

- Set up these machines quickly
- Schedule the machines effectively
- Purchase high-quality components
- Reduce the number of parts
- Design products that are easy to manufacture

Each of these items can be measured independently. Your set of measurements should help you triangulate *all* of the key business functions needed to reduce inventory and increase profits without disturbing the customer. The inventory example is taken from the manufacturing world, but the same principles apply to service industries.

Your system of measures should include both leading and lagging measures. *Leading measures* show the immediate results of a completed operation, such as defects, cycle time, throughput, and break-even time. *Lagging measures* show the results of completed operations over time, such as stockholder value creation (e.g., earnings, cash flow, revenue), customer satisfaction and retention, market share gain, new product successes, and inventory. A balanced set of performance measures should include *both* the leading and lagging categories.

A balanced set of performance measures should include *both* the leading and lagging categories.

A balanced set of measures will also support an organization's internal and external environments. While *internal measures* such as backlog, revenue, profit, cash flow, and asset management measures may remain important, you should also include measures that provide an *external perspective* on the business environment—measures that reflect the company's performance in relation to its customers, competitors, suppliers, and the marketplace. In addition, there should be both cost-based and non-cost-based measures. Many of the cost-based measures (e.g., design cost, manufacturing cost) are result measures. They should be supplemented by measures reflecting the underlying cost drivers, most of which are non-cost-based (e.g., design cycle time, product complexity).

Figure 12.2
Supportive (Balanced) Measures

A balanced set of measures will support an organization's internal and external perspectives and will include both cost-based and non-cost-based measures.

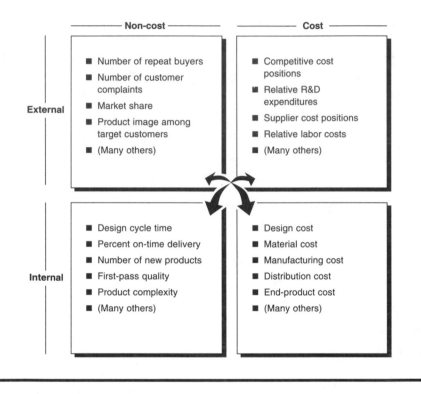

The measures should encompass the organization's entire value chain, and they should be interrelated and applied with consistency. The traditional hierarchical measures (e.g., headcount and budget attainment) should be augmented by vertically linked interunit measures (e.g., customer service response time) that link functional groups together to meet common objectives. Improving customer service levels requires teamwork from procurement, sales, logistics, and engineering. To meet a product development schedule, marketing, manufacturing, and engineering have to cooperate. These cross-functional relationships are often overlooked in traditional approaches to measurement.

Making Measurements Work for You

Developing performance measures today requires balance, synthesis, and integration. Tension and trade-off are everywhere. The best measurement systems help managers analyze and interpret data, anticipate results, synthesize what's occurring, and rationalize resources. A good system of measures promotes both thoroughness *and* decisiveness. A tall order.

Now add the need for flexibility. Decisions made with data from the set of measures must support the organization's strategies. The goal is to create a symphony from all the diverse and potentially discordant contributors in the organization. Just when harmony has been achieved, the strategies change and call for change in the measurement set to develop a *new* harmony. Now the order has become even taller.

Combining our collective experience with insights from our interviews with managers, we offer the following guidelines to help you achieve a better measurement system.

1. Use Fewer and More Balanced Measures

In the post–World War II industrial expansion, companies created new ways to measure their success. Each process change, each new information system, each wave of management—and, in some cases, each new question asked at the executive level—produced new measurements. However, what a company really needs to measure performance is a small number of items that everyone should concentrate on, important things that make the company successful. Most of the data available in computer files just don't help very much. They are not focused on clear business issues. They are just data.

When we say "fewer" measures, we mean a handful—maybe 50 to 60. In 1994, we visited a *Fortune* 100 company that created monthly over 100,000 profit and loss statements. *Over 100,000 P&Ls!* They existed on "formal" MIS systems and in a profusion of spreadsheet models across the company. The P&Ls

were awash in allocations, so much so that the term "actuals" on many of these reports had little or no meaning. Nearly every well-established line executive employed a small army of financial samurai to ensure that allocations were favorable—to him or her, of course.

What happens to a company with thousands of measurements? Answer: It loses its way. Managers begin to spend much of their time fighting over allocations. Focus gives way to chaos.

We recall a company where well over 1,000 measures were reported at various organizational levels. Managers, overwhelmed with data, were pleading for information they could act on. Overhauling its information system, the company replaced data with measurement.

General Motors also spotted the need for focused measures. The company reduced its measures to well under 100, giving managers at all levels of the organization clear direction about what is important. The GM 1991 annual report stated:

> Another priority involves the implementation of a new performance measurement system, which will facilitate the basic changes taking place. The system covers all aspects of the business, including people development, product development, manufacturing and shareholder satisfaction. The system includes a focused set of measures that deal with the primary factors influencing quality, customer satisfaction and financial performance . . . *With full system implementation, we expect a more consistent application of common performance benchmarks across the organization.* [italics added][1]

2. Measure Processes as Well as Results

Historically, financial measurements have been broad gauges of overall company success. The trouble is that by the time they turn red it's too late. While result measures like this tell us how things are, they seldom tell us what is going wrong. Recognizing this limitation, companies are now developing measures that indicate whether business processes are working. The premise is that if the company's strategies are right and

Better Measures

Figure 12.3
Gyroscope

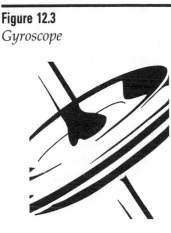

The gyrocompass is a very accurate compass, unaffected by magnetic influences, which came into wide use during World War II. It consists essentially of a rapidly spinning, electrically driven rotor suspended in such a way that its axis automatically points along the geographical meridian. It provides a very accurate measurement of your position.

Do your measures do as well?

its processes are working, results will follow. Such companies have not abandoned result measures, which make clear whether current strategies are improving financial outcomes. But management supplements this historical data with process-oriented measurements. Top managers derive their measurements from objectives and strategies. Process measures tell them whether they are *implementing* their strategies; result measures tell them whether company objectives are being met.

For example, a customer satisfaction index is a process measure. If this measure begins to go sour, managers can count on subsequent loss of market share and a red-zone P&L (result measures). Companies are rapidly adjusting their measurement system to let them know what is coming by augmenting results measurements with probes into company processes.

3. Measure Teamwork as Well as Functions or Departments

To measure both processes and results, companies are supplementing their reliance on performance measurements of functional "silos" with measures indicating whether separate parts of the organization are pulling together.

Consider order fulfillment cycle time, a key measure of customer satisfaction. Many functions within the organization have to work in tandem for cycle time to improve. Engineering must design the product quickly, logistics must order needed components rapidly, manufacturing must cut its operational lead time, marketing must accurately forecast sales, order fulfillment must pick the right items, and transportation must get the product to the customer when wanted.

Labor efficiency reporting in manufacturing companies is a good illustration of the change taking place. Historically, efficiency reports were prepared to pinpoint the manufacturing departments and individuals not producing to standard. But with automated machine tools and cellular manufacturing, such reporting merely makes work for the industrial engineers. The labor efficiency report is expensive and doesn't measure anything very well. A blip in the efficiency report usually indicates that there was a heavy snowfall, a machine was scheduled for maintenance, the plant called a team meeting, or the standard was wrong. (See the "clock time" discussion on the next page for a discussion of standards.) Of course, sometimes a manufacturing worker is inefficient—we all have good and bad days—but having this information is hardly worth the cost of getting it. Besides, hasn't the team already noticed most of what's in the report?

Many efficiency measures of the past are obsolete today. Machine utilization, once used to help drive production at ever-increasing throughput levels, provides another example. Now that we better understand the dynamics of supply chain processes, we have grasped that we cannot examine efficiency measures in isolation. Viewed in a vacuum, efficiency measures such as machine, department, or plant utilization have actually contributed to unnecessary build-up of inventory. A balanced set of measures is more likely to focus upon things that calibrate the "synchronicity" of production. Are inputs, efforts, and outputs in harmony? If we're an auto company, are we producing about the same number of transmissions as we are steering wheels?

"Clock Time" in the Goal-Setting Process: *Personal Reflections by Dan Keegan, Price Waterhouse Partner and Contributing Author*

When I was young, I often stayed with my cousin, who lived in a large house surrounded by woods. We explored that countryside with as much dedication as any 16th-century Spaniard discovering the world beyond. And sometimes we would just sit in the kitchen, planning the day's adventure or reliving some past experience.

Wristwatches were a luxury in those days. From another room we would hear an occasional call: "What time is it?" My cousin would glance at the clock over the stove and shout back, "8:40, clock time." Later in the day, the same question would echo through the house: "What time is it?" Once again, my cousin would look at the clock and call out, "5:10, clock time."

I observed this dialogue repeatedly during many visits. Eventually I began to wonder why the response always ended with the phrase "clock time." Finally it dawned on me. The kitchen clock was set 15 minutes fast. My aunt, a kindly woman who wanted to spare us the pains of hell, used this little deception to get the family to church in plenty of time for Sunday service.

Of course, everyone *knew* that the clock was set 15 minutes fast. That's why the shout from the kitchen invariably included "clock time." Without these words, the response would have been hopelessly ambiguous. Had the informant in the kitchen adjusted the answer to real time? Or was he consistently reporting clock time?

I see a lot of "clock time" in performance measurement systems. In the belief that the organization will be "inspired" by patently unrealistic goals, management uses my aunt's little deception to motivate the company. "Clock time" has many forms: budgets that are too tight, standards that call for unobtainably high performance, gross margins that are wildly optimistic, sales discounts that don't reflect market realities, "hockey stick" sales forecasts that no one believes.

By changing the clock, my aunt successfully rallied the churchgoers—at first. Similarly, unrealistic measurement goals can achieve their purpose for a time. Pretty soon, however, everyone mentally thinks "clock time" when they look at their performance charts.

Would it not be better to set demanding but achievable goals?

Mine Safety Appliances, an innovative company in Pittsburgh, threw out its labor reporting system and resolved to concentrate on unit cost. The company quickly discovered that very little has been lost except the expense of reporting the labor information. Unit cost is a far better measure of overall company efficiency, and reduced cost will allow management to price more surgically. To reduce cost, the engineers, purchasing managers, and production supervisors have to work together. What does it matter if none of these groups gets credit for cost savings through improved efficiency? The customer is better off, as is the company. The team knows it did a good job. And management knows.

Mine Safety Appliances has *54 measurements in total,* nine of which deal with product development. John Ryan III, the company's chairman, has consistently maintained product development budgets in good times and in bad. In his company, executives meet regularly to review some or all of the following product development measurements:

- Average time to market for new products
- Design for manufacturability (a series of factors that indicate how easy it is to make the new product)
- New product sales dollars as a percentage of total sales dollars
- Number of engineering changes after production release
- Number of part numbers (and percentage of parts standardized among products)
- Concept-to-customer *time* milestones met
- R&D investment as a percentage of sales
- Planned and actual return on new product investment
- Target product cost achievement

4. Measure Activities as Well as Departments

While measurements should be balanced, oriented toward process and results, and both inward- and outward-looking, cost control always remains important. Increasingly, management is turning its attention to the cost of *activities* and augmenting its traditional budgetary view of departmental costs with this new information.

We recently visited a very large company in which management was asking, "What do the 4,000 people classified as members of the Selling, General and Administrative Departments *actually do*?" This company had gone through a painful downsizing, creating problems it did not want to repeat. Management knew that it had to take a more precise approach to realign additional resources—and the company's accounting system offered no help. The account system could tell management *how much* was being spent by each department, but it contained next to no information about *why* it was being spent.

The functional organization reflects a management style rather than the way a company builds its products or does its work. As a result, relying on the functional organization as the only vehicle for measurement is often counterproductive. The measurement scheme is typically a cost-based reporting budget versus actual, but this approach can't measure effectiveness and can rarely link functional contributions to products or outputs. Most of us have seen, however, that work does not actually follow a functional structure; it flows cross-functionally through an organization's processes. This suggests that measurement should focus on the outcomes of these processes. Measuring and managing outcomes allow you to better measure and manage key processes and their related activities. Along these process lines, costs accumulate and value is added to customer solutions. Accumulating costs by outcome will at long last allow you to understand the true cost of complexity in your business model. The answers will both alarm you and arm you. You will have both the incentive and the tools to become more competitive.

Effective cost management today obliges you to understand the link between functions (departments, etc.) and processes. The link is individual activities—each performed *by a department* but also *part of a process*. Each activity in your organization ought to provide an output that supports a process goal (eliminate those that don't!). The functional organization provides resources to the process, which in turn produces the required outcome. By measuring and managing costs at the activity level, links from the traditional functional structure to the horizontal process can be recognized.

In its initial attempt to organize around products, Chrysler created product teams. Although the K-car platform was a successful result of this approach, the team members struggled with their measures because they were mostly judged on the basis of budget versus actual and from the perspectives of their functional managers. The current approach—vastly more successful—is rooted in activity-based costing, which links activities both to the functional organization and to the horizontal product team. Using Chrysler's activity-based costing system as the foundation, measures are created at the activity level and linked back to the horizontal team and the functional organization. The functional manager is required to provide a capable resource at a given unit cost, while the teams are responsible for their consumption of that resource.

5. Be Creative in Developing Measures

In designing a new measurement system, creativity is the watchword. For example, where cross-functional harmony is important to achieve objectives, the company may wish to establish a teamwork index. As an adjunct to the yearly budget, important units could rate themselves on how well they interact with other units of the company—and could in turn be rated by the other units. Where gaps appear in these ratings, extra effort may be in order.

Creative measures might include such things as a design for manufacturability index, an employee satisfaction index, a customer loyalty index, and a training goals achieved index. The principle is to carefully categorize company strategy and determine the types of measures that are needed to promote and assess strategy implementation. Then install them.

While developing the system of measures, it is important to remember the big difference between measurements and data. Data are fleeting units of information that can be invaluable for decision making, but they are not monitored regularly and do not command periodic attention. Gross domestic product is an example of useful data. GDP tends to indicate the overall state of the economy and might set the tone for a capital expenditure plan. But it is only a backdrop to the *management* process. Data points are not actionable.

Measurements, on the other hand, should reflect things that we want to do. As such, measurements always have a goal, and they are carefully monitored. Measurements say to the organization: This matter is important, pay attention. Measurements should be probes into key aspects of the company, which help executive management understand how well processes are operating and whether or not the processes are bringing about their intended objectives.

Developing creative, effective measurements is more important than analytical perfection. Restrain the tendency to push for mathematical precision. Establish measurements based on your strategy—even if there is only an imprecise relationship to near-term profits.

6. Tear Down Old Measures

Most corporate measurement systems have been set up to track static performance. Unless they are reshaped, old measures will hamper your effort to create a more effective organization. Innovative companies alter their measurements from time to time because they recognize that measures drive behavior in a fairly predictable manner, and they understand that measures can speed the pace of change. These companies are moving away from things that can be *controlled* to things that can be *influenced*. Through measurements, management influences the organization.

Old measures will sustain the old company.

Figure 12.4

Filter Measures

In selecting measures, filter them using your objectives and strategies.

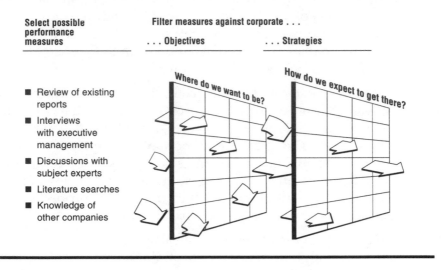

Select possible performance measures	Filter measures against corporate . . .	
	. . . Objectives	. . . Strategies

- Review of existing reports
- Interviews with executive management
- Discussions with subject experts
- Literature searches
- Knowledge of other companies

Where do we want to be?

How do we expect to get there?

Managers attempting to do something about their measurements find that old measures do not fade away, they must be dismantled. Too often companies layer new measures on top of the old. This always undermines the objectives of the new measures. The old measures will sustain the old company.

Performance measurements need to evolve with the company. Like any other part of the organization, they have a life cycle. Old measures should be killed when they no longer support what the company wants to do—symbolically beheaded in public.

7. Make Your Measures Talk

Companies have found that measurements should be presented graphically. A graphic approach has several attractions:

- Graphs shows trends, seasonality, and attainment. You don't get jumbled in the numbers.

- Graphs prevent too much data from being displayed. There is no room on the page.
- Graphs provide simple, important messages. They are easy to understand.
- Graphs conform to the picture-rich world in which we live; data tables don't.

A measurement chart should contain several lines of commentary, penned by the individual who can either influence the measurement result or influence those who can. The reason that most executive information systems failed is that they merely presented data, not commentary. And too much of it. They were too complex, providing "drill-down capability" useful to an analyst but not to a busy executive.

An executive wants to know, "How are we doing?" If we are doing poorly, "What steps are being taken to correct the problem?" Measurement charts are the stepping-off point for additional communication. In themselves, the charts simply indicate progress toward goal achievement. Effective measurement usage implies communication.

Ideally, the chart should be prepared by the individual who will supply the commentary. For efficiency, however, chart construction may often be delegated to a different organizational unit, often finance or perhaps the operating manager's assistant. Who prepares the chart is much less important than who creates the commentary. That person is the *de facto* owner of the measure. As such, he or she will influence measurement results. In complex organizations, this creates, in effect, a horizontal structure.

For example, the director of order management might prepare the divisional on-time shipment chart. To explain a deteriorating trend, the director will comment upon a missed vendor delivery date, a quality glitch in manufacturing, or a wildcat strike. The individual may not directly supervise all these parts of the organization. Unimportant. What *is* important is that a business process is not working properly and steps need to be taken to correct it. If there is an impasse somewhere in the organization, the commentary writer may

Figure 12.5

Components of a Measurement Chart

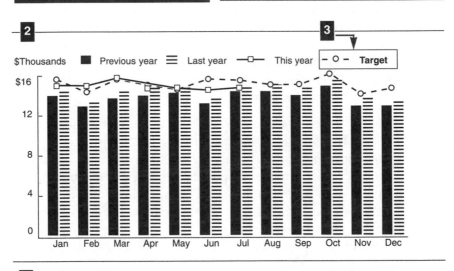

1

Previous Year	Last Year	This Year	Target
$xxx	$xxx	$xxx	$xxx
xxx	xxx	xxx	xxx
xxx	xxx	xxx	xxx
xxx	xxx	xxx	xxx
xxx	xxx	xxx	xxx
xxx	xxx	xxx	xxx
xxx	xxx	xxx	xxx
$xxx	$xxx	$xxx	$xxx

A robust measurement chart will:

1. Display the data

2. Include a graphic (chart) for visual impact

3. Include a goal

4. Include an explanation of the results and or trends

2   **3**

$Thousands   ■ Previous year   ≡ Last year   —□— This year   – O – **Target**

Jan Feb Mar Apr May Jun Jul Aug Sep Oct Nov Dec

4

Although sales remained on target for early months of the year, there has been a fall-off during each of the last months caused by unfavorable publicity in the business press concerning product A.

We are aggressively countering the incorrectly reported competitive statistics by mounting a comprehensive advertising campaign that gets under way next month.

We do not expect to turn around the situation this year, but our next-year sales should be even higher than our preliminary estimates.

be unable to state that the condition has been rectified. In such a case, higher-level executive action could be required.

8. Make Measurement Your Organization's "Glue"

Get the measures into executive forums. Seldom can one individual or even groups working together correct a *pervasive* business problem. Missing a goal usually means that a business process is ineffective for a complex reason. It can't be fixed at the local level or it would already have been fixed. The need may be more capital or new technology. And, of course, on occasion a personnel change may be in order.

One technique for changing an organization is to change the content of key planning and performance review meetings. A good place to start is to look at the periodic "operations" or performance review meetings as opportunities to introduce new measures and to motivate action through them.

The performance measurement system is a critical *integrating mechanism* that provides information and commentary that fosters communication. It is critical to incorporate the company's performance measurements into important managerial forums. These operational review meetings turn measurements into an important part of the management process. By filling the agenda with measurement charts and encouraging dialogue, management ensures that the information conveyed by the charts will be carefully prepared. Here is an axiom: The measurement system gets better when it is used.

Discussing *new* measures at executive meetings helps make *old* measures go away. If no one ever talks about labor efficiency anymore, there is not much reason to collect it.

Fact-based measurements leave turf jockeys at the gate.

Additionally, incorporating performance measurement charts into operational review meetings helps to maintain focus. If well designed, measurements report the workings of key company processes that cut across the formal organizational structure. Executives can concentrate on *fact-based business issues,* signaling to the company that goal achievement is important. And fact-based measurements leave turf jockeys at the gate.

9. Build Consensus around a Few Best Measures

Consider using a Delphi technique to build awareness and agreement around a reduced set of measures. A good set of measures for your organization may already exist—among so many other measures that they are ineffective. To agree upon new measures or simply to select the best existing ones, even a modified Delphi process helps.

To provide functional knowledge of the various organizational units, representatives from throughout the company should be included in the selection team. A questionnaire is prepared asking team members to rank each preliminary performance measure by the following criteria:

- *Relevance:* the degree to which the measure is linked to the company's strategies and objectives
- *Usefulness:* how well the measure helps to identify the strengths and weaknesses of underlying business processes
- *Understandability:* how easily the measure can be understood
- *Availability of data:* how easily the necessary data for the measure can be obtained.

The questionnaire results are compiled and discussed among the project team members in a workshop that typically lasts two to three days. Various viewpoints are voiced and debated to arrive at a new performance measurement set.

10. Use Caution When Tying Measures to an Incentive System

A revised incentive system may be necessary to link the new performance measures to appropriate rewards. The system of measures will inform you about the effectiveness of business processes by measuring the processes themselves and by

Delphi Process

Originally developed at Rand Corporation in the 1950s, the Delphi process is a forecasting technique. It's based on repeated polling of the same experts and the exposure of all participants to evolving group opinions as a basis for later polls. The questionnaire rounds are designed to achieve consensus by allowing the participants to modify their responses in each round in light of the collected responses received in the previous rounds. The process is anonymous; the participants interact only through the published findings of the questionnaire circulated by the Delphi coordinator. The intention is to assure that changes in responses reflect rational judgment rather than the influence of high-profile opinion leaders.

The basic premises of the Delphi process are that repeated polling will decrease and converge the range of responses and that the emerging consensus will move toward "correct" answers. The feedback mechanism, designed to stimulate the participants' thinking, reveals to them factors or developments they might otherwise overlook. Because the participants remain anonymous, they feel more comfortable if and when they change their earlier responses in light of new knowledge or insights accumulated by the process.

A modified Delphi process can be effectively used for the selection of performance measures. Instead of repeated polling, the results of the initial questionnaire survey are organized and discussed in a workshop to arrive at an agreed set of performance measures.

---

measuring the ultimate results of these processes. The system should not be designed to gauge the effectiveness of an individual. Major corporate processes (e.g., new product design, parts and components manufacturing, customer order fulfillment, and maintenance of the product distribution chain) are simply too complex to be controlled by one individual or one group of individuals.

As Robert Eccles has pointed out, aligning incentives to performance by means of an objective formula is quite difficult:

> If the formula is simple and focuses on a few key variables, it inevitably leaves some important measures out. Conversely, if the formula is complex and factors in all the variables that require attention, people are likely to find it

Figure 12.6
Selecting Measures Using the Delphi Process

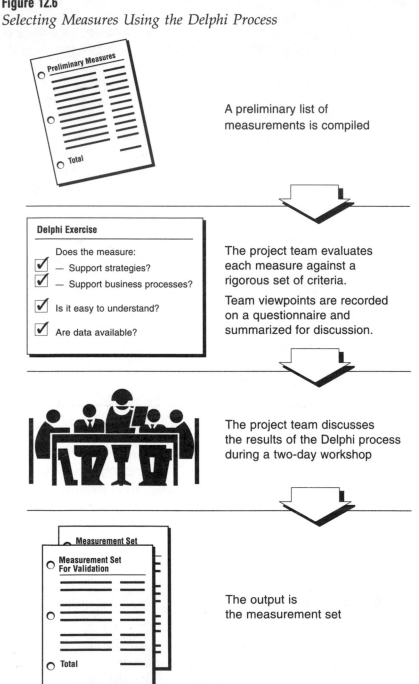

A preliminary list of
measurements is compiled

The project team evaluates
each measure against a
rigorous set of criteria.

Team viewpoints are recorded
on a questionnaire and
summarized for discussion.

The project team discusses
the results of the Delphi process
during a two-day workshop

The output is
the measurement set

confusing and may start to play games with the numbers. Moreover, the relative importance of the variables is certain to change more often—and faster—than the whole incentive system can change.[2]

Managers should be allowed to determine their subordinates' rewards on the basis of all relevant information, both qualitative and quantitative. As one manager said to us, "Judging a manager's value and contribution takes a great deal of 'adult supervision.' Tying compensation to specific measures is sketchy, at best."

What about Results?

Within the last few years, it has become clear to most executives that their efforts to revise company strategy and change the organization are insufficient if they do not also *align measurements with revised strategies*. One of the first companies to fully recognize this need was General Motors. GM began to revise its measurements in 1989. Full rollout started in earnest during the 1992 business year.

It seems to be working. *Fortune* magazine, in an article entitled "The $11 Billion Turnaround at GM," reported the following:

> GM has a worldwide payroll of 710,800. Slightly more than half, or 361,000, work in car and truck operations in the U.S. and Canada—enough to fill Yankee Stadium six times over or the ranks of Microsoft 31 times over . . . After losing $4.5 billion in 1991 and a spectacular $23.5 billion in 1992 [mostly because of accounting changes], GM earned $2.5 billion last year. . . . At the old GM, financial yardsticks were used to measure everything—whether the measurements were meaningful or not. . . . There is no better demonstration of GM's turnaround than the remarkable improvements in the design and manufacture of new models. . . . The front door of the 1995 Chevrolet Cavalier has 50% fewer parts than its predecessor and costs 13% less to build . . . Every new car or truck has to hit one of the 26 precisely defined market segments . . . Carefully manipulating the internal machinery of a giant corporation—coordinating, realigning, simplifying—to get it running smoothly requires the skills of a master

mechanic. . . . There's more excitement around here than we have had for a long time. . . . It is more than morale; it is a real feeling that people can make a difference.

A table from the article says something about measurement:

	1988 Midsize Cars	1997–98 Midsize Cars
Investment costs	$5.9 billion	$1.6 billion
Development time	72 months	37 months
Assembly hours per vehicle	39.0	18.9
Number of parts	3,200	2,300
Number of plants	5	3
Number of combinations	1,900,000	1,000
Unit volume	600,000 per year	700,000 per year

Fortune goes on to say: "Initial models of the Chevrolet Lumina, Pontiac Gran Prix, Oldsmobile Cutlass Supreme, and Buick Regal lost money. Their successors will be very profitable."[3]

John Ryan III, the CEO of Mine Safety Appliances, puts it this way:

There is much we can learn from Carl von Clausewitz. His theory of war is just as applicable to Desert Storm as it was when written 200 years ago. It states that the *key to success is correctly identifying those few crucial, limited areas on which the outcome depends.* And then concentrate overwhelming, superior force at those decisive points while being defensively protected elsewhere. In modern business life we know that most attention is paid to those things that get measured. Therefore, once an organization recognizes its key focal areas and what portions of its overall strategy are at risk, management must recognize, watch, and take action relative to the company's performance on those key factors.

Notes

1. *General Motors Annual Report* (U.S.A.: The General Motors Company, 1991), p. 12.

2. Robert G. Eccles, "The Performance Measurement Manifesto," *Harvard Business Review,* January–February 1991, p. 135.

3. Alex Taylor III, "The $11 Billion Turnaround at GM," *Fortune,* October 17, 1994, p. 54.

PART SEVEN

FIFTEEN RULES:

A Manifesto on Managing Paradox

Every coin, I now realize, has at least two sides, but there are pathways through the paradoxes if we can understand what is happening and are prepared to act differently.

Charles Handy
The Age of Paradox

C haos, complexity, and contradiction—enemies all, each an obstacle to performance. But none insurmountable. We must accept them, but without allowing them their consequences. This may be the greatest paradox: We must simultaneously embrace them and deny them their due.

Some rules are in order.

Drawn from the foregoing pages, the following 15 rules add up to a manifesto on managing the chaos, complexity, and contradiction that will challenge us all. Applying these rules has made a difference for the executives who contributed through interviews to this book. While many evergreen fundamentals underlie them, their relevance today shows in the success of those who employ them.

We hope that you will choose to keep these rules close at hand. They are the best map we know for the course ahead. Remember that you will need to use them steadfastly. Knowledge is never enough. It is through resolute application that the successes of the next decade will be determined. Embrace the paradoxes you face. Manage them. Learn from them. Derive from their energy and intricacy the winning insights that will set your business apart from all others.

Rules for Managing Chaos, Complexity, and Contradictions

Rule 1: Fortify Change with Stability

Rampant change without key elements of stability is chaos. Uncontrolled change generates turmoil, not performance. Managers need stakes in the ground to guide change. Buoys mark the course for sailboats, constellations provide fixed points for navigation, the lighthouse on shore guides the ship into port. All are stable points of reference. In the absence of such stability, change is a free-for-all—significant activity but far from enough real and positive change.

Rule 2: Build a Formidable Enterprise, One Individual at a Time

Create a global enterprise using the fundamental building block and most critical component of your organization—the individual employee, each one of them. To do this you will need to integrate your thinking about the individual, unique among all others in skills and aspirations, and about the organization as a whole. The greatest leaders in the decade ahead will look upon the majority and see the one. They will set a vision for the whole that engages the many. They will understand the organization by knowing its people. And they will optimize performance in the aggregate by maximizing the potential of each one.

Rule 3: Make Learning More Important than "the Answer"

A continuing parade of management doctrine is developing a form of attention deficit disorder in managers today. Little time is given to introspection, reflection, and learning. The pressure to be fast is overwhelming the opportunity to be effective over the long term. Make continuous learning a goal of redesigned processes. Create a culture that values initiative, resourcefulness, judgment, common sense, the insatiable desire to learn, and balance.

Rule 4: Create a New Culture by Focusing Not on the Culture but on the Forces That Shape It

Managers now understand the powerful leverage to be gained when the way people behave and the decisions they make reinforce the organization's strategy. But the effort to change a culture must be as powerful and deep-seated as the culture itself. Culture change does not result from training programs, wish lists of values and beliefs, or instructing people to care about customers. No amount of wishful talk regarding the characteristics of a new corporate culture will change yours. Because culture drives performance, you *must* work with your culture. But do so indirectly, through the factors that create and shape culture.

Rule 5: Drive Organizational Change through Personal Change

Personal change is the prerequisite to organizational change. All the restructuring, reengineering, process change, compensation change, and communications programs in the world won't change a thing unless individual behavior changes. Organizational transformation occurs one individual at a time. Involve the total person in making change happen. Build real incentives for desirable behavior change; coach and train; measure results. And keep only those who adopt and adapt.

Rule 6: Empower with Strong Leadership

Without forceful, directed, and purposeful leadership, empowerment will not happen. New Age theorists are wrong when they advocate that employees run the workplace. Employees want and expect leaders to set direction and determine the business focus. But they also want new latitude in achieving objectives. A new interactive model of leadership is emerging. It relies more on the power of *influence* than on command and control. It is based on mutual respect, and reinforced by effective communication skills. Its aim is to balance an increasing need for bold leadership with the instinct for freedom and initiative.

Rule 7: Foster Vigorous Debate and Steadfast Commitment

Today's environment demands that you balance leadership with employee involvement. Employees want to be involved in the business. Engaging them in decisions and forging consensus is growing more important every day. On the other hand, the need for speed, initiative, and responsiveness has never been greater. High-performing organizations manage to have it both ways: healthy, creative conflict in generating ideas and exploring alternatives coupled with decisiveness and dutiful commitment to initiatives once they're blessed.

Rule 8: Decide Who Decides

In the command-and-control hierarchical model of the past, decision rights were clear to everyone. This is not the case today. Thus, decision rights—the combination of authority and responsibility, and an awareness of where the real limits lie—must be spelled out and clearly communicated. High-performing organizations understand the importance of the question: "Who decides who decides?" They create an architecture for decision making and thereby bring clarity and consensus to key decisions and decision rights. The mechanism for decision making must be explicit and continually reinforced. The idea is to ensure that decisions are good ones, taken swiftly and based on real data and credible assumptions. Reality looks different from different levels. Realistic decisions, swiftly taken, are necessarily the purview of those with the appropriate perspective. Your decision architecture must reflect this.

Rule 9: Reignite Middle Management

After a decade in which it has been fashionable to bash middle managers as non-value-adding coordinators who block change, a very different view is emerging about those who remain. Smart executives have begun to value midlevel managers for their unique 360 degree perspective. Acting as the power train between strategy and execution, they can be the greatest integrating force of the corporation. As our organizations become flatter, these individuals will operate at the nexus of hierarchy and horizontalness. They will be structural linchpins.

Rule 10: Make Strategic Planning a Line Responsibility

Good strategic planning is built on objectivity, analytical and creative skills, and a broad base of experience. While value can be drawn from the creative and objective insights of a good planner, the best companies now recognize that effective strategic planning requires the involvement and commitment of those running the business and those closest to the market. Fusing these skills and experience is not easy. But the best managers now understand the need for better synthesis of strategy and execution, better integration of planning and operations, better balance between thinking about the future and being clear about conditions today.

Rule 11: Connect the Dots

The term "strategic alignment" has come to mean a condition in which all of the disparate elements and resources of an organization are bound and energized by a common strategy. Strategic alignment is (or should be) a principal concern of all CEOs. From which follows the importance of connecting the dots. Effective leaders work relentlessly to focus all actions and behaviors toward organizational goals. They encourage good decisions, enlightened decisions, decisions that reflect and further the established strategy and objectives. Strategic alignment requires balance, the integration of collective efforts, the synthesis of seemingly contradictory objectives. A good strategy and poor alignment subject the organization to untold inefficiencies. Avoid this.

Rule 12: Institutionalize Project Skills

The need to manage change has given new importance to the discipline of project management. The effect upon managers will be (and must be!) profound. In the decade ahead, your ability to effect continuous transformation will depend upon your ability to complete successful projects. You cannot be a 10 in operations and a 4 in project work. Yet this is the case in many companies. Project skills—both project management and project work skills—must be made an important learning objective.

Rule 13: Remove Threats. Reinforce Incentives

Leaders managing those who take responsibility for major risks have a special charge. Empowering those managers and employees who must stick their necks out in the course of their jobs requires special care and uncommon skill. Large-scale project management—particularly when it involves developing sophisticated technologies—is one such hazard. Project managers, with their reputations and careers on the line, walk a razor's edge between openness and discretion. Savvy leaders understand risk and the psychology of those who manage it. Through enlightened and forceful leadership, they empower their managers to act boldly—but intelligently. They work hard to remove the threat of failure when their best and boldest people attempt the impossible. They do everything they can to reinforce incentives to achieve the impossible.

Rule 14: Use Fewer, Broader, More Balanced Measures

Most companies today are awash in measures, enduring unchanged in the face of new strategies, revised structures, new markets, and new products and services. Measures developed to support strategies and initiatives long since discarded result in inefficiency and waste. They lock managers back into yesterday's framework. Without a limited, intelligent, and balanced set of measurements, many actions taken by your organization are of no value to customers, to shareholders, or to employees themselves. The worst measures (and there are many) destroy value. Measurements provide tangible guidance in dealing with paradox. Correctly designed, they are one of the most powerful tools to shape culture and deploy strategies.

Rule 15: Measure Activities as Well as Departments

Effective cost management obliges you to understand the links between functions (departments, etc.) and processes. Work does not follow the structure of the functional organization but flows cross-functionally through an organization's processes. By measuring and managing costs at the activity level, linkage from the functional structure to the horizontal process can be made. The measurement scheme should focus on the outcomes of these processes. Attention to outcomes allows you to better measure and manage key processes and their related activities. Along the process lines in your organization, costs accumulate and value is added to customer solutions. Accumulating costs by outcome will at long last allow you to understand the true cost of complexity in your business model. The insights gained will both alarm you and arm you. You will have both the incentive and the tools to become more competitive.

Afterword

B efore closing this book, we have a paradox of our own to deal with and some important words of encouragement. Our paradox is this: We have warned against quick fixes, ideas-of-the-month, and fads-of-the-year. But aren't the concepts in this book at least *a little* like all of these things? As authors, wouldn't we be satisfied to ignite a management fad of the year and then retreat to our condos when something else comes along?

We want to call attention to these ideas. But, we honestly hold that the concept of managing paradox with understanding, firmness, and creativity is beyond a fad; it is more fundamental than that. It is, we believe, a concept that needs to be restated by each generation of managers in the terms imposed by their own experience (Mary Parker Follett, in the quote that follows, will show you just what we mean). We hope to bring about focused consideration of the ideas in this book and steady application of their substance to the needs of individual businesses, which does not describe a fad rocketing past.

This book is about managing complexity, battling chaos, and facing the paradoxes in our environment head-on. It is full of ideas but is not a cookbook. You will filter these ideas through the lens of your own experience; they will enrich and change as you apply them. And here is the basis for a final thought on courage and good reason for hope. Through their evolving, but very real mastery of paradox, the managers discussed in this book have found new sources of strength and competitiveness. They created better organizations because they struggled with the contradictions inherent in each paradox and found a way forward that integrates the energies of paradoxical situations. They didn't try to destroy the paradox, coerce it into submission, ignore it, or give it Prozac. They faced it and worked with it.

As they confronted the paradoxical relationship between leadership and empowerment, for example, they became stronger, better leaders, while distributing new authority and accountability to employees. They did not feel reduced by their extensions of power to the workforce, because they had analyzed all of the newly empowered roles, their own and those of employees, and they liked what they saw. It made sense for each and all. At the next stage of the empowerment process, they did not worry unduly over employees' complaints about the burdens of empowerment—and there are many complaints when the exercise is real. Nor did they grow discouraged when employees resisted or failed to grasp the initial attempts at empowerment. Instead, they assessed the contradictions of empowerment and rose to the challenge. Leading their teams forcefully and exercising power intelligently, they more fully enabled their people.

The managers we interviewed talked freely about tension and frustration, not to complain but to put before us what they learned. As we spoke with them, it became clearer than ever that mature business judgment has a fabulous power to coordinate contradiction into a positive pattern. You have met a new kind of manager in these pages—the ex-POW full of courage fashioned out of his memories of Vietnam; the planner at a multinational oil company whose team of futurists developed an uncanny match between their predictive concepts and the actual course of events; the British utilities executive who moved from classic London to the not-so-classic industrial North to prove by his actions that change really was happening. Each of these managers faced conflict. Each made no compromise. Yet each changed in perspective and effectiveness. Each helped create a new kind of organization, and a new kind of success along an unexpected path.

More than 70 years ago, a management thinker, who happens to have been a woman, captured in her own way and for her era the theme of this book. Mary Parker Follett was a management consultant before there were management consultants. Her writings and observations are so powerful that Peter Drucker has called Follett a prophet of management. Henry Mintzberg holds that most of the innovative ideas in the field of human relations had their seeds in her work. Warren Bennis has said that just about everything written today about leadership and organizations comes from [her] writings and lectures.

While Follett did not use words such as strategy, empowerment, or culture, she wrote about the realities these now-common words point to and explored to remarkable depth, the characteristics of organizations and management. For that reason, she understood and wrote often about the paradoxical nature of business—even then.

Follett understood what was necessary to get past these paradoxes into a new dimension of management. What she grasped—indeed, what each of the managers we interviewed has grasped—is that trying to subjugate the contradictory forces of a paradoxical situation is not the point and that compromising between those forces is also not the point. In her vision, the point is to find a different way or to emphasize a different variable. Then, the organization can move forward. A paradoxical solution to a paradoxical problem.

In one of her most persuasive essays on the nature of conflict, Mary Parker Follett wrote:

> As conflict—difference—is here in the world, as we cannot avoid it, we should, I think, use it. Instead of condemning it, we should set it to work for us . . . So in business, we have to know when to . . . try to capitalize [on conflict], when to see what work we can make it do . . . [In that light] it is possible to conceive of conflict as not necessarily a wasteful outbreak of incompatibilities but a normal process by which socially valuable differences register themselves for the enrichment of all concerned . . . Conflict as the moment of the appearing and focusing of difference may be a sign of health, a prophecy of progress.

Paradox can be confronted. Complexity can be managed. Conflict can stimulate innovative solutions. Enjoy the contest. With it comes a new sense of purpose and new fulfillment.

Index

Other books of interest to you from Irwin Professional Publishing . . .

BETTER CHANGE

Best Practices for Transforming Your Organization

Price Waterhouse Change Integration® Team

Based on the Price Waterhouse Change Integration Team's experiences with hundreds of clients, *Better Change* takes managers into the real texture and "feel" of change projects. This is the first-ever, four-color tool kit for change with specific, practical advice on every page, supported by case studies and checklists.
ISBN: 0-7863-0342-5

SECURE YOUR FUTURE

Your Personal Companion for Understanding Lifestyle & Financial Aspects of Retirement

Price Waterhouse LLP

Completely rewritten and revised to reflect consumers's new attitudes toward retirement, this unique book focuses on the lifestyle and financial issues involved in planning for retirement. As economic factors change, as personal goals change, as life expectancy changes, so do retirement goals. *Secure Your Future* helps readers determine where they are now, where they want to be, and how they can get there.
ISBN: 0-7863-0526-6

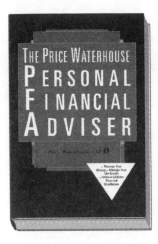

THE PRICE WATERHOUSE PERSONAL FINANCIAL ADVISER

Price Waterhouse LLP

This practical guide helps readers face their financial reality and plan for the financial impact of life events such as marriage, children's education, divorce, disability, and retirement. Numerous Price Waterhouse examples, stories, and cases will help readers see how other people have benefitted from solid financial planning.
ISBN: 0-7863-0461-8

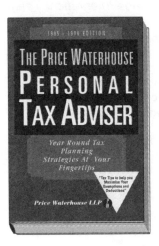

THE PRICE WATERHOUSE PERSONAL TAX ADVISER

Year Round Tax Planning Strategies at Your Fingertips, 1995–1996 Ed.

Price Waterhouse LLP

This best-selling guide, from one of America's most trusted professional service firms, is packed with up-to-the-minute information, valuable tips, and proven strategies that help everyone save money, **now and in the years to come.**
ISBN: 0-7863-0500-2

Available in fine bookstores and libraries everywhere!